Supporting
Young
Learners 3

Other Books in Series:

Supporting Young Learners:
Ideas for Preschool and Day Care Providers

• • • • • •

Supporting Young Learners 2:
Ideas for Preschool and Child Care Providers

Available from

High/Scope® Press
A division of the High/Scope Educational Research Foundation
600 North River Street, Ypsilanti, MI 48198-2898
ORDERS: phone (800)40-PRESS, fax (800)442-4FAX
e-mail: *press@highscope.org*
www.highscope.org

A third collection of articles from Extensions,
the Newsletter of the High/Scope Curriculum

Edited by
Nancy Altman Brickman

Supporting Young Learners 3

IDEAS FOR CHILD CARE PROVIDERS AND TEACHERS

HIGH/SCOPE® PRESS

Ypsilanti, Michigan

PUBLISHED BY

HIGH/SCOPE® PRESS
A division of the
HIGH/SCOPE EDUCATIONAL RESEARCH FOUNDATION
600 NORTH RIVER STREET
YPSILANTI, MICHIGAN 48198-2898
734/485-2000, FAX 734/485-0704
press@highscope.org

Editors: Holly Barton, Linda Koopmann, and Lynn Taylor
Cover design, text design: Judy Seling of Seling Design
Photography: Gregory Fox

Library of Congress Cataloging-in-Publication Data
Supporting young learners 3 : ideas for child care providers and teachers / edited by Nancy
    Altman Brickman.
      p. cm.
    "A third collection of articles from Extensions, the newsletter of the High/Scope curriculum."
    Includes bibliographical references and index.
    ISBN 1-57379-101-6
    1. Education, Preschool--Activity programs--United States. 2. Day care centers--Activity
programs--United States. 3. Active learning--United States. 4. Children and adults--United
States. I. Brickman, Nancy Altman. II. High/Scope Educational Research Foundation.
III. Extensions (Ypsilanti, Mich.) IV. Title: Supporting young learners three.
LB1140.35.C74S875 2001
372.13--dc21
                                                                                00-054089

Printed in the United States of America

10 9 8 7 6 5 4 3 2 1

Contents

Preface

The articles presented in *Supporting Young Learners 3: Ideas for Child Care Providers and Teachers* originally appeared in various issues of *Extensions: The Newsletter of the High/Scope Curriculum*. This book is High/Scope's third compilation of *Extensions* articles. The first, *Supporting Young Learners: Ideas for Preschool and Day Care Providers*, was published in 1991 and included articles appearing in *Extensions* from fall 1986 through spring 1991. The second, *Supporting Young Learners 2: Ideas for Child Care Providers and Teachers*, was published in 1996 and included articles appearing in *Extensions* from summer 1991 through spring 1996. The selections in this new collection span the period from fall 1996 through summer 2000.

Extensions is designed primarily as a professional development tool for early childhood program staff who are interested in the High/Scope Curriculum. The newsletter contains articles of interest to teachers, aides, staff of home- or center-based child care programs, special educators, administrators, trainers, and curriculum specialists.

The High/Scope approach to early childhood education was originally developed in the 1960s by former High/Scope President David P. Weikart and his colleagues, who at the time were working in the Ypsilanti Public School District in Michigan. Since 1970 the development of this approach has continued under the auspices of the High/Scope Educational Research Foundation, founded by Dr. Weikart. (Dr. Weikart retired as President of the Foundation in December 2000 after 43 years of work in curriculum development and research on the education of children and youth. He remains on the High/Scope Board of Directors.)

While the preschool level (ages 2½ to 5 years) is the primary focus of *Extensions*, we have gradually added articles on working with infants and toddlers, since many programs serving preschoolers are now also serving this younger age group. *Extensions* also includes some material aimed at early elementary school teachers.

The approach to early childhood education and care that is presented in the newsletter is continuously evolving. In recent years, High/Scope staff and field consultants have developed new strategies and practices in such areas as arts education, adult-child interaction, conflict resolution, and infant/toddler care. A major purpose of

Extensions, which is published six times yearly, is to keep readers informed of such new developments. Because this evolutionary process continues even after the publication of new material in Extensions, the articles in this collection have been edited to reflect the latest developments in the approach.

As a collection of brief articles from an eight-page newsletter, this volume does not claim to present an in-depth picture of the High/Scope educational approach. For a more comprehensive treatment of preschool curriculum issues, we refer the reader to the High/Scope preschool manual *Educating Young Children: Active Learning Practices for Preschool and Child Care Programs* by Mary Hohmann and David P. Weikart and to other High/Scope Press publications that are listed in the Appendix. In addition, for those with an interest in implementing High/Scope practices in their early childhood programs, High/Scope offers a range of training opportunities. High/Scope training and consulting take place at Foundation headquarters and at sites throughout the United States and overseas.

We would like to thank all those who have contributed over the years to the *Extensions* newsletter and the publication of this book. In addition to writing their own articles for *Extensions*, the authors—many of whom are past and present members of High/Scope's Program Division—have also been helpful in reviewing the content of the newsletter and have made many useful suggestions for improving it. While he was High/Scope president, David Weikart also found time to carefully review each issue of *Extensions*. In addition, we appreciate the contributions of High/Scope practitioners from throughout the United States and overseas, including teachers, child care providers, field consultants, teacher-trainers, and administrators. These individuals have written articles for the newsletter or have suggested many of the ideas and strategies reported in it. Finally, we would like to acknowledge the efforts of Holly Barton, Linda Koopmann, and Lynn Taylor, who helped to edit parts of the newsletter and this entire collection, as well as those of our editorial assistant, Pattie McDonald, who formatted each issue of the newsletter for the printer and helped to prepare the manuscript of this book for typesetting.

Chapter One

Supportive Adult-Child Interaction

· ·

*H*igh/Scope teachers and caregivers are trained to interact with children primarily as partners in their activities, rather than as instructors. On any given day, this interaction includes sharing control with children, focusing on their strengths, forming dependable relationships with children, supporting their play ideas, and adopting a problem-solving approach to social conflict. How we watch, listen to, and talk with children and the ways in which we respond to and participate in children's play have a powerful effect on how comfortable children feel in following through on their own ideas. The articles in this chapter illustrate how teachers interact with children throughout the day in a High/Scope setting, supporting their interests and helping them understand their world.

In the first article, "Children's Problem Solving: When to Step In, When to Stand Back," Michelle Graves describes the role we play in supporting children's efforts to find solutions to everyday problems. In the High/Scope approach, children's efforts to follow through on their own choices and plans are seen as central to learning. Graves points out that by giving children time to solve problems on their own—stepping in only when frustration levels are too high or when children cannot continue with their plans without help—adults help children learn a problem-solving process they can use in future situations.

In the second article, "Encouraging Group Problem Solving," Michelle Graves expands on this theme by describing how High/Scope's six-step conflict resolution process can be used to help children resolve the problems that often arise during group play. Using a situation that occurred at the High/Scope Demonstration Preschool as an example, Graves shows how the problem-solving process can help keep children's group play moving forward.

In the next two selections, "A Child Development Approach to Rules and Limits," and "Going Beyond 'Follow the Rules,'" Graves discusses High/Scope's approach to setting rules and limits, and provides some basic guidelines for adults to use when applying this approach in their preschool setting. Using examples from the High/Scope Demonstration Preschool, Graves also illustrates how teachers can help children share control of the process of maintaining a safe and secure classroom or center.

In the next two articles, Debbie Handler introduces the idea of persona dolls (dolls with fixed identities designated by the teacher). In "Storytelling With Dolls: A Powerful Way of Communicating With Children," Handler explains how she combines the power of storytelling with the use of persona dolls to help young children identify and process feelings they have about particular issues, experiences, and situations, such as being new to a classroom or separating from their parents. In "Persona Dolls as Discussion Starters," Handler retells an experience shared with her by a Head Start teaching team that used two persona dolls with disabilities as a teaching tool to encourage children to discuss social skills and health issues.

The last two articles in this chapter show how teachers can build on children's interests, even if those interests conflict with the teacher's personal belief system. In "Ban It, Ignore It, or Join It? What to Do About Superhero Play," Beth Marshall walks us through the thinking and research process she uses to deal with difficult classroom issues, in this case the issue of how to approach superhero play in the classroom. In her efforts to maintain a supportive social climate in the classroom, Marshall re-examined her attitudes about superhero play in general and decided to focus her attention on helping children move from imitation of their favorite superheros to the richness of representational play. Marshall also provides five general High/Scope strategies for adults who want to help support children's pretend play. In the last selection, "Supporting Children's Interests 'Moment to Moment,'" Michelle Graves reviews adult-child interaction strategies that encourage children to expand on their play interests.

Children's Problem Solving: When to Step In, When to Stand Back

By Michelle Graves

• •

Takeisha, one of the younger 3-year-olds in an all-day preschool, runs to the slide as outside time begins. She gets to the top of the slide, slides partway down, stops, and begins kicking her feet. She shouts for the teacher to come and help her. Looking over at the slide, the teacher notices a small puddle of water on the sliding surface near the bottom. The teacher pauses for a moment, wondering how best to support Takeisha.

§

In High/Scope settings, children like Takeisha have many opportunities to make choices and decisions throughout the day. Takeisha's problem with the slide is typical of the many stumbling blocks inevitably encountered as children follow through on their initiatives. In this article, we will discuss these everyday problems and examine the role adults play in supporting children's efforts to find solutions.

Determining just how to support a child who has encountered a problem during play is a delicate balancing act that requires sensitivity. In the High/Scope approach, children's efforts to follow through on their own choices and plans are seen as central to learning. So when children get "stuck" as they carry out these efforts, it's only natural for teachers to want to help them complete what they've set out to do. But sometimes the best way to help a child who is encountering problems is to stand back and let the child solve the problem independently.

Everyday Problems Preschool Children Encounter

Knowing when and how to provide assistance will help you find a balanced approach to supporting individual children in solving problems. The first step is to recognize when a child is having problems. In addition to Takeisha and the slide, let's consider the following examples:

Raina is painting at the easel. She has covered most of the paper with color. She steps back from her work, looks at it for a moment, then begins to tug at the clothespins that are holding the paper on the easel. When the clothespins don't come off, she pushes at the bottom of one of them with the end of her paintbrush. When it moves slightly, revealing white paper underneath, she paints over the white spot with blue paint.

Bobby takes a long piece of blue fabric from the supplies in the art area. He walks to the house area with the fabric, stands in front of the mirror, and wraps the material around his head. When he turns around, it slips off. He picks it up and puts it back on his head. Holding the fabric in place with his hand, he walks up to an adult and says, "Will you tie this for me so I can be a shepherd?"

Jenna, in the block area, is making a tower with hollow wooden blocks. She starts by putting two small blocks on the bottom, then begins to stack larger ones on top of those. After she puts the fourth block on the stack, it topples over. She walks away from the pile and starts drawing a picture with markers.

Terrell is working at the water table. He repeatedly dips his hands in the water, lifts up a handful of bubbles, then brings his hands to his face to look at the bubbles more closely. After several minutes, he begins swishing the water in the table with his hands, producing more bubbles and splashing water on the tile floor. As the floor gets wetter, he begins to slip on it.

Jacob is working at the computer, using an animated story program. During the part of the program where the screen changes to a new page (creating a delay of about 6 seconds), he bangs the mouse repeatedly on the table, saying "Hurry up, hurry up."

§

The opportunity to independently solve the problems involved in getting dressed builds the child's confidence and competence.

Play scenarios like these are familiar to adults who work daily with young children. In approaching children who are experiencing such problems, it's important for adults to remember that **these problems arise from children's own decisions.** In each of these cases, children have made a choice based on personal interests and the materials available. Whether the choice is to paint at the easel, to dress up like a shepherd, to slide down the slide, or to build a block tower, a problem results when the child's goal-oriented play is interrupted. From an adult's point of view, the problem may seem trivial, but to the child, the obstacle faced is important. Realizing this, adults should recognize that within such problem situations lie opportunities for learning. By providing sensitive support when children encounter problems, adults help them learn a problem-solving process they can use whenever obstacles stand in the way of completing personally important goals and tasks.

Strategies Adults Use in Support of Young Problem Solvers

Following are some guidelines to help adults frame their thinking about how to support young problem solvers.

Before selecting a strategy, observe individual children and the way they approach problem situations. Ask yourself: Is the child aware that a problem exists? If so, does he or she attempt to solve it? If the child makes an unsuccessful attempt to solve the problem, does he or she give up or persist in trying to find a solution? For example, the observant adult will see that both Raina and Bobby seem aware that they have problems and are using strategies of some kind to solve them. In contrast, it appears that Jenna has already given up on solving her problem, possibly without even realizing that she has one. Similarly, Terrell may be aware that he is slipping and sliding, but he probably doesn't see that his own actions are the cause of the problem.

Common Problems Preschoolers Face

- Pouring glue from a glue bottle
- Getting a tower of blocks to balance
- Spreading cream cheese on a bagel at snack time
- Opening up an individually packaged granola bar
- Turning the bottom of a glue stick to raise the glue surface, and stopping before it breaks off
- Passing out one napkin for each person at snack
- Singing an adult-planned song at large-group time when he or she would rather sing "Jingle Bells"
- Stapling together two pieces of construction paper
- Hanging up a piece of art work to dry
- Turning the sink faucet on to get warm water
- Figuring out which shoe goes on which foot
- Putting on snow pants and coat in the right order
- Finishing snack before the next activity starts
- Pedaling a bicycle up a slight incline

Watch children as they interact to solve problems on their own.

Based on what you observe, choose one or more of the support strategies shown below. When choosing a strategy, remember that individual children approach problems in a variety of ways. Understanding these differences will help you select the strategies that best support each child. Sometimes your choice of strategy will be affected by the child's developmental level. For example, developmentally young children like Terrell and Jenna may not perceive that spilling water on the tile floor makes it slippery or that stacking large blocks on top of small blocks will make the tower collapse. For these younger children, you might choose the first strategy. On the other hand, a developmentally older child like Bobby has more advanced verbal skills and a sharper awareness of what his problem is. When working with a child like Bobby, you might choose to wait and let the *child* describe the problem (strategy 4).

1. **Instead of making judgments, describe children's behaviors in a matter-of-fact way.** Comments like "I noticed your blocks fell over, and then you left them on the floor" or "When you swish your bubbles like that, water spills on the floor and makes you slip" give children like Jenna or Terrell an opportunity to see the relationship between cause and effect in their situations.

2. **Give children time to solve problems on their own, without your help or interference.** As you observe Raina, it may become clear to you that she wants to paint under the clothespins. Resist the urge to rush over and take the clothespins off for her. Allow her to be successful without the help of an adult. Sometimes an additional 30 seconds of waiting gives children the time they need to move a clothespin, button a button, or open a heavy door.

3. **Comment on (rather than praise) children's efforts and accomplishments.** "You worked hard to paint under the clothespin, Raina. First you tugged it with your fingers, then you pushed it with the paintbrush." Comments like this send children the message that they can generate and follow through on their own solutions.

When Adults Help Children Too Much

I recently attended a workshop on supporting children as they encounter problems in the classroom. Before this, I had always felt that the things I did for children were a big help to them and showed them how much I cared about them as people. Now I see that encouraging children to solve such problems for themselves will help them become more confident in their abilities. My problem is that I have a co-teacher who didn't attend the workshop and who constantly does things for children. I'm seeing the same thing with some of the parents. How do I tactfully get these other adults to stop helping children so much?

—A preschool teacher

Congratulations on your determination to continue to stretch yourself and to encourage those around you to examine their own attitudes. It sounds like the other people on your team are doing things for children because they see this as nurturing and helpful.

The High/Scope model encourages adults to use people's strengths as the starting point for encouraging change. Using this perspective, focus on the fact that the adults you work with truly care about the children. Then, consider the following concrete suggestions for helping them gain the awareness you now have:

- Share with your co-teacher and the parents your observations of the children as you see them grow in confidence. Make sure these stories are simply descriptions of what you see—avoid anything that could sound judgmental. For example, "Today Japera threw her own napkin away. Then she came to me and said, 'Look, the table is ready for small group.'" Contrast this with a comment like "There you go setting the table for kids again. You do too many things for them that they could do themselves."

- Try to remember the specific information from the workshop that inspired your new approach to working with the children. Share this information with the others, making it as concrete and visual as possible. For example, suppose the workshop participants matched a list of common problems preschoolers face with corresponding adult strategies for encouraging independent problem solving. Post these lists and refer to them during the class day, in your team meetings, or in conversations with parents.

- Comment on the times you notice yourself or the other adults practicing the strategies. Acknowledge that the change is awkward, but continue to focus on the benefits to the children: "Sometimes I really have to hold myself back from wiping the table off after snack time, but I've noticed that if I wait, a couple of children usually volunteer to do it. The table doesn't get as clean, but they're so proud of themselves for helping."

- Plan with your team to look for children engaged in problem-solving situations (again, use a common-problems list, such as the one on p. 7, to guide you). Make an observation sheet for parents to use at school, and ask them to sit down for a few minutes during the school day and write down what they see. This will help to keep them from doing so many things for children and will help them begin to notice how children independently approach and solve problems.

4. **Rather than make assumptions or interpretations, wait for children to describe their problems to you. This is important, even when you're sure you know what the child's problem is.** When Takeisha, midway down the slide, shouts for your help, it is a safe bet that she has seen the puddle. However, saying "One moment, let me get a towel" has a very different impact on her development than calmly walking over to the slide and giving her the chance to tell you what is wrong. Young children need to be allowed to first *observe* and *describe* a problem, so they can then move on to decide what step they will try first to complete their plans. Since Takeisha wants to complete her trip down the slide, her motivation to think of solutions herself is strong.

5. **Identify the times when it is appropriate for you to step in and help—for example, when a child's frustration level is too high, or when a child can't continue with his or her ideas without some assistance.** Not every stumbling block needs to be turned into an opportunity for the child to solve problems. It's important to strike a balance between providing too little and too much intervention. If you think Bobby might become so distracted by his efforts to tie on the fabric piece that he will abandon his plan to be a shepherd, then tie the fabric for him, describing the way you are doing it as you work. If Raina is not persistent with the clothespin, assisting her might be an appropriate way to help her complete her plan of painting the entire paper. In addition, giving children this kind of assistance provides an opportunity for you to model a solution that they may be able to refer to in the future.

6. **Enlist the support of other children, and help them communicate with one another.** When a child is wrestling with a problem, children who are developmentally older, or who are less involved in the excitement or frustration of the moment, may be helpful. Although Terrell may not be worried about the water on the floor because he is so focused on swishing bubbles, another child might be able to offer a towel to dry the floor or a tool Terrell could use to swish without spilling. Likewise, you may find a child quite willing to help Takeisha deal with the water at the bottom of the slide. A simple request ("Erica, Takeisha is calling for help. Can you

Adult Support for Problem Solving: General Guidelines

- Observe closely.
- Acknowledge the problem and the child's feelings.
- Encourage children to describe their own problems.
- Allow time for children to solve their own problems.
- Assist children when they are frustrated and in danger of abandoning their ideas.

Cleanup time is full of problem-solving opportunities.

find out why?") is often all that is needed to put children in touch with one another. Acting as a bridge between children is another way to support them in their efforts to rely on their own abilities to confront obstacles. This also sends a message that children can rely on one another instead of always calling for adults to help.

7. **Recognize that in some cases you will want to step in and provide a limit on the child's actions, while still offering some choice to the child.** In the case of Jacob, it is important not only to acknowledge his

Children often face problem situations when working and playing together.

desire to speed up the computer but also to establish that banging the mouse on the table is not an acceptable solution to his problem: "I can see you really want the next page to come sooner, but banging the mouse could break it." In addition, you can offer problem-solving ideas to the child: "You can sit with me and watch the runner (an animated character that slowly moves across the screen as the page is changing) or get up and jump around until the page changes."

• **Adopt a group problem-solving approach when it is appropriate.** All the above examples involve individual children facing problems, but small groups of children working or playing together also face problem situations. In these cases, many of the strategies already described are useful, but the group context often requires some additional strategies.

§

The following article offers a useful process for dealing with group problem-solving situations.

Encouraging Group Problem Solving

By Michelle Graves

· ·

As children play together in groups, they invariably encounter problems and disputes. To help them resolve the difficulties that arise in the natural course of their play together, High/Scope offers a six-step process derived from the literature about conflict resolution. We've introduced and described this process in other High/Scope publications*—primarily in the context of one-time, on-the-spot problem solving. This process, however, is also useful in resolving longer-term issues that arise as groups of children play.

An example of such a long-term problem occurred at the High/Scope Demonstration Preschool one year. Over the course of the school year, three children—Elia, Jake, and Zachary—often made plans that involved playing together. This play usually occurred in the wide-open space of the block area and often reflected sports- or dinosaur-related themes.

In the beginning of the school year, the play was relatively simple; for example, the three boys often imitated dinosaurs by making sweeping arm and leg movements and loud roaring noises. As the school year progressed, however, the children's play became more and more detailed—they often built elaborate block structures to house the pretend dinosaurs or to

Steps in Conflict Resolution

1. Approach calmly.
2. Acknowledge feelings.
3. Gather information.
4. Restate the problem.
5. Ask for ideas for solutions, and choose one together.
6. Give follow-up support as needed.

---

*See *Educating Young Children: Active Learning Practices for Preschool and Child Care Programs,* by Mary Hohmann and David P. Weikart (Ypsilanti, MI: High/Scope Press, 1995), p. 405; *Supporting Young Learners 2,* edited by Nancy Brickman (Ypsilanti, MI: High/Scope Press, 1996), pp. 30–34; and *You Can't Come to My Birthday Party: Conflict Mediation With Young Children,* by Betsy Evans (Ypsilanti, MI: High/Scope Press, in press).

serve as arenas for football, hockey, and wrestling games. As time passed, other children in the class joined the sports and dinosaur games. Many of these new players were developmentally younger than the original three boys, who by this time were close to 5 years old.

With these developments came a wave of problems that needed to be resolved so that the group play could continue to move forward. The most difficult challenge the children faced was coordinating their play so that no one would get hurt and younger children could participate, even though they did not yet grasp the concept of games with rules.

These issues came to a head with an incident that occurred late in the school year:

Elia, Jake, Zachary, and Michael (a 3½-year-old) had made a pretend wrestling ring by laying blocks around the perimeter of the oval-shaped rug in the block area. As Michael watched, the three older boys took their shirts off and began rolling around together inside the ring. Before long, Zachary started to cry. "Jake kicked me in the face," he said through his tears. Then Elia shouted to Jake, "That's not fair! You fouled! Go to the penalty box."

To respond to this incident, the classroom teacher used High/Scope's six steps in problem solving. Through this process, the children worked out a solution that addressed both the immediate problem and their longer-range play needs. Here are the steps as the teacher used them.

This teacher is beginning the six-step problem-solving process by approaching the children calmly and staying neutral.

1. Approach calmly. While it is often easier or more comfortable for teachers to favor one child's perspective over another's, it's important to stay neutral. This sends the message that you're respectful of all children and able to listen to all points of view.

Hearing the crying and the argument that followed the kicking incident, the teacher, Eileen, walked calmly to the block area and positioned herself on the floor with one arm around Zachary (who was still crying) and the other around Jake. Jake stood near Elia, looking at the floor. Michael stood nearby, watching with interest.

2. Acknowledge feelings. This step must not be skipped! Keep it simple, but do call attention to the children's feelings. This will free them to think more clearly about what they need to do to resolve the problem.

"It looks like a lot of people are upset here," Eileen said.

3. Gather information. Give all children the chance to express their points of view. You need the information, the children need to have a say, and all will benefit from hearing what others feel they need.

Zachary said, "I won't play if you hurt me," to which Jake replied, "Well, I'll be more careful, but real wrestlers get hurt sometimes." Elia said, "Yeah, but you're not allowed to play when you mess up." The discussion continued in this vein for a while.

4. Restate the problem. Echo the children's words, rephrasing any hurtful language if necessary. This will help them understand that you've truly listened and that you aren't taking sides or imposing a solution on them. Give them a chance to add additional details to your restatement.

Eileen said, "Zachary says he won't play if he's going to get hurt, and Jake says he's willing to be more careful, even though he knows real wrestlers do get hurt. Elia says he thinks you shouldn't be allowed to play if you mess up."

5. Ask for ideas for solutions, and choose one together. Start by accepting everyone's ideas, even when you know some of them are not realistic. Help children think through the consequences of their proposed solutions. Once the children choose a solution, check with each child to confirm that the solution works for him or her.

"It sounds like you still want to play the game. How can we work it out so people stay safe?" Eileen asked. After some discussion, Elia said, "I know—we can make up rules, and write 'em down. Then we hang them over there on the

wall." Zachary and Jake agreed. They left to get paper and markers from the art area, then returned. The three children sat down and generated a list of "Wrestling Rules," which Eileen wrote down. Though not suggesting any rules, Michael continued to watch with great interest throughout the discussion. Following are the rules the children developed:

1. Don't cry for your mama.
2. Only pretend punching or slapping.
3. Only pretend kicking.
4. You have to wear cool stuff.
5. You cannot play with weapons.
6. Try to keep guys on the mat.
7. No being wild. Be wild at home.
8. People can choose their own person to be.
9. You have to get introduced. (At the start of a match, a child would announce the pretend names of each wrestler, using a block or a hand to represent a microphone.)
10. No yelling at other people.
11. No teasing other kids.
12. First kid hurt, and the game is over. They forfeit the game.
13. No picking people up and throwing them.
14. No picking on other wrestlers.
15. If it is warm enough, wrestlers can take shirts off (if you want to).

Once the conflict appears to be resolved, watch to see if the children need help in acting on their decisions.

The children also asked the teacher to list their special wrestling names and to include the list of names in the rules. Michael, who up to this point had watched silently, asked the teacher to add his special name, "The Cat," to the list. A while later another child, Jacob, added his name.

Zachary—Macho Man
Elia—Hollywood Hogan
Jake—Ultimo Dragon
Jacob—Action Jackson
Michael—The Cat

6. Be prepared to give follow-up support. As children return to their play, stay nearby. Watch to see if they need help in carrying out their solution.

Eileen became a part of the "audience," positioning herself on the outskirts of the wrestling match. When children broke the rules they'd developed, she stopped the play and referred them to the rule, pointing to the specific words on the list. As the play continued over the next several days, more children joined in the matches and asked to have their names added to the list. As Eileen observed them in action, she recorded the times when the children themselves stopped the game and pointed to a rule.

❧

The above steps can be applied to many short- and long-term problem situations. Group problem-solving experiences like this one can help to resolve recurrent problems that keep children's play from moving forward.

A Child Development Approach to Rules and Limits

By Michelle Graves

· ·

When dealing with any classroom issue, the guiding principle for High/Scope educators is to look first at children's development: how they think and reason, what their physical and social abilities are, and how they tend to view everyday situations. Teachers then use this understanding to develop support strategies attuned to each child's capabilities and way of experiencing the world.

With this guiding principle in mind, in this article we'll explore how early childhood teachers and caregivers can develop a more effective approach to setting rules and limits in their childhood settings. We'll begin by identifying some of the characteristics that affect preschoolers' ability to understand behavioral expectations. Then we'll look at some concrete ways in which teaching adults can apply this child development knowledge in their daily work with children.

Rules: The Child's Viewpoint

Young children often don't follow the everyday rules of behavior that seem so sensible and necessary to adults, primarily because children and adults approach rules and limits from very different perspectives. Though older children and adults can keep several things in mind at once, young children tend to focus on **one thing at a time.** And this is just one of several **developmental factors** that affect how children experience classroom rules. In addition (and partly because of this one-thing-at-a-time thinking), young children are **present-oriented.** They rarely reflect on their past experiences or the future consequences of their actions; instead, they live in the **here and now.**

This here-and-now orientation and the preschooler's inability to consider several things at once can lead to clashes and problems in the classroom, especially in programs (like High/Scope's) that place a high value on

One way children learn about social rules and expectations is by assuming pretend roles and acting out everyday situations with their playmates.

children's decision making and choices. When children feel free to express and follow through on their ideas, they often become totally absorbed in their plans, to the exclusion of everything else. For example, let's consider the following interchange between a teacher and preschooler:

Teacher to a preschooler at work time: "Use your walking feet inside, please. Remember, we can run when we get to the playground." Child to teacher: "My walking feet are just pretending to be running feet."

In this example, although it is work time, Alicia might be engrossed in carrying out her plan to "play Batman and run around to catch the bad people." Alicia's class may have a no-running rule, and she may at other times seem aware of this rule. But at this particular moment, something else—her plan to be Batman—is uppermost in Alicia's mind. Her intention to be Batman and save people includes, in her thinking, running.

This example is typical of many situations that arise as young children play. When children are following through on their own ideas, they often have difficulty thinking about other things—what the rules are or how their activity affects others around them.

An observation shared with us by an early childhood teacher new to the High/Scope approach illustrates this point. Her classroom had always had the rule, "No hitting allowed. We use our words instead." Yet, even though most of the children in her classroom could verbalize their understanding of this rule, they frequently forgot it in situations where their activities overlapped with those of another. The teacher related an incident she observed in the toy area, where Claire was carrying out her plan to build a castle for the plastic knight she had brought from home. Next to her, Callahan was using a toy bulldozer and dump truck to knock down small block towers he was creating (he had recently watched a work crew demolish a large building near his home). In his enthusiasm about knocking over his "buildings," Callahan knocked over some of Claire's castle blocks. Claire then grabbed a Tinkertoy® stick and hit Callahan, who immediately pushed her down. The teacher entered in time to separate them, stop the hitting and pushing, and remind them of the "Use your words" rule.

Claire and Callahan's behavior in this incident is a good example of the one-thing-at-a-time, present-oriented thinking already discussed. It also illustrates another related characteristic of preschoolers: They often **express emotions physically.** While Claire and Callahan undoubtedly *know* that hitting and pushing are not permitted in their classroom, in this incident their emotions got the better of them. Eventually, Claire and Callahan's social and verbal skills will develop to the point where they will usually express their feelings in words rather than with their bodies. However, since these abilities are not yet firmly established, in moments of high emotion they will likely fall back on less mature ways of behaving.

Even when children *do* express their emotions verbally, the language they use is often unacceptable to us. Insults like "You're not my friend anymore!" are familiar to early childhood teachers. Young children use such extreme language because they're just developing the ability to *classify* (sort into categories). Since their classification abilities aren't yet fully developed, they often sort things according to **rigid either/or rules.** At any given moment, the child may see a playmate as all friend or all enemy, all good or all bad, all right or all wrong. Although preschool children's thinking will become more flexible in time, at this stage it doesn't matter to them that the children they now classify as all bad were friends just a few minutes before.

Preschoolers often exhibit one-thing-at-a-time, present-oriented thinking, and they often express emotions physically in moments of high emotion.

Understanding that the preschooler's rigid categories are a normal part of development is helpful to many adults because it frees them to hear and accept children's hurtful statements without feeling as much emotional tension. The adult understands that the child isn't deliberately trying to hurt another person's feelings; this makes it easier for the adult to gently assist the child in restating his or her thoughts.

The fact that young children are **egocentric (self-centered)** also affects their ability to carry out rules. By saying this we do not mean that young children are selfish, but simply that they have difficulty seeing things from another person's point of view. They are more likely to consider how a rule affects *them* at any given moment rather than how it affects the whole class or community. Consider this example:

In an effort to conserve juice at snack time, teachers in one early childhood classroom had a rule that children could pour their own juice up to the halfway mark on the cup. The teachers had explained to the children that this rule would prevent juice from being wasted and ensure that there would be enough juice for everyone. One day, as the children were passing around the juice pitcher, Elia loudly pointed out that Terrell had poured his juice all the way to the top of his cup and that now there wouldn't be enough for everyone. Yet a few minutes later, when it was Elia's turn to pour, he poured his own juice to the top of his cup. When the teacher commented on his behavior, Elia's explanation was simple: "Well, I can do it because my throat hurts and I need it."

In this and similar situations, many young children simply don't see how a rule applies to their own behavior. Because of Elia's egocentric thinking, he did not see the contradiction in his statement and his own behavior.

From a child development perspective, Alicia, Claire, Callahan, and Elia aren't defiant, disrespectful, or "bad" because they failed to comply with classroom rules. Rather, they behaved as they did because their social, language, and thinking skills aren't yet fully developed. Gradually, with adult support, young children will learn the everyday rules and customs of appropriate behavior. Meanwhile, here are some suggestions for supporting children as they develop the skills they need to meet these social expectations.

What Teachers Can Do

As with most situations, a plan of action for dealing with rules and limits in the classroom starts with an examination of our own personal feelings about our roles as teachers of young children. Some adults feel comfort-

An Alternative to "Teaching" Rules

I recently attended a High/Scope workshop on using a problem-solving approach to conflict. I have always had a list of rules posted in my classroom, with cute sketches next to them that children can "read." I think it is important for children to learn the rule "Share and be friends," and I have always been successful in getting my preschoolers to follow it by reminding them of the rule when they are not sharing and by pointing out the happy smiles of the children pictured playing together on the posted rule chart. Why should I change, and what are the easiest first steps to take if I decide to try out some of the ideas?

—*A Head Start teacher*

We agree with you that it is important for children to learn positive ways of relating to others. However, we don't believe this can be achieved simply by telling them the rules and showing them pictures of what adults think they should feel and do. We believe children learn through *experience*. Thus, children develop an understanding of social rules by solving real social problems and by trying out social behaviors through pretend play. When we just tell children the rules, they may comply out of fear or simply to please us, without having any real understanding of why the rules are important. As a result, when our backs are turned they may try to evade rules that are not meaningful from their point of view.

If you agree that "experience is the best teacher," your next question is where do you start. We would suggest

Rather than make a rule against climbing and jumping, the teachers provide materials and support so children can climb and jump safely.

two guidelines. **First, observe children closely.** You will see lots of instances in which children are learning social rules through their play experiences. For example, children often create pretend play scenarios in which they take responsibility for others around them. As children assign roles to peers and adults ("You be the mommy, and I'll be the sister" or "I'm the bad guy, so catch me and take me to jail") they are using rules they've agreed on together to organize their play. They are learning to cooperate and to understand another person's point of view.

Second, when sharing issues do arise in the classroom, begin by practicing just the initial steps in problem solving. Approach the children calmly, and focus on acknowledging children's underlying feelings and describing their behaviors ("Tamara, you really want all the blue teddy bear counters. You want them so much your arms are crossed over your chest and your forehead is all wrinkled up." "Ramon, you really want the blue teddies, too!"). While this kind of language may at first seem stilted, keep in mind that it helps you really look at the situation from the children's point of view rather than attributing your own meanings to their behavior. If you continue to practice acknowledging children's feelings, it will begin to feel more natural to you, and the other steps in problem solving will come more easily.

able deciding on a list of rules before the children even arrive—for example, "Everyone has to share and take turns," "No running inside the classroom," "No hitting, throwing toys, or name-calling," "Be respectful and polite at all times." The adult's role in such a classroom is clear-cut: Whenever children violate a rule, the adult will step in and remind the child about it.

Some adults find this policing role to be a comfortable one because it gives them a clearly defined way of interacting with children. As High/Scope educators, we approach these issues from a different perspective. Our primary goal isn't the enforcement of rules but the development of children's *empathy* (understanding the feelings of others) and *divergent thinking* (learning that situations can be viewed from many different perspectives and that there are many solutions to problems). Acting within this framework, we don't view problem situations as opportunities to "teach the rules"; rather, we see them as occasions to encourage children to reflect on their actions and learn effective problem-solving skills. This doesn't mean there are no rules and limits in High/Scope classrooms. Our rules and limits are an outgrowth of our interactions with children. As we assist children in developing more mature social behavior, we take into consideration the important developmental information outlined earlier.

Basic Guidelines for Adults

Here are some guideposts to keep in mind when applying High/Scope's approach to classroom rules and limits:

• **When considering whether to set a rule or limit, ask yourself whether the unacceptable behavior affects people's physical or emotional safety or is destructive to the classroom or materials.** If so, it's necessary to stop the behavior and set firm limits with children. **When you state the limit to the child, always give the reason for it.** Use concrete terms the child can understand: "Stop hitting, it hurts his body," "I'm asking you to stop calling Adam 'Poo-poo-head' because I notice it's making him cry," or "I'm stopping you from tearing the book; other people won't be able to use it if the pages are torn."

• **Accept that children will express strong feelings in the classroom, including anger, sadness, irritability, joy, and excitement.** Sometimes these strong feelings are expressed in behaviors that are socially immature. A child who's frustrated or angry may hit, throw things, or yell so loudly that it's uncomfortable for adults and other children. A child who's excited may run and jump around, laugh and shout out loud, or hug another child or adult in a way that knocks them over. To help children develop empathy, we need to show acceptance for *their* feelings, by making a comment that helps the child separate the feeling from the unacceptable behavior: "I can see you're very upset, but you're hurting him when you hit. I'm going to hold you so we can all be safe."

• **As children deal with problems, help them remember similar experiences they dealt with successfully.** Remind children of past solutions that have worked for themselves or for others: "I remember that the last time you felt sad about your daddy leaving town, you went to the art area and drew him a picture." These simple reminders empower the child to look for positive ways of expressing uncomfortable feelings.

• **Encourage children to think of alternatives to unacceptable behavior that don't threaten people's safety or harm materials.** For example, throwing items in the classroom could become part of a child's plan if the child considers how throwing an item might affect the materials being used or the safety of others. Thus, if Lucy is throwing blocks, the teacher would stop her and encourage her to think of a safe alternative, such as throwing beanbags into a basket.

To help children develop empathy, we need to show acceptance of their feelings by making a comment that helps the child separate the feeling from the unacceptable behavior.

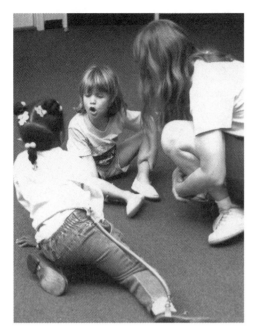

Remind children of past solutions that have worked for themselves or others. These reminders empower children to look for positive ways to express uncomfortable feelings.

• **Use a familiar part of the routine to raise and discuss behavior issues that affect the class as a whole.** As the need arises, encourage children to think of rules they can successfully keep or ways in which they can make a specific behavior safer or less destructive. For example, if riding-toy behavior is causing a problem, at greeting circle or small-group time, discuss safety guidelines that children can remember when using riding toys.

• **Plan safe ways to accommodate children's needs by modifying the environment or daily routine.** For example, if you have a group of children who like to climb and make noise, extend the time you spend outside, add materials children can use to build things they can climb on and jump off of safely, provide musical instruments or woodworking materials to make noises with, and plan large-group times that allow for large and loud movements.

• **Use concrete, visual reminders to help children remember safety rules.** For example, to remind children not to run in front of the swings, lay a railroad-tie boundary around the space a safe distance from the swings.

• **When possible, use High/Scope's steps in conflict resolution to deal with conflicts between children (see p. 13).** Then, at non-crisis times, use some of the other strategies recommended here to deal with underlying issues that contribute to similar conflicts.

❧

In summary, we recommend that adults look at the rules and limits in the classroom from the perspective of children. Children live in the here and now, in the moment. Their emerging abilities affect the ways in which they react to problems and relate to others. Understanding these developmental issues helps adults support children in learning more mature approaches to everyday problem situations.

Going Beyond "Follow the Rules"

By Michelle Graves

• •

Unlike early childhood settings in which teachers approach classroom behavior issues primarily by teaching and enforcing rules, in High/Scope classrooms the emphasis is not on rules themselves but on helping children explore and understand the issues that lead to rules.

We recognize that a list of rules may be too abstract for concrete-minded preschoolers to grasp. Instead of imposing rules on children, we encourage children to *share control* of the process of maintaining a safe and secure classroom or center. Therefore, we invite children to participate in developing rules and expectations and in finding ways to meet their own needs without harming themselves, other people, or the materials in the classroom.

In the following section, we illustrate this approach to rules and limits by listing four rules that are common in early childhood classrooms. Following each rule is a description of an incident from the High/Scope Demonstration Preschool that illustrates an alternative way to approach the same issue.

↪ **Instead of the "Use a tissue" rule.** A number of children in the classroom had colds. The teachers were concerned that many of the children were spreading their infections by coughing and sneezing without covering their mouths, sneezing into their hands without washing them afterwards, and wiping their noses on their clothes or hands. To spark a discussion of this issue, the teachers taped a facial tissue to the message board next to a sketch of a face with a drippy nose and lines coming out of the mouth to indicate coughing and sneezing. Next to this drawing they sketched a "sad face" symbol.

At morning greeting circle, they asked the children to guess what the message meant. A discussion followed in which several children shared their knowledge of what to do if you have a cold and why these health practices are important. Everyone agreed to use a tissue when coughing, sneezing, or wiping noses. After this discussion, the teachers observed that those children who understood this rule often reminded other children who had colds to use tissues or to cover their mouths when they coughed or sneezed.

⇸ **Instead of the "Be friends" rule.** Preschoolers Myles and Humza had built a block structure they called a "tank." Ben, a third child, joined them, immediately kicking over the tank. The children began arguing loudly. Myles called for a teacher, saying to her as she joined them, "Ben knocked over our tank on purpose!" Ben replied, "It was an accident, you poo-poo-head."

The children argued back and forth like this for a while, with the teacher acknowledging their feelings, rephrasing their harsh language, and helping them identify the underlying problem, namely that Myles and Humza wanted to play by themselves and Ben was angry about being excluded. None of the children budged from these positions, so after some discussion, the teacher helped them resolve the situation by proposing that Ben find someone else to build with. Later on in the same work time, when Myles had hurt himself with a block, Ben went to get an ice pack for him without any prompting from the teacher. Myles accepted the ice pack from Ben.

Thinking to herself that Ben was now interacting with

High/Scope teachers encourage children to share control of the process of maintaining a safe and secure classroom or center. The emphasis is not on rules themselves but on helping children explore and understand the issues that lead to rules.

Myles in a more empathic way, the teacher was pleased that she had not tried to force Myles and Humza to be friends with Ben but instead had helped all three children discuss their needs and feelings.

⇸ **Instead of the "No weapons" rule.** At work time the same day, children were playing on the steps inside the classroom, pretending that it was a cliff. Holding "guns" (long wooden unit blocks) in their hands, they shot "bullets" (plastic construction blocks) at imaginary sea monsters. Although nobody had been hit with the "bullets," some children playing nearby called to the teacher, saying they didn't want to be shot.

The teacher privately observed that although the nearby children were complaining, they were clearly excited and were enjoying the other children's game. She pointed out to the group on the stairs that the flying construction toys could hurt somebody and encouraged the game players to discuss how they could continue their game while keeping everyone safe. Soon the children began a safer activity of "shooting" soft foam balls at one another, still using the long wooden unit blocks as pretend guns.

The children then added a new element to their play. After children were "shot," they would fall over and play dead until another child revived them by sprinkling "magic dust" on them. Eventually the children dropped the pretend shooting, but the magic-dust play continued at outside time in a new variation: "Dragons and Rescuers." The teacher noted that had she called an initial halt to the weapons play, it might have prevented the children from developing their play scenario further. Based on similar experiences, she also felt she wouldn't have succeeded in getting the children to stop their weapons play altogether—they probably would have simply become more careful about when they displayed this type of play.

➦ **Instead of the "At this school we share" rule.** For small-group time, the teacher had prepared a small basket containing different colors of felt-tipped markers for each child. As the children began drawing, Jamal asked to use the blue marker that was in Greg's hand. Greg refused to give it to him. Jamal began crying. Sue, the teacher, acknowledged his feelings, saying "You're upset because you want to use Greg's blue marker, and he won't give it to you." She then turned to Greg and said, "Jamal is having a problem because he wants to use the marker." Instead of insisting that Greg share the marker, Sue paused.

Then Erica, who was sitting across the table, offered her blue marker to Jamal. He refused to accept this substitute. The discussion went on like this for a while, with Greg continuing to refuse to share his blue marker and Jamal insisting that he had to have **that one.** Sue continued to acknowledge the children's feelings, pointing out how very upset Jamal was about not getting the marker. But Greg still was not interested in sharing. Finally, Greg noticed that the other small group was starting snack time. He pointed this out to Sue, who said, "That's right, but I'm not comfortable starting snack while Jamal is still so upset." At this point, Greg handed the marker to Jamal, who put one blue stroke on his paper, and then handed the marker back to Greg. Greg then quickly finished his picture. With the tension dissipated, snack time began uneventfully.

Reflecting on this later, the teacher remembered that the year before she would not have been able to sit quietly and listen when Greg and Jamal's dispute seemed at a stalemate. She now realized she'd learned to wait through uncomfortable moments like these, giving children the time they need to take over the responsibility for solving their own problems.

§

All of the above incidents would have unfolded much differently if the teachers had seen their role as one of simply stating, enforcing, and reminding children of rules. Instead, they took the time to challenge children to think about the feelings of others, to explore the impact of their own actions, and to generate alternative ways of meeting their own needs. Over time, this control-sharing approach to classroom problems often teaches children the same things teachers hope children will learn from the quick-fix method of imposing a rule. In addition, the lessons learned through this more reflective approach are more likely to stick with children because they have freely chosen the outcome of the situation.

A teacher learns to wait through uncomfortable moments to give children the time they need to take over the responsibility for solving their own problems.

Storytelling With Dolls: A Powerful Way of Communicating With Children

By Debbie Handler

• •

Stories are magical to children. Throughout history, parents and grand-parents have used storytelling to hand down family and cultural information from generation to generation.

Early childhood educators, too, have found storytelling to be a powerful tool for communicating with children on a wide variety of topics, such as dealing with human differences and other uncomfortable topics. One effective approach for discussing such issues with young children is to tell stories using *persona dolls* as props. Persona dolls are dolls with specific identities designated by the teacher. These fixed identities make them different from other dolls found in High/Scope classrooms whose identities change frequently as children use them to pretend in various ways.

Stories made more concrete by the presence of persona dolls model an attitude of acceptance and provide children with a means of exploring their fears and other emotions. They also help children anticipate new experiences and situations and talk about ideas for dealing with them. In the pages that follow, we'll explain how adults introduce this special kind of doll and how children use persona dolls and their stories as a tool for making sense of their world.

The following excerpt from a discussion with children illustrates the process of using persona dolls.

"Persona dolls" have specific identities. Children can use these dolls and the stories they make up about them to make sense of their world.

The discussion occurred in a Texas Head Start classroom that I was involved with as a teacher-trainer. I led the activity as a way of demonstrating the storytelling/discussion process to the other teachers and introducing the process to children.

In our teacher-planning session, we had decided I would tell a story that would include elements and themes familiar to children. The goal was to introduce children to the process of talking about a problem and coming up with solutions. The doll character, Rosie, was intended to be Hispanic, like several other children in the classroom. At the beginning of the school year, several of the children, including Rosie, had experienced difficulties separating from their parents. Although the children were now comfortable in the classroom, the teachers felt that the topic of being new in school would still be of interest to children. Here's how part of the discussion went between the children and me:

Teacher (Debbie Handler): [holding up the doll] "I would like you to meet Rosie. Rosie lives in Dallas. She lives with her father, mother, grandmother, aunt, uncle, and cousins. Rosie's mother is a nurse at a big hospital. At home, Rosie and her family speak Spanish most of the time, but Rosie likes speaking both English and Spanish with all of us at school. Rosie is my friend. This is her first day of school, and she is a little nervous. When she gets nervous her stomach feels tight. Maybe some of your stomachs feel like that when you're nervous."

Maria: "Yeah."

Hector: "No."

Steve: "Yeah!"

Teacher: "Rosie has a mother and a father like some of you."

Steve: "My dad brought me to school."

Maria: "So did mine."

Teacher: "Why do you think Rosie is afraid?"

Tammy: "I know. She doesn't know about school."

Hector: "She's scared."

Maria: "She misses her parents."

Stacy: "She's afraid. She doesn't know what we do at school."

Jennifer: "She doesn't know where we eat lunch, or the toys we have to play with."

Teacher: "That's right, she doesn't know about those things."

Steve: "She doesn't know how to open things."

Stacy: "She's too little, she can copy her teacher."

Teacher: "She can copy her teacher. Rosie told me that when her parents leave, she is afraid of being alone because she doesn't have any friends yet. Does someone want to be her friend?"

Maria: "I'll be her friend!"

Hector: "I'll be her friend too!"

Teacher: "We can all be her friend."

Hector: "I love being her friend."

Teacher: "Maybe some of you can show her our room."

Maria: "She doesn't even know where the bathroom is. She can't even brush her teeth."

Selena: "I'll show her where to brush her teeth."

Steve: "I'll share toys with her."

Teacher: "So who would like to show her our room?"

Hector: "Me!"

Steve: "Me!"

Andrea: "Me!"

Teacher: "We will put her in the circle for the rest of greeting time, and maybe during small-group time she could sit with some of you. Would you like to hold her?"

Author Debbie Handler introduces the Rosie doll.

Maria: "Yes."

Teacher: "Remember, her name is Rosie, and she's a little nervous. Do you want to tell Rosie who you are?"

(The children passed Rosie around the circle, introducing themselves to her. As Rosie was being passed around the circle, a child poked Rosie. Andrea, who was watching the doll, said to the child, "Don't scare her.")

Andrea: (pointing to Rosie's belly) "She eats a lot of food."

Hector: "Can she sit down with me?"

Maria: (talking to Rosie) "I love your hair."

Andrea: (replying for Rosie) "Thank you."

Teacher: "So, Selena, you're going to show Rosie where to brush her teeth, and Steve, you're going to share toys with her. Then, Rosie will sit with Hector. I think Rosie is going to enjoy our class."

After children had heard and discussed Rosie's situation, many of the children "cared for" Rosie during the rest of the day. The Rosie doll spent most of her time that day with Hector. He took her to small-group time with him, reminding other children to be nice to her because she was scared. During work time, other children included Rosie in their play. After recall time, Rosie "said goodbye" to the children and left with me. Later, the regular teachers used the process I had modeled to introduce other persona dolls who then became a permanent part of the classroom.

As this example illustrates, persona dolls are a valuable tool in helping children discover their place in the world and how their actions affect others. Following are general steps in the process of introducing and using persona dolls and their stories in your classroom.

Giving the Doll an Identity

First, choose a doll and define its identity. The doll's identity should include such characteristics as culture, language, gender, ethnicity, appearance, personal history, home and community, personality characteristics, and family structure (parents and siblings, extended family, names and ages of family members). As you develop the identity of your doll, be sure to reflect characteristics of the children in your classroom, including special issues that you may want to address with them. Be on the alert for any stereotypes that you may be including in the doll's history and characteristics. Choose doll clothing and accessories that reflect the personal qualities you wish to emphasize.

To illustrate how to develop a doll's identity, I'll use the example of a friend's child who is in a wheelchair because of cerebral palsy. As a young child, my friend's son felt isolated at school. He had been mainstreamed in a regular classroom, and the other children avoided interacting with him. As a teacher concerned about such a child, I might create a doll, Bob, who has curly brown hair, is a baseball fan, and who uses a black wheelchair. He loves to wear tee shirts and baseball caps from his favorite team, the Texas Rangers. He wears black tennis shoes, and his wheelchair is decorated with Rangers bumper stickers.

In Bob's case, the doll's features correspond to the characteristics of a single child. However, while it might be ideal to have one doll to represent each child in the classroom, creating that many dolls may be difficult or impossible because of limitations on your time and budget. Instead, you may want to start with one or two dolls

The doll's identity should include such characteristics as culture, language, gender, ethnicity, appearance, personal history, home and community, personality characteristics, and family structure (parents and siblings, extended family, names and ages of family members).

whose identities reflect general qualities of some of the children in the classroom. Teachers should keep in mind, however, that although a single persona doll may be used to highlight multiple situations in their classrooms (for example, ethnic characteristics shared by several children or the fact that some children have disabilities), the identity of a particular doll should not change; that is, Bob should remain in his wheelchair for the entire school year.

When used as props for storytelling, persona dolls help children develop awareness of important real-life issues. Some issues that may be approached through storytelling with a persona doll include the following:

• Everyday classroom conflicts, for example, problems sharing space or toys

• Classroom situations, such as separating from parents at the beginning of the school year, that involve strong emotions

• Preventing bias, for example, dealing with a child who has a leg brace or thick glasses or whose parents speak a foreign language at home

• Family events, for example, new siblings, death or illness of a relative

• Different family situations, for example, two-parent families, single-parent families, families headed by another relative or by a guardian

Telling the Story

To encourage discussion about your real-life issue, bring the doll out at small- or large-group time and tell a story with it, using the following steps:

1. Begin the story by introducing the doll. The first time you bring out the doll, give the doll's identity and life history. Once the children are familiar with the doll, you will only need to remind children of a few characteristics.

2. Continue the story by letting children know that the doll has a problem. Encourage children to discuss this part of the story. Help the children identify feelings that might exist for the character represented by the persona doll or for other children in the classroom who may be experiencing similar problems.

3. Encourage the children to discuss possible solutions to the doll's problem. Avoid imposing your own ideas in this step. Remember, the process of discussing feelings and solutions is more important than finding a perfect solution for the character in the story.

4. Bring the group activity to a close by ending the story, possibly referring to future plans for the doll character. Be sure to incorporate some of the ideas suggested by children in your ending statement, choosing solutions that are realistic. Be attentive to the message that your story is delivering to the children. Following the story, you may return the persona doll to its shelf or, at the children's request, keep it out for play.

Though using persona dolls may be a new strategy for many High/Scope teachers, this storytelling process has several elements that will be familiar to those experienced in using the High/Scope educational approach. For example, High/Scope adult strategies for encouraging conversation (see next page) are used throughout the storytelling process to engage children in a discussion of the story as it is being told. Using these strategies, the teacher lets children take the lead in identifying the doll's feelings and in suggesting ideas for making the doll character feel welcome and comfortable. Note, too, that the steps in storytelling are similar to the steps in High/Scope's conflict

Encourage children to discuss possible solutions to the doll's problem. The process of discussing feelings and solutions is more important than finding a perfect solution for the character in the story.

resolution process (see "Steps in Conflict Resolution," p. 13). In both processes, children participate in identifying and discussing feelings related to a problem situation and, following this, in suggesting and sorting through ideas for possible solutions. In one situation, however, the conflict is a real one, involving feelings that are fresh and strong; in the other, the problem is part of a story told about a pretend character. Both processes have the same results for children: improved social and language skills and a greater sense of control over life's difficult experiences.

Locating the Doll in the Classroom

Because persona dolls are different from other kinds of dolls in High/Scope classrooms, you will have to find ways to convey their special status to children. You can explain to children that these dolls are to be treated more like real people than the other dolls, which are toys. Like real people, persona dolls have names that do not change, and playing with them is like playing with another child—children need to ask first. Similarly, just as we wouldn't undress a child in the room, we wouldn't undress the persona doll. Persona dolls are usually kept on their own shelf or other special spot, not in the dramatic play or house area, where other dolls are kept. At first, you may want to keep the persona dolls in a place that is visible but out of reach of children—an adult would get the persona doll out to tell a story or at a child's request ("Can I have the Rosie doll to play with in the block area?"). As time passes, if you observe that children are playing appropriately with the persona dolls, you can change to a system in which children get the dolls out themselves.

As is the case with many classroom issues and conflicts, the outcomes of storytelling with persona dolls will vary. Our goal in telling the story is to encourage children to identify their feelings about particular issues and then, through conversation, to process the feelings in a nonthreatening and accepting way. As the above discussion of Rosie's problem illustrates, children usually respond very thoughtfully to these stories, dealing with feelings, ideas, and solutions with an attitude of acceptance and caring.

In this article, we've outlined a process in which an adult—who has listened to children, watched children, and played with children—tells a story about an issue children are experiencing. Storytelling is a powerful way of communicating with children, and the use of dolls as part of the storytelling process makes it easier for children to connect the story with

Conversing With Children: Adult Strategies

- Look for natural opportunities for conversation.
- Join children at their level for conversation.
- Respond to children's conversational leads.
- Converse as a partner with children.
  - Stick to the topic the child raises.
  - Make comments that allow the conversation to continue without pressuring the child for a response.

- Wait for the child to respond before taking another turn.
- Keep your comments fairly brief.
- Ask questions sparingly.
  - Ask questions that relate directly to what children are doing.
  - Ask questions about the child's thought process.

their own lives. Each child who listens to a story is unique, physically and cognitively. The family cultures, values, and expectations each child has experienced are varied. Using dolls as part of the storytelling experience empowers children to reflect on who they are and on the identities and feelings of those around them. In this way, children gain an opportunity to explore relationships with others in a nonthreatening setting and to learn skills that will allow them to handle problems and conflicts in a positive way.

REFERENCES

Fullerton College Child Development Department. (1996, November). *Storytelling with persona dolls.* Presented at the National Association for the Education of Young Children Conference, Dallas, TX.

Weatherby, P. (1997, January/February). Using dolls to build disability awareness. *Extensions: The Newsletter of the High/Scope Curriculum.*

Whitney, T. & Stauber, D. (1996, Fall). Good reasons to tell a doll a story. *Educational Doll Plans* (newsletter produced by doll manufacturer People of Every Stripe, P.O. Box 12505, Portland, OR 97212).

Persona Dolls as Discussion Starters

By Debbie Handler

• •

*T*he following experiences with using persona dolls in the classroom were
shared with me by a Head Start teacher in Texas, several months after I had
*demonstrated their use to her and her staff. Persona dolls can become valuable
tools for communicating effectively with children about many challenging issues.
These examples illustrate only a few of the possible applications. The actual range
is virtually unlimited—your children provide the frontiers.*

ş

Our Head Start class was introduced to our first persona doll at the
beginning of one school year. I was excited about using this new teaching
tool to encourage children to discuss social skills and health issues. I chose a
doll whose light skin, blond hair, and blue eyes resembled one of the students in my classroom. However, unlike the real child, the doll had two
hearing aids behind his ears. I named the doll David.

Introducing David

After the first days of school had passed and most of the children were
comfortable at school, I decided to introduce David. Two of our students, a
boy and a girl, were still unhappy about being left at school by their family
members, so I decided to discuss the issues of being afraid to come to
school and making friends. I began,

> *"This is David. He lives with his mother and grandmother. His mother has just
> had a new baby, and David is learning about being a big brother. This is his first day
> of school. He is really afraid of being left by his mother. He doesn't know his teachers
> very well and he hasn't made any friends yet. How can we help David?"*
>
> *Almost all of the children were eager to give suggestions and advice. Two
> of the more reticent children were sitting at the edge of the group. One of them,
> Corbin, excitedly said, "We have snakes!" (That day, he had made a long line
> of pop beads and pretended it was a snake.)*

Allen, the other reticent child, said to the David doll, "We'll go outside and play!" Tyla, joining in, said, "We have fun at school."

As I was holding David, Corbin was touching him and found the hearing aids behind his ears.

Brooke informed us, "He has something behind his ear to help him hear us."

Tyla noticed a black spot in the David doll's mouth where he was missing a tooth. She said, "David has a toothache," pointing at the spot.

Brooke joined in, "He has a loose tooth. When a tooth falls out a new one comes in. That means you're growing up." Dean added, "He got money from the tooth fairy."

Then we discussed how we would treat David: like any other child in our classroom. Later, at work time, Brooke carried David around carefully and remarked, "This is my brother."

More "Doll Talk"

Another time we met to discuss an issue I saw occurring at lunch with several of the children. Holding the David doll, I began,

"David has been getting his clothes dirty at lunch time. Sometimes his food falls in his lap or on the floor and makes a mess. And his sleeve gets dirty from wiping his mouth. Can we help David?"

Erica said, "Use a napkin," to which Kelsey added, "Eat over the plate."

"Use a spoon, not your fingers," Dean suggested.

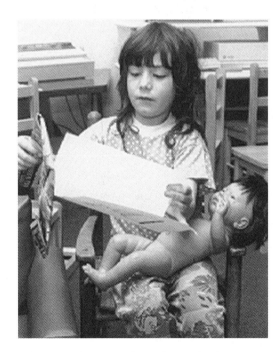

Children explore their relationships with others through pretend play with dolls.

A few months later I acquired another persona doll. We named this doll LaShantell. The LaShantell doll used a walker and was African-American in appearance. I told the children,

"When LaShantell was born, she was very sick. Now that she is older, she uses a walker to help her walk. She is the same age that you are. She lives with her grandmother, two brothers, and a sister. She is the youngest."

More About Persona Dolls

Where can I purchase persona dolls?
—Early childhood teacher

Many early childhood educational supply companies carry a variety of dolls that can be used as persona dolls. Look for dolls with hairstyles, skin coloring, and facial features that resemble children in your classroom. In choosing dolls, keep in mind that because they represent the children in your classroom, they should be treated differently from other dolls used for dramatic play.

One teacher bought commercial dolls and then dressed them in clothes similar to those worn by the children in her classroom. For example, one doll wore a jean jacket, a baseball cap, and tennis shoes. She even cut another doll's hair and dyed it red to match the hair of a child in her class. By the end of the year, the teacher had a doll representing each child in her classroom.

When you are using a persona doll that represents a particular child in your classroom, are there problems when the children recognize that the doll represents that child?
—Preschool teacher

Young children do not mind this. Teachers discover that children find comfort and support in having a doll similar to themselves in the classroom. To illustrate, let's use the example of Craig, a child who has been in the classroom for a month. Craig has just gotten glasses, and the children are making fun of him. Craig's teacher might decide to get a persona doll with glasses and to tell a story about him. On the morning she plans to tell the story, the teacher might say to Craig (showing him the persona doll, Juan, wearing glasses), "Today, I am going to talk to the children about Juan. He is upset that people are making fun of his new glasses. I thought I would ask the children to help me solve this problem, so Juan won't be sad."

Craig might respond to this statement in various ways. For example, he might say that the children are also making fun of him. This would be an opportunity to talk to Craig about his feelings. The teacher could then ask Craig how he would feel if she asked the children what the class could do to make Juan feel better.

Later, as the teacher introduces the Juan doll to the children, a child might make a comment like "Craig wears glasses." The teacher might respond by repeating back and acknowledging the child's statement: "That's right, Craig does wear glasses." The teacher would then continue to listen to and acknowledge what Craig and the other children were saying.

When I asked the children if they had any questions about our new friend, there was much discussion:

"She could fall down and cut herself," Michael said.
"What does she use so she won't fall down?" I asked.
"The blue bag," Dean answered.
I explained, "She uses the blue bag like a backpack to carry things so she won't fall down. She uses this walker to help her walk."

"She has black hair," Erica said.

Then Cindy said, "I want to see her walk."

"When she walks, she picks up the back of the walker and takes a step, while the wheels on the front roll," I explained. "Both young people and older people use this to help them walk," I added. "Do you think that she can run very fast?"

Everyone answered with a loud "No!"

"She has a problem. If someone pushed her, she could fall down," I went on. "What can we tell people to help?"

"Don't shove, hit, or bite her, and don't mess up her hair," Erica answered.

Sharon suggested, "Don't kick or jump in front of her."

"Dean, how does it make you feel if someone pushes you?" I asked.

"It makes me feel sad and mad."

Kelsey joined in: "My brother pushed me down on the bike and made me cry."

Since we introduced the dolls, they've been the focus of many more lively discussions. Our students have really enjoyed having David and LaShantell in our class. They often ask to play with them and to take them along on our field trips. Our teaching team feels that these dolls have been beneficial in dealing with many social and health issues.

Persona dolls are valuable tools for communicating effectively and comfortably with children about many challenging issues.

Ban It, Ignore It, or Join It?
What to Do About Superhero Play

By Beth Marshall

• •

Working with preschoolers—what an interesting, challenging, and constantly changing experience! Because of the dynamic nature of preschool children, teachers are often faced with classroom issues and problems that are neither simple nor clear-cut. In seeking solutions, they often ask, "What does High/Scope say about _____?" You can fill in the blank with any issue you are currently wrestling with in your classroom: what to do when children bring toys from home, whether to involve community volunteers, or how to work with a child who always plays in the block area.

This article deals with a question that makes many teachers and parents uneasy: How do we handle children's superhero play? Drawn from my experiences as both a teacher and a trainer, this article follows the development of my thinking as I used the High/Scope approach to find answers to this question. My purpose here is not only to offer my insights on the superhero issue but also to present an effective *process* for dealing with any classroom issue.

Like many preschool teachers, I can trace my career by naming the superhero characters I've seen children transform themselves into, beginning with the Incredible Hulk and memories of children with glazed expressions and puffed-up chests stomping around the playground. New characters would take the Hulk's place, but children's interest in power-oriented play persisted.

Over the years, I have tried several methods for dealing with this challenging play. First, I tried banning it, telling children they couldn't play that way at school. However, this approach wasn't very satisfying, for me or for the children. It felt like I'd turned into a classroom policeman, constantly on the lookout for superhero characters. Rather than comply with my new rule the children became more deceptive about their superhero pretending, quickly changing roles and props if I came near. Next, I tried ignoring the classroom superheroes, letting children pretend to be those characters if they chose to, but not doing much to support this sort of play. Unfortunately, this didn't work either; I still wasn't comfortable with their actions. As children ran through the classroom and high-kicked other children (we were into Ninja Turtles by now), I wondered what my next move should be.

Fortunately, around this time I started to attend a High/Scope Training of Trainers course. I began the process of re-examining all my teaching practices and beliefs, measuring them against the new concepts I was learning. Although my problems with superhero play didn't magically disappear, at least I now had an educational philosophy to help me make some decisions about what to try next.

One thing I found particularly helpful was the curriculum's framework for creating a supportive social climate. My High/Scope training helped me distinguish between **directive climates,** which are directed and controlled by adults; **laissez-faire climates,** in which children have most of the control; and **supportive climates,** in which adults and children share control (for more information on these three classroom climates, see p. 45). Armed with this new perspective, I recognized that my previous try at banning superhero play fell into the directive-climate category. I also saw that by ignoring this play, I was providing a laissez-faire climate for my classroom superheroes. Since I knew that I wanted to move toward a supportive classroom climate, I decided that my new response should be one of supporting superhero play in constructive ways.

Re-examining Attitudes

Before I could begin to generate support strategies, however, I had to overcome one major obstacle—I still felt uncomfortable about children pretending to be the characters Batman and Robin. I realized that for me to be comfortable with this type of play, which often had themes of violence, I would have to re-examine my attitudes.

As I thought about this, a scene from a video that we had viewed in the High/Scope training played out in my mind. The video was about caring for infants, and I remembered the caregiver stating, "I don't believe that we know what a baby needs better than that baby . . . so I want to learn from that baby." To me, those same sentiments applied to preschool children. I realized I had to respect children's need to play out issues that were important to them (even though I might not choose those play themes myself or even fully understand why they were important to the children).

Contrasting Climates for Children

To deal more effectively with children's superhero play, consider it in the context of the social climate you are currently providing for play in your classroom. Do you take a hands-off attitude toward superhero pretending? Do you support and participate in this play? Do you ban it or attempt to control it? These three approaches to superhero play reflect three social climates that are typical of early childhood programs. Some programs offer a consistent social climate throughout the day, while others use a mixture of these approaches. Below are summaries of the three climates. (The descriptions are taken from the High/Scope preschool manual, Educating Young Children: Active Learning Practices For Preschool and Child Care Programs, *by Mary Hohmann and David P. Weikart, p. 49, Ypsilanti, MI: High/Scope Press, 1995.)*

Laissez-Faire Climate
- Children are in control most of the time, with adults as bystanders who provide supervision.
- Adults intervene to respond to requests, offer information, restore order.
- Curriculum content comes from children's play.

- Adults highly value children's play.
- Adults use various approaches to child management.

Supportive Climate
- Children and adults have control.
- Adults observe children's strengths, form authentic partnerships with children, support children's intentional play.
- Curriculum content comes from children's initiatives and key experiences for child development.
- Adults highly value children's active learning.
- Adults take a problem-solving approach to social conflict.

Directive Climate
- Adults are in control.
- Adults give directions and information.
- Curriculum content comes from learning objectives set by adults.
- Adults highly value drill and practice for children.
- Adults use correction and separation as predominant child management strategies.

So I decided to set aside for the moment my issues with the violent side of superhero play and instead look at its meaning to children. Since this type of play is really just a form of pretend play, I realized I had to do some thinking and research about the development of pretend play in general.

From Imitation to Representation

I was now a graduate student teaching in the High/Scope Demonstration Preschool. In the readings I did for my coursework, I found that Jean Piaget talks about the development of pretend play as a progression that starts with **imitative play** and progresses to **representational play.** Imitative play is often seen in younger children or children trying something new. They imitate or replicate actions that they have observed as a way of interpreting reality and figuring out how and where they fit in. I recognized this kind of imitation in 3-year-old Bryant, whom I had observed imitating the actions of other children as they pretended to go on a car ride. Bryant, a new player, watched carefully as each child got a hollow block, sat on it, and bounced up and down. Soon, he was doing the same thing. A while later, Bryant had grown comfortable with this imitative play. He was now moving to actually "owning" the play and adding different elements to it. "Hey, we need to stop and get some gas," he said, adding, "and I'm gonna stop at Taco Bell,

too." Then he brought back several blocks and passed them out to the other children, saying they were "tacos and pop." At this point, I understood that Bryant had moved into what Piaget calls **representational play.**

Representational play is defined by Piaget as play in which children take their perceptions of reality and fit them into their own inner understanding and needs. In a sense, children are taking images of reality and playing with them. As this happens,

Superhero play doesn't have to be violent.

children's play scenarios become rich and complex; they add all kinds of elements to their pretend play. They use one item to stand for another, talk in voices appropriate to their roles, and elaborate on and extend their original ideas.

This perspective on how pretend play develops over time helped me understand some of the difficulties I'd had with superhero play. I realized that my frustrations stemmed primarily from the imitative nature of much of this play—children mostly ran through the classroom and high-kicked into the air. When I watched several superhero programs as part of my research, I found they were very repetitive. There is a problem with a villain; the superheroes respond with lots of flying, chasing, or fighting; and finally, the superhero wins. Children in my classroom were *imitating* the flying, chasing, and fighting, but were not moving beyond that into the richness of *representational play.* While I really wanted to support them at whatever level they were at, I thought that perhaps children **couldn't** move on, in part because they didn't have *real experiences* to draw from. The only experiences they had were those they saw on television.

I wondered if there were additional materials or experiences I could provide to help children move forward in their play. For ideas, I looked in the chapter on creative representation in High/Scope's preschool manual, *Educating Young Children: Active Learning Practices for Preschool and Child Care Programs,* by Mary Hohmann and David P. Weikart (Ypsilanti, MI: High/Scope Press, 1995). I found the following **general strategies** for supporting pretending to be particularly helpful for my classroom Power Rangers.

General Support Strategies

1. Observe children's play over time. Document your observations of your superheroes to help evaluate what is going on. Watch for actions and details that seem to be important to the children. For example, Jennifer seems to enjoy running. Mark seems to love dressing up in a cape, boots, and long gloves. Next, observe how the play changes or develops over time, if at all. What variety occurs with characters, their actions, the story, or the materials? For example, I noticed that Jack and Raina planned each day to be Batman and Robin, and the resulting play mainly consisted of putting on scarves and darting back and forth across the room. Over time, this play stayed pretty much the same: in other words, it was *imitative* in nature. On the other hand, when Rachel pretended to be a Power Ranger, she made a "hiding spot" under the table and stocked it with pretend food.

2. To encourage more complex play, add related materials. Be flexible in how and where these materials are used. In "'Super-Strategies' for Superheroes" (*Extensions: Newsletter of the High/Scope Curriculum.* [1995, March/April, Ypsilanti, MI: High/Scope Press.]), author Betsy Evans recommends that teachers develop a list of the characteristics of superheroes that children find appealing (she suggests *strength, speed, appearance changes, scary situations,* and *emergencies*). Then teachers list materials that could be added to the classroom that correspond to each characteristic (see sample list at left). When I evaluated my own classroom in terms of Evans's list, I decided to add more materials for *appearance changes* and *scary situations.* I started by adding some long, brightly colored gloves donated by a local bridal shop, and some colorful lengths of fabric that children often used as capes. When I saw children often incorporating the activities of hiding and finding into their play, I added working flashlights to the house area. We also added a cassette recording of the *Jurassic Park* soundtrack that had some eerie-sounding selections. Children often chose this scary music as a backdrop for their play. Other teachers have found that children use the materials they have provided (such as masks, paper towel rolls, and tin foil) to make their own superhero costumes and props as they begin to focus on the details of the characters. This tends to slow down the play, and children move more carefully. As a result, rougher play diminishes. In addition, the ensuing superhero play is more complex, lasts longer, and involves more conversation among the children.

3. Enter children's superhero play as a co-player, just as you would with any other type of play. This allows you to experience this play through the eyes of a child, rather than as an adult looking on. When I tried this with my superhero preschoolers, I found that their play *was not as wild and violent as it looked* when I observed it from the outside. When co-playing with children, remember these three important guidelines: **Imitate the child's actions at first, take your cues from the child about how to play,** and finally, **make sure the child retains control of the play.** For example, as a way of entering children's play, I tied a scarf around my neck and imitated their actions of "flying" through the classroom. As we "flew," I watched and listened to children and tried to make the same sounds they were making. It was important for me to remember to follow and respect what the children were doing. Once they were comfortable with me as a co-player, I could try the next strategy.

4. Add to the complexity of play by offering ideas for extensions. If you find that children's superhero play is very imitative,

Observe your superheroes at play to help evaluate what's going on. Watch to see if the play develops over time.

Add to the complexity of children's play by offering ideas for extensions. Remember to respect children's responses to your ideas.

you may want to try extending it. Staying within your role as a player, try **posing a problem to extend children's thinking.** When I was the "bad guy," I kept escaping from jail. James ("Batman") had to do some problem solving about how to keep me in there. He decided to make some paper hand-cuffs he called "bat cuffs." Now, in addition to pretending, he was cutting paper strips, taping them around my wrists, and figuring out how to make the cuffs the right size (so I couldn't escape again). You can also **make a comment that extends children's ideas.** At one of the rare times I was allowed to pretend to be Batgirl, I yawned and said to my co-players, "I'm rather sleepy." They jumped on the idea and told me it was nighttime and we all had to go to bed. Where do Batman, Robin, and Batgirl sleep? Why, in the Bat Cave, of course! By now we were making a bat cave out of large hollow blocks and stocking it with pillows, blankets, and food. Once children had this new idea, their play spiraled in all kinds of directions.

When making suggestions for play extensions, remember to **respect children's responses to your ideas.** One time, children were running down the hill outside, and I ran with them for a while. When I asked where our bat cave was (thinking perhaps we might construct one outdoors), I was told, "Beth, we're just running and flying now." Remembering that children should retain the control of their play, I went right back to running and fly-ing with them.

5. Add to the children's store of related real-life experiences by planning field trips and inviting visitors to the classroom. Although there are no superheroes in real life, there are field trips or visitors that might build on the interests children are expressing through this kind of play. Decide what seems to be most interesting to your children, and then look around your community for inspiration. If your children seem to be

Not Comfortable Supporting Superhero Play?

It is important to examine your own beliefs about this type of play for children. Perhaps you have already made a commitment to support children's interests (an important first step), but you are just not comfortable playing along with children in this type of play because it feels too much like condoning it. You may want to look at what children are doing in your classroom and see if there are any elements of their superhero play that you **would** be comfortable participating in. For example, you may decide that you are comfortable with dressing up like a superhero and "flying," but are **not** comfortable with pretending to shoot. With your co-teacher, generate strategies for handling situations in which children play in ways that make you feel uncomfortable. It is fine to give children genuine feedback on what **you** feel comfortable doing. Remember to use "I" statements when explaining this to children. You might decide to say something like "I don't want to shoot him because I don't like to use guns or fight. I don't like to hurt people and I don't like to get hurt myself. Is there another way I could help you catch the bad guy?" This type of feedback is simply an honest statement of how **you** feel. You are not placing a value judgment on the child's play; thus, you are still supporting his or her choice of play theme. You may find that children are initially curious about your decision not to participate in certain kinds of activities, and that they are quite willing to help you find something else to do so you can still participate. They might even become quite involved in these new ideas themselves!

interested in the rescuing aspect of superhero play, invite an emergency medical technician to visit your classroom or arrange for a field trip to the local fire station. If you think it's the changes in appearance that interest children most, arrange a visit to the local community theater and look at their costume collection. In one setting, children were involved in imitating the kick-fighting of television characters, and their play was often rough and disruptive. The situation improved, however, when a child in the class who had been taking karate lessons became a resource for the other children. This child would often tell the others that they were only supposed to fight to defend themselves, not to hurt others. He would occasionally demonstrate karate movements; later, his family members were invited to the classroom to do the same. As the other children learned about the appropriate uses of karate and practiced some of the specific movements, their play became more focused and less disruptive.

I found that as I used these five strategies, I became comfortable with superhero play in my setting. I realized that it made sense to approach children's play with power characters just as I would any other form of pretending. What would I do if a child were pretending to drive to Georgia, to be a

It makes sense to approach children's play with power characters just as we would any other form of pretending—by supporting and encouraging the play, regardless of its theme.

kitty, to feed a baby, or to be Batman? My response would be the same: to support and encourage the play, regardless of its theme. As I became more relaxed with superhero play and allowed it to grow and develop, I could see its richness and complexity.

Although I am not teaching in our classroom at present, superhero play is still an issue I'm dealing with. As I conduct training sessions for other teachers, I find it to be a popular topic. In working with teachers concerned about this or any other classroom issue, I recommend the *general process* described in this article. First, define your particular concern. Then take a step back and look at your issue from a broader perspective. Next, delve into the High/Scope approach. How does the approach guide us in general? Are there pertinent High/Scope books, articles, or videos that you can consult? What about your own personal belief system? What strategies are you willing to try in your classroom? When and how will you re-evaluate the situation with your team members? Using this process with your team members will help you develop useful strategies for dealing with any classroom issue.

Supporting Children's Interests "Moment to Moment"

By Michelle Graves

. . . .

Teachers who plan around children's interests (instead of around weekly themes like dinosaurs, spring, colors, or numbers) often wonder how to interact with children to support the interests they are expressing through their play. In the High/Scope approach, teachers use a variety of **interaction strategies** to encourage children to expand on their play interests. These are on-the-spot communication techniques that teachers use to respond to what children are doing from moment to moment. Here are some suggestions for making the most of such interactions:

• **With your team member, begin by examining your own interests, preferences, and attitudes about working with children during different kinds of play.** For example, in one classroom where some children were pretending to be dogs and planning a pet show, teachers Laila and Sue discussed some of their attitudes about different kinds of play during their team planning session. Laila said she felt quite comfortable crawling on the floor and imitating animals with the children, while Sue was less comfortable with this kind of play and preferred to interact with the children who were making the prize ribbons with various art materials. Thus, when the pet-show play arose several days later, Laila assumed the role of a dog, barking and howling with the other "dogs" while Sue sat and worked side by side with children as they made their prize ribbons. Though Laila and Sue often assumed these respective roles while working with the children, each teacher also gradually learned new interaction techniques by watching her teammate's enthusiastic and skilled support of a particular kind of play.

• **Wait until children invite you to be a part of their play.** Start by simply observing a child at play. **If you wish to join the child, try playing alongside, imitating the child's actions.** This simple technique sends children the message that their play has value and opens the door for children to invite you into their play when the time seems right to them. Consider the example of Rachel, a child who often enjoyed acting out part of the movie *Home Alone* by winding string around classroom structures. To support Rachel's actions, her teachers took turns working next to her, winding string around other nearby objects. Often the only verbal interactions that occurred were simple requests from Rachel, such as "Pass me the scissors"; sometimes, however, Rachel would suggest to the teacher, "Let's make a big trap together."

• **Talk to children in ways that relate to their chosen activity, waiting until there is a natural opening before jumping in and beginning a conversation.** Rather than ask questions, make a specific comment or observation about the child's work. This will communicate your interest in the child's ideas without pressuring for a response. For example, in the classroom where children were playing "dogs," Alex announced his idea for a dog show and came back to the block area with art supplies to complete his plan. His teacher said, "Alex, I heard you say you wanted to have a dog show, and now I see you carrying a lot of art materials."

• **Don't jump to conclusions about the nature of children's play. Instead, encourage children to clarify their ideas.** Then listen carefully, acknowledging what they say. In this way, you'll **avoid taking the play in a new direction not intended by the child.** When Rachel asked for her teacher's help in making a crib mobile for her brother, her teacher simply asked, "A mobile, you want to make a mobile?" The teacher then paused for a moment, waiting for more information about Rachel's understanding of what she needed. This encouraged Rachel to explain, "Yeah, that stuff that hangs over his head."

• **Encourage children to discover ways to find their own solutions to the problems that will naturally occur as they pursue their ideas.** Rachel's teacher saw that Rachel had created all the hanging pieces for her mobile and had attached strings to them, but needed to hang them on something. Instead of taking over by instructing Rachel in the next step, she elicited Rachel's explanation of what she meant by a mobile ("that stuff that hangs over his head"). As a way of encouraging Rachel to think further about the problem, Rachel's teacher then commented, "So, you need to hang these things from something?" "Yes," Rachel answered, "you find it." The teacher then suggested that they look through the room together to find something that might work, and Rachel eventually decided to tie her creations to a paper towel tube.

• Rather than praise children ("Oh, what beautiful ribbons—you did a good job"), make a specific, nonjudgmental comment on a child's effort ("You worked a long time on making the ribbons"). Comments like these convey your support for children's efforts; at the same time, they encourage children to evaluate their own work rather than rely on the adult to judge its value.

§

In her article "Planning Around Children's Interests" (p. 349), Michelle Graves provides an outline for incorporating children's interests into every aspect of the preschool day.

If children invite you to be a part of their play, play alongside them and imitate their actions.

Chapter Two

Materials and Environments for Active Learners

· ·

*H*igh/Scope educators are guided by the belief that young children learn best when they interact directly with people, materials, events, and ideas. As they engage in and reflect on these direct experiences, children build knowledge and make sense of the world around them. This process of action and reflection is called **active learning.** Active learning is central to the High/Scope approach to learning. The space and materials in a High/ Scope environment are carefully selected and arranged to promote active learning. The center is divided into "interest areas" organized around spe- cific kinds of play, and materials in each area are organized so children can get them out easily and put them away independently. The articles in this chapter focus on how materials and environment support the active learning process for children.

In the first article, "Materials and Space for Drawing and Painting," Mary Hohmann discusses how to equip and arrange an art area that pro-

vides children with enough space and accessible materials—paints, brushes, paper, work surfaces, and other art materials—to support a wide variety of two- and three-dimensional drawing and painting experiences.

In the next article, "'My Way'—Children at the Computer Area," Beth Marshall discusses some of the concerns teachers have about the use of computers in the preschool setting. Do they provide too "programmed" an approach to learning? Does too much time in the computer area deprive preschoolers of social experiences with their classmates? Based on a series of observations she made and anecdotes she recorded about how preschoolers actually use software, Marshall concludes that computers can support children's initiatives and choices if the right software is chosen. Throughout the article, Marshall provides strategies for supporting children's learning in the computer area.

In the next selection, "Materials for Infants and Toddlers," Jackie Post and Mary Hohmann review how to create a learning setting that supports the ingredients of active learning (manipulation, choice, communication and language from children, and adult support) by making use of the abundance of everyday materials that support infants' and toddlers' sensory-motor approach to active learning.

The last two articles in this chapter highlight gardening as an enriching way to support an active learning environment for children. In "How Does Your Garden Grow?" you will learn how teachers at the High/Scope Demonstration Preschool helped children plant a garden and the important lesson the children gained from this endeavor—respect for nature. In "A Garden Journal," Linda Clegg Hawkins, Director of Clervaux Nursery (an early childhood learning center affiliated with High/Scope UK) in South Tyneside, England, shares with us seasonal journal entries she made as her teaching team (with the help of children, parents, and other volunteers from the community) created an outdoor classroom for their center.

Materials and Space for Drawing and Painting

By Mary Hohmann

• •

In a High/Scope early childhood setting, the art area is arranged and equipped to provide children with enough space and accessible materials to support a wide variety of two- and three-dimensional art experiences. Children use the art area during work time to explore and create with art materials. They also use it as a supply depot for work time activities in other areas—for example, they may get paper and markers to make signs for buildings they are constructing in the block area. Adults and children use supplies from the art area at other times of the day, too, including recall time and small-group time.

In the following section, specific art area materials and work surfaces that are particularly supportive of children's **drawing and painting** are described.

Paints. A basic stock of paint includes tempera or poster paint that is smooth, workable, and thick—"the consistency of heavy cream," Nancy Smith (Smith et al., 1993, 20) advises. Novice painters have more control when working with thick paint, and it is less likely to drip when children paint at an easel. In addition, thick paint can be used for finger painting as well as for brush painting. For more experienced painters, thick paint can be easily thinned by adding water. Keep the art area stocked with paints in the primary colors—red, yellow, and blue. As children begin to mix these colors they will discover how to make the secondary colors— orange, green, and violet. Children will also need

Keep the art area stocked with paints in primary colors as well as with sturdy brushes in a variety of widths.

white, black, and brown paints. As they become familiar with poster or tempera paints, consider adding watercolors and watercolor paper, which allow them to create different painting effects.

Young children need low, sturdy, spill-resistant paint containers that will stay firmly in place as they dip their brushes in and out. Plastic containers that sit firmly in the easel tray can be purchased from a hardware or variety store. For children working at tables or on the floor, fit shallow cups or containers inside a plastic box, use muffin tins, or cut holes into the top of a sturdy box and fit small, empty yogurt containers into the holes. It is important to have enough of these containers in holders to allow individual children and groups of children easy access to the paints. Also, maintain a supply of paper plates or small metal trays for finger paints. These kinds of wide, shallow containers enable children to dip their whole palms and all their fingers into the paint.

Brushes. Stock the art area with sturdy brushes in a variety of widths. With enough brushes, young painters can use a different brush for each color; this prevents the colors from becoming muddy. More experienced painters can learn to dip and wash their brushes in clean water when using the same brush for more than one color of paint. If you are using this system, it is helpful to provide each child with a sponge for wiping off the brush after rinsing. According to Smith, the sponge "is very effective in reminding the children to wipe the brush and [it] also absorbs the remaining water" (Smith et al. 1993, 21). Artists' brushes, available from any art supply catalog, have paint-holding bristles that make them the best choice for young painters. However, since such brushes are expensive, you can supplement them with less expensive and thicker 2-inch and 3-inch household paintbrushes that are available at discount or hardware stores. Just be aware that the softer and fuller the bristles, the more satisfactory they are for conveying paint from container to painting surface.

In addition to brushes, provide more experienced painters with nontraditional painting tools, such as combs, toothbrushes, sticks, and feathers. Children will enjoy the kinds of lines and effects they can create when they apply paint with these tools.

Markers, crayons, chalk, and oil pastels. If possible, provide children with all of these media, each of which creates different effects and provides different drawing experiences. **Colored felt-tipped markers** enable children to apply color smoothly without applying much pressure. **Crayons** respond to differences in pressure and enable children to create a wide variety of effects and express a broad range of emotions and ideas. When using

What About Art on the Computer?

Computer drawing and painting programs make it easy for children to create "perfect" shapes, lines, fill patterns, and color blends. Do these "gain-without-pain" features impair or enhance the development of children's drawing and painting abilities?

With artwork as with language, tools that allow children to focus their energy on **communication** help to encourage the overall process of self-expression more than they promote specific skills and techniques. In this sense, computer drawing and painting tools can enable children to use artistic expression in accomplishing everyday communication tasks. In addition, while it may be relatively easy to use a computer to create and manipulate lines, shapes, colors, and fill patterns, it takes practice to create a pleasing composition with these elements. The child still has to work at the sense of balance and composition that makes an artistic product.

What features should I look for in computer programs for drawing and painting?

Nearly all of the drawing and painting programs available for children are open-ended, providing a wide range of drawing and painting tools. Look for large icons that make it easy for young children to select and use colors and drawing tools. Stamps and stickers (icons for pre-drawn items that children can click on and use) should be clearly visible on the drawing screen. Also look for a slide show component that will display children's completed artwork on the computer screen. Nearly all drawing and painting programs include output to the printer. To make the most of drawing and painting software, we recommend you invest in one of the newer, relatively inexpensive color printers, which provide printed output of stunning quality.

The stamps, stickers, and other clip-art features available in many programs offer children the option of inserting pre-made drawings and animated figures into their artwork. Does this prevent children from developing their own skills in drawing and painting?

Children's use of the pre-made pictures in drawing and painting programs is not a replacement for experiences in creating original drawings with pencils, charcoal, brushes, pastels, paints, and other artistic media. Yet working with the pre-made images provided in computer programs offers children **another kind of artistic experience.** Children often use computers as **image processors,** that is, as tools for integrating illustrations from a variety of sources into their own creative projects. Some computer programs make it easy for grade-school children to incorporate computer-made graphics, scans of photos and drawings, and so forth, into their presentations. Learning to appreciate and use artwork for such aesthetic and communicative purposes is a valuable art lesson in itself.

Children in High/Scope settings have enough space and accessible materials to support a wide variety of drawing and painting experiences.

chalk, children can easily blend colors. **Oil pastels** also blend well, respond to varied pressures, and enable children to apply rich, intense colors to their artistic creations.

Paper. A paper supply for painting and drawing begins with a large roll of white butcher or craft paper that can be torn or cut into whatever lengths are needed. This paper is wide enough to provide novice painters and drawers with the large surface they need for their whole-arm motions. Once you have an ample supply of white butcher paper or craft paper, add wide rolls of red, yellow, or blue craft paper. The effects provided by the more saturated colors and smoother surfaces of this paper are different from those allowed by the rougher surfaces, and muddier colors, of construction paper. Colored cellophane also presents a unique painting surface that produces surprising effects. Children also enjoy experimenting with the textures and effects of inexpensive drawing surfaces such as newspaper, paper bags, cardboard, paper tubes, and boxes.

Work surfaces. Easels allow children to paint on a fairly vertical surface. Side-by-side easels allow children to paint together as well as to observe and get ideas from their peers. Many children feel more in control of their efforts, however, when they can paint on a horizontal surface, such as a table or the floor. For painting and drawing experiences at small-group time, it may be necessary to move shelves and tables to make room for children to paint on the floor. Another option is to plan painting and drawing experiences for the outdoors, where children can spread out large sheets of paper or put their paper on boards they can hold themselves.

These ideas for tools, paper, and work space are just a few things to consider as you plan your art area to encourage young children to draw and paint. As you carefully observe children's painting and drawing activities, you will come up with many other ideas that are geared specifically to your group of children.

REFERENCE

Smith, N., Fucigna, C., Kennedy, M., & Lord, L. (1993). *Experience and art: Teaching children to paint* (2nd ed.). New York: Teachers College Press.

"My Way"—Children at the Computer Area

By Beth Marshall

• •

Although computers have become quite common in early childhood classrooms and centers, educators continue to have questions and concerns about their impact on young children's learning and development. Teachers and administrators who believe in an active learning approach may wonder whether computers primarily provide a "programmed" approach to learning. They may ask how computer programs can possibly provide opportunities for child initiation and control like those offered by traditional preschool materials, such as blocks, art materials, dress-up clothes, and props for pretend play.

Two friends share a thoughtful moment as they try out a computer program for the first time.

Another common concern is that computer activities may be *too* appealing to children. Having observed the almost addictive appeal of video games and other electronic toys, many teachers fear that computers will tempt children away from books, block play, pretend play, and explorations with clay, sand, paints, and crayons—activities considered necessary to a well-rounded preschool experience. Another worry is that too much time in the computer area will deprive preschoolers of social experiences with their classmates.

These and other concerns were on my mind as I began a series of observations of how young children actually use computers in active learning settings. The observations were conducted over a 3-year period in the High/Scope Demonstration Preschool and at four preschool sites participating in High/Scope's IBM Technology Demonstration Partnership Project. To document these observations, I collected numerous anecdotes—brief descriptions of what children said and did in the computer area on a given day. The anecdotes provide a wealth of information about both the interests and the abilities of individual children, as well as general issues surrounding the use of computers by young children.

The anecdotes provide vivid evidence that **children often use computers to express their intentions, preferences, and interests.** Because computers support children's initiatives and choices so effectively, we can rest assured that **computers do have a place in active learning classrooms.**

This article provides a representative sampling of these anecdotes, along with a discussion of the insights they reveal about the uses of computers in active learning programs. The anecdotes are grouped according to key trends we've noticed in children's computer use. With each set of anecdotes, related strategies are included for supporting children's learning in the computer area.

Children's Initiative With Computers

Sept. 16: At planning, Stone said he was going to work on the computers. He spent most of work time figuring out how to help the lion cub in the Zurk's Learning Safari *program (Soleil Software) find her way home by getting help from the various animals on the screen.*

Oct. 23: At planning, Asia and Cirra decided to work on the computers together. They went over to the computers, turned them on, and clicked on the picture menu to select the drawing program KidPix *(Broderbund Software). Then they worked together to make a picture using the whale stamps. When it was finished, they printed it out.*

Feb. 18: At work time in the computer area, Adam and Lizzie were using the program Thinkin'Things *(Edmark). Adam said to Lizzie, "Hey, want to see something funny? Watch these chickens." Then he showed her how to turn the xylophone on the screen into chickens that clucked at different pitches when he touched them.*

Wait to see how children are using a program, then make comments that refer to children's actions and ideas.

Mar. 11: At work time, after watching Lizzie and Adam work together on the computer for several days, Kevin joined them and used the computer for the first time.

Besides illustrating children's initiatives in the computer area, the preceding anecdotes also suggest the wide variations we can expect in the ways in which children use computers. And, as is true of most active learning materials, at any given time some children will have a strong interest in computers while others will have no interest at all.

Children have many different purposes in mind as they use computers. Some children, like Stone, are drawn to computers right from the start of the school year and may spend a good deal of time working on them. For such children, computers seem to offer a nice transition into the preschool setting. They find the computer area to be a comfortable place—a good place for playing alone or perhaps gradually easing into interactions with other children.

Stone, for example, enjoyed helping other children latch and unlatch the keyboard tray on the computer stand. Eventually he began to converse with children as they arrived to use the computers, and he would sometimes work at a computer with one or more of the other children. Still later, he began to spend work time in other parts of the room, often playing and interacting with classmates.

Computer Conflicts

High/Scope recommends that we don't regulate children's use of computers with turn charts or sign-up sheets. But we find that children are having a lot of conflicts about getting a turn at our classroom computers (we have two). What should we do?
—*A Head Start teacher*

You are wise not to use sign-up sheets or turn charts in your computer area, just as you wouldn't ask children to sign up to use the easel or water table. As with any other item in the classroom, we try to let children's own interests and choices determine how materials should be used. If you are encountering conflicts about using the computer, here are several things to consider. First, look at your computer area to see if your equipment is arranged to **promote social experiences** (see p. 73). Are you inadvertently encouraging solitary use of the computers by having only one chair at each computer, or are there several chairs by each? Second, remember to treat conflicts about computer use as you would

any other problem in your classroom—**use the six-step problem-solving approach (see p. 13) to help children negotiate their own turns.** During problem solving, children often decide to work together: "You pick the heads, and I'll pick the bodies, okay?" "I get to finish this mouse game, and then you can do the next one." Sometimes, children decide to resolve a conflict by leaving the computer and going to play somewhere else. When children really want to work alone at a computer, we have found that sand timers often help them agree on an acceptable time interval for turns. We have made several different-sized sand timers available in an area adjacent to our computer area, and children often use them to negotiate turns: "Okay, three flips of the big sand timer and then I get to try that game." Again, the strategies that we use here are no different than the ones we would use with children negotiating turns on the swings, with the cooking pot, or with any other classroom material.

Other children, like Kevin, may not be interested in the computers at the beginning of the year. Kevin preferred instead the materials he found in the art and block areas. Not until halfway through the school year did he "discover" the computers and try them out for himself.

Like the materials in other areas of the classroom, computers are most rewarding for children when they are free to use them in their own ways. Yet adults often feel uncomfortable giving children the same free access to computers that they have to other classroom materials. They may feel that some children are using computers too much, and others not enough, or that the program's investment in expensive computer equipment isn't justified unless each child gets his or her fair share of computer time. As a result, they may feel the need to regulate children's use of computers with sign-up sheets or turn charts, forgetting that

The ways children use computers are just as unique as their ways of using other kinds of materials.

children get the most out of computers (or any other classroom material) when they choose to use them in ways that are personally meaningful.

Should a teacher be concerned about a child like Stone, who has a strong interest in computers? At the beginning of the year, even though Stone spent most work times playing alone in the computer area, his teachers wisely realized that work time was only one part of Stone's day. Stone had many contacts with his classmates during planning, recall, small- and large-group times, and outdoors. Small-group time offered him experiences with a variety of other classroom materials: paints, plastic construction toys (such as LEGO®), puppets, play dough, musical instruments, and so forth. Stone's teachers concluded that he was getting a well-rounded preschool experience. They also knew that as Stone became more comfortable in the classroom his interests would probably expand to include other children and other materials. Likewise, the teachers accepted Kevin's lack of interest in the computers until the time was right for *him.* The actions of these teachers highlight an important support strategy: to make the most of computers as an active learning tool, we need to **accept children's choices of when and how to use them.**

Interacting With Software: Child Control

Feb. 18: At work time in the computer area, Donald and Steven played the "Mousehole Game" from the software program The Playroom *(Broderbund Software). When it was his turn, Donald deliberately chose game-losing strategies, for example, always picking the lower-numbered dice or choosing the dice that would send his player, the mouse, backwards. At the end of the game, Donald said "Yes!" when his character, the mouse, lost. When I commented that it looked like he wanted the other character, the robot, to win, he said, "Yes, we hate the mouse to win—the robot does the cooler dance."*

Nov. 4: At work time in the computer area, Asia and Cirra were using the program Millie's Math House *(Edmark). They consistently matched the smallest character with the largest shoes, each time giggling and laughing at how funny the small character looked wearing large shoes or boots.*

Jan. 29: At work time, on the "Fribbles" screen of the Thinkin' Things *program (Edmark), Carleen consistently chose the Fribble with the characteristics that the game was NOT asking for. When the only Fribble left was the "correct" choice, she said, "Nope, you can't have him. He's mine." Then she replayed the game the same way, again keeping the desired Fribble until last.*

In choosing materials for High/Scope active learning classrooms, an important guideline is to **seek materials that allow children to control results and outcomes.** This principle is behind our recommendation that adults choose materials that can be used in a variety of ways, rather than materials like worksheets that lock children into one activity.

Because many computer programs have a game or activity format that points children toward certain desired responses, some educators worry that these materials are not compatible with an active learning approach. However, observations like the preceding illustrate that good computer programs give children plenty of latitude to manipulate results and outcomes. Even if a game is designed to be played a certain way, children can be ingenious in devising their own ways to play.

To support this process of invention, adults in active learning settings should keep in mind that **children will use software in unique ways that make sense to them.** Choosing to be the loser in a game so you can see the "coolest dance" makes perfect sense to a child (even though the teacher or software designer might not see this as a logical move). Similarly, choosing the "wrong-sized" shoe does not mean the child doesn't understand the concepts of *small, middle-size,* and *big.* In this instance, it means that the children are expressing *their* choice of how they want the characters to look—they don't feel obligated to follow the formula set out by the software designers.

Instead of telling a child how to use a program, invite the child to explain what he or she is doing.

As Children Use Computers: Support Strategies

Here are some interaction strategies for supporting children in the computer area. Use them as children are learning a new program or whenever children are working at the computers.

- **Observe what children are doing with the software.** How are they using it? What are they saying to each other while they work?

- **Look for natural opportunities to converse with children.** Be aware that they probably aren't going to want to hold long conversations with you. Any conversation they do make will most likely center on what they are doing or want to do with the program.

- **Make a simple comment that acknowledges a child's actions with the software** ("You're making the chicken cluck"). This is a nonintrusive way to invite children to talk with you about what they are doing. Be sensitive to children who are focused on their work and are not ready to talk to you.

- **Resist the impulse to show a child the "right" way to use a program.** Instead, observe and make comments that invite the child to show you how he is using the program and why: "Jason, I see you keep clicking on the castle over and over."

- **If a problem arises, make comments that encourage problem solving:** "So you want to get rid of the whale stamps, and the paintbrush doesn't seem to work? What else looks like something you could use as an eraser?" **Or you could refer the child to another child for help:** "I just saw Kevin erase some things on his picture. Maybe he could show you how he did it."

As adults, how can we both support and learn more about children's unique ways of using software? First, **choose good software that will allow children to have control over the program.** Remember, in a good software program, there should be many choices for a child to make and more than one way to use the software. Then, **become very familiar with the software yourself.** Sit down and play with it after the children leave. Explore it as a child would. Do things the "wrong way" and see what happens. If this is difficult for you, invite children to play with you, watch what they do and then try it yourself.

It's also important to use nondirective support strategies when you are working with children at the computers. **Resist the urge to show children the "right" way to use a program.** Instead, comment on what you see happening on the screen ("Erica, I see your person is going backwards") and wait to find out what the child thinks she is doing and why she is doing it that way. **Use a problem-solving approach to work through any difficulties encountered on the computer:** "You want to make big dots in a lot of different colors, but they are all the same color. Where else might you try clicking?" You can also **refer one child to another for help:** "I saw Stone

Placing computers side by side so children can look from one screen to another will allow them to talk with each other and work together.

printing out a picture yesterday; maybe he knows how to get the printer to work." Remember, it often makes no difference to young children what an adult might see as the "point" of a computer program. Children want to make their own "point" by making the software do the things that make sense to them.

Computer-Area Social Experiences

Mar. 12: At work time in the computer area, Daniel and Carleen were working together, trying to find the hidden treasures in the "Sandbox Treasure Game" from The Backyard *program (Broderbund). Jack, another child who was in the nearby house area, heard their struggles and joined them. Jack explained to Daniel and Carleen how to find the treasure. "You see the digger by the cup? You have to find the cup on the map, and go over here (he pointed to the X on the map) and then dig." They all worked together for 20 minutes.*

Jan. 21: At work time in the computer area, Kelly and Leah worked together constructing a city scene using The Playroom *program (Broderbund). As they worked, they conversed about things they saw around their own neighborhoods.*

July 15: At work time in the computer area, Cirra sat at the computer next to Adrianna and watched her. Then she chose the same program Adrianna was using and used it in the same way.

Adults are often fearful that children will not interact with other children while they are using the computer. However, we have not observed this happening, either in our own classroom or in other classrooms throughout the country. When it comes to social play, we find the computer area is

Software for Toddlers— Too Much, Too Soon?

Recent findings from brain research have increased our awareness of the toddler period's importance to learning and development. One result of these findings has been the release of computer software designed specifically for children aged 3 years and under. Though we've been supportive of computer use for children of preschool age, we wonder whether computers are appropriate for *toddlers*.

Interactive computer use doesn't make sense until children can grasp a cause-and-effect relationship between moving or clicking the mouse and the events that take place on the computer screen. Typically, children can move the mouse pointer to an on-screen target and click on it successfully by late toddlerhood (that is, between the ages of 2 and 3 years). Most younger toddlers are capable of operating programs that require mouse movement only. These younger toddlers can readily appreciate the animation, color changes, and noises that result as they move the mouse, much as they might enjoy the effects created by manipulating the buttons, wheels, and levers of a busy box.

But what about the *content* of computer activities for toddlers? Even a bargain-basement computer priced at under $1,000 is an expensive (and delicate) toy for a toddler. In programs or families where toddlers will be sharing a computer intended mainly for older children or adults, program staff and parents might want to consider purchasing some toddler-oriented software. To evaluate the appropriateness and quality of software designed for toddlers, let's look at some typical features of these programs.

- **Many of the programs focus on letters, numbers, and shapes.** Though there's nothing harmful in these activities, this is not what toddlers are really about. We'd be discouraged to see toddlers and their caregivers focusing their time and energies on this type of pre-academic content.

- **Many programs use music**, either for its own sake or to accompany the activities. There are sing-alongs and animated activities accompanied by music. In some of these programs, though, the musical content isn't much different from a music box or a cartoon with a musical soundtrack.

- **Peekaboo games** are another theme shared by many software programs for very young children. Unless an adult is present to enliven the game, however, these computer versions of peekaboo pale compared to the real thing.

- **Creative art activities** are popular in programs designed for toddlers. Some allow children to use stickers, paintbrushes, and other tools to draw and paint. Others employ a coloring-book-style activity that is too simple even for toddlers.

For content other than mouse training, toddler software may hardly be worth the investment, though it can provide some appropriate activities for toddlers and slightly older children who are using computers together. Perhaps the one clear contribution of much of the toddler software is that it provides some computer activities that really are appropriate and fun for early preschoolers.

no different from other areas of the classroom. The above examples illustrate that children's experiences at the computer range from being solitary to highly social. Sometimes children work alone at computers, sometimes they play in parallel, and sometimes they work together with several children sharing one computer. Many children use the computer area as just another place to spend time with friends. They could just as easily be in the block area, using the dress-up clothes, or at the water table. Computer use often spurs conversation among children, much as the city scene did with Leah and Kelly. Children's social interactions at the computer area also often encourage learning and problem solving. A child like Jack may have mastered a particular program and can serve as a natural "expert" in helping other children who encounter problems.

Here are some things that adults can do to facilitate children's social experiences in the computer area. First, **if you have more than one computer, place them side by side** so children can look from one screen to another to both see and talk with the children at the other machines. Second, to avoid setting the expectation of only one child per computer, **place several chairs in front of each computer.** Finally, **place the computer area near another active area,** such as the block area; don't isolate it from the rest of the action in the classroom. One year in our classroom, the computer area was next to our very active house area. Often children in the house area would stop by the computer area just to chat or to check out what was happening there.

§

The preceding anecdotes illustrate that children's ways of using computers are just as unique as their ways of using other kinds of materials. We can conclude that computers in High/Scope settings should be treated like any other material that invites children's choices, initiatives, and social experiences. Resist the temptation to treat the computer as a "special" material that requires special rules and teaching strategies, and instead encourage children to "do it their way" in the computer area.

Materials for Infants and Toddlers

By Jacalyn Post and Mary Hohmann

• •

Infants and toddlers, active learners from birth, use all their **senses** and the **actions of their bodies** to construct an understanding of the world in which they find themselves. They make discoveries about themselves and their immediate environment by watching their hands, turning over, kicking, reaching out, grasping, banging, poking, smelling, looking, listening, touching, and tasting. This combination of **sensory experience** and **physical action** is so characteristic of the ways in which infants and toddlers relate to their world that developmental psychologist Jean Piaget (1952, 1966) used the term *sensory-motor* to describe this period in children's lives.

Adults working in infant and toddler programs look for ways to lovingly and creatively support these very young children as they explore materials with their whole bodies and all their senses. To ensure an environment in which infants and toddlers can flourish as active learners, caregivers give thoughtful, ongoing attention to the **ingredients of active learning** (Post & Hohmann, 2000):

• **Materials**—Abundant, age-appropriate materials exist for infants and children to use in a variety of ways. Learning grows out of the child's direct actions on these materials.

• **Manipulation**—The child has opportunities (using his or her *whole body* and all the *senses*) to explore, manipulate, combine, and transform the chosen materials.

• **Choice**—The child chooses what to do. Since learning results from the child's attempts to pursue personal interests and goals, the opportunity to choose activities and materials is essential.

• **Communication and language from children**—The child communicates his or her needs, feelings, discoveries, and ideas through motions, gestures, facial expressions, sounds, and words. Adults attend to and encourage the child's communications and language in a give-and-take manner.

• **Adult support**—Adults strive to establish and maintain trusting relationships with each child in their care. Adults recognize and encourage each child's intentions, actions, communications, explorations, problem solving, and creativity.

Keeping these ingredients of active learning in mind, infant and toddler caregivers can create a learning setting that meets the changing needs of their children and supports and stimulates children as they explore their world, the nature of its inhabitants, and the properties of its objects.

This article examines how infant and toddler caregivers think about and provide one particular active learning ingredient—**materials** that support infants' and toddlers' **sensory-motor approach to active learning.**

Guidelines for Providing Materials for Infants and Toddlers

In active learning programs:

• **Materials for infants and toddlers are** *varied* **and** *plentiful.* Offering a variety of materials supports infants' and toddlers' natural curiosity and their ongoing need for objects on which to try out their emerging skills. For example, for very young children a grapefruit or bright yellow ball can provide interesting opportunities for looking, reaching, grasping, mouthing, rolling, finding, banging, and carrying. Some **everyday kinds of materials** that appeal to infants and toddlers and spur their active learning explorations are *household objects; natural and found materials; soft, cuddly materials; easy-to-handle materials; squishy, messy materials; materials that children can set in motion; materials children can climb on and use to pull themselves up; and materials children can use to make noise.* (These kinds of materials will be discussed in more detail later in this article.) In addition to providing a *varied range* of materials for infants and toddlers, caregivers also ensure that supplies of materials are *plentiful*—that is, there should be many similar materials, as well as duplicates of some objects. Having an abundance of materials is important because infants and toddlers live in the present. What they see is often what they want *at that moment.* The concept of sharing and taking turns with an attractive, much-prized object means nothing to them. Moreover, having a plentiful supply of materials allows adults to remove batches of playthings for routine cleaning and maintenance.

• **Children explore and play with materials in a variety of ways.** Infants and toddlers use materials in many different ways, sometimes in ways adults expect (when Devawn wakes up and coos to the teddy bear he sees in the corner of his crib) and sometimes in ways that surprise them (when Ada crawls from the rocking chair to the window carrying her teddy bear in her mouth, sits in front of the window, and bangs her bear against the window saying "Dahw, dahw!"). **Whenever possible, adults, understanding the importance of this kind of exploration, support all the ways in which children use materials,** even when they play with the materials in unconventional ways.

Everyday materials often make the best toys.

• **Children have a safe place to explore and play with materials.** Caregivers ensure that infants and toddlers are safe from environmental hazards, such as electrical outlets, wires, and cords; stairs; hard and slippery surfaces; medicines; cleaning materials; poisonous plants; and sharp objects, corners, and edges. They do this by thinking about the physical exchanges that occur between children as they explore. Because infants are immobile before they begin to creep and crawl and the balance of most toddlers is precarious, caregivers take measures to protect infants and toddlers from one another. They survey the play space, considering such questions as: Can a nonmobile infant sit and explore objects without being crawled over by a more mobile child? Can an older toddler stack a tower of blocks in a place safe from a child who is just learning to walk? Is there enough room between children? For example, can a baby who is exploring sounds by hitting two rattles together do so without poking or striking another baby nearby? While caregivers encourage infants and toddlers to interact with one another, they are also sensitive to each child's need for safety and freedom from the unintended disruptions that may be caused by peers who are busy exploring materials.

• **Caregivers respect children's need for time to explore and play with materials.** Infants and toddlers acquire and practice many new skills as they go through significant developmental changes within a relatively short span of 2½ years. For example, Sam may steady himself by hanging onto furniture, his caregivers, and other children for many days and weeks

By cuddling and rocking her "baby," this toddler mimics the way her mother rocks and cuddles her new baby sister.

as he cruises around the room. Then one day he suddenly stands unaided and tentatively takes a few steps toward the outstretched arms of his caregiver. Sam has arrived at this point because over time he has *practiced* the prerequisite physical skills—crawling; pulling himself up to a stand; cruising; balancing his weight on one foot, the other foot, and both feet; and leaning on anything and anyone within reach. At each stage along the way, his caregivers have patiently given him the time and space he's needed to repeatedly practice each new skill. They've done this because they understand the developmental sequence of walking and know that children develop this skill at their own individual rates.

In an active learning setting, caregivers grant children the practice time they need—not only as they move through the stages of motor development but also as they explore and play with materials. For example, Alison's caregiver notes that Alison is very intent on seeing how many blocks she can stuff into a cloth bag, so she delays Alison's diaper change for a few minutes until Alison comes to a natural pause in her play. Joey's caregiver has planned to bring out water in tubs for water play. She sees, however, that Joey has just managed to get all of the small cars out of the multi-level toy garage and has begun to put them back one at a time. She waits until he completes this self-initiated task before she introduces the water play. These caregivers realize that most infants and toddlers can't yet express in words a thought like "I'll be with you as soon as I finish this" or "I need just a few more minutes to get this to work!" By observing children's actions and nonverbal cues, caregivers come to understand and respect children's intentions. Rather than interrupt them to introduce a new activity, adults try to allow children the extra time they need to explore and play.

• **Children have access to materials throughout the day.** An issue closely related to providing *time* for exploration is giving children *access* to materials throughout the day. If we expect sensory-motor children to become successful, self-confident learners, we must strive not to limit their access to materials (to designated times such as "choice time," "activity time," or "exploration time"), but to provide interesting materials for them to explore *throughout* the day. For example, in active learning settings caregivers may provide picture books or photographs for children to look at during diaper changes. For napping, children may have favorite comfort items in their cribs or on their cots. At mealtime, adults will understand that as infants and toddlers eat they will also take time to explore their food and eating utensils. Similarly, caregivers may offer nesting blocks in a variety of sizes to use in the sandbox at outside time or an assortment of interestingly shaped pieces of wood to spread with paint at small-group time.

• **Children have access to materials over long periods of time.** Once caregivers introduce materials, they make sure infants and toddlers have access to them for an appreciable period of time. They do not remove them the next day, week, or month simply because they are no longer novel. Keeping materials available allows children to rely on known and favorite materials for practice and comfort. While caregivers continue to introduce new materials based on children's interests and developmental needs, they add them to the materials children already have, rather than routinely removing familiar materials to make room for the new.

• **Finally, as they plan and equip play spaces and interact with sensory-motor children who are using materials, adults are mindful and supportive of the characteristic ways in which infants and toddlers manipulate materials.** They understand that infants and toddlers need to explore materials with their eyes, hands, feet, and mouths; experiment with materials to find out how they work; and use their whole bodies to climb on objects and move them from place to place. They are also aware that children in this age range use materials both to imitate what others are doing and to do things independently, and that they like to use materials as tools. Adults expect, encourage, and plan for these typical infant and toddler behaviors.

Everyday Objects for the Infant and Toddler Center

Providing infants and toddlers with a variety of materials does not mean that you must have a large budget for this purpose. Many of the materials of most interest to very young children are common, everyday objects. Here are some general kinds of materials—many of them free or inexpensive—that are appealing to very young children.

As they collect everyday materials, caregivers will need to use good judgment about the appropriateness and safety of individual items for the particular young infants and children in their care.

• **Household objects.** Infants and toddlers are fascinated by many objects adults take for granted: toilet paper rolls and empty boxes; the lid from a jar of baby food; a washcloth; a spoon, cup, or spatula; a lemon; various types of brushes; keys on key rings; clothespins without springs; pots and pans. The fact that these common objects are used daily by adults adds to their value in children's eyes. Important people use these objects—they *must* be worth getting hold of!

The primary caregivers themselves are another kind of "household object." Important adults are objects of intense interest to infants and toddlers who are exploring their environment. Infants study their faces, listen for and respond to the sounds of their voices, know how they smell, and settle into the comfort of their arms and bodies. Toddlers use adults as supports to lean on and relax against or to brace themselves as they pull to their feet to stand. In addition, their caregivers' shoelaces, jewelry, glasses, and clothing provide a variety of shapes, textures, and colors to explore by looking, stroking, or grabbing. Adult caregivers are every bit as interesting and useful for exploration as many other objects in the environment—and generally more responsive!

• **Natural and found materials.** Materials readily available in the children's environment are not only practical and economical but they also draw children's interest. Objects such as stones of different colors and textures (safely secured in non-breakable jars for the youngest children), shells large enough to handle easily, pine cones, wrapping paper and computer paper for crumpling and tearing, paper bags, wicker baskets, boxes of various sizes, and food storage containers with lids provide children with many opportunities to try out emerging skills and construct knowledge about what things do and how they work. And don't overlook water, a soothing and accessible natural material. Infants like to sit and splash in water and feel its coolness on their hands, legs, and feet. They experiment with dropping objects into water and fishing them out again. Toddlers like to play in wading pools, pour water from one container to another, push floating objects across the water's surface, squeeze water from sponges, and drip water on sand or on paper sprinkled with powdered paint.

• **Soft, cuddly materials.** Young children associate soft things with feelings of comfort and security. Therefore, it is important for caregivers to provide children with soft, washable materials, such as cloth pieces, scarves, stuffed animals, rag dolls, blankets, quilts, and pieces of fleece that children can finger, stroke, crawl on, wrap around themselves, cuddle, drag from place to place, and snuggle with at nap time or whenever they need them throughout the day.

• **Easy-to-handle materials.** Infants and toddlers are developing their grasping, pulling, reaching, and manipulating skills at a rapid pace. Caregivers support the development of these important skills by providing children with materials that are easy to grasp and handle. With "handle-ability" in mind, here are some things to consider: Do the objects infants want to explore have surfaces they can easily grasp? Do the books you provide have thick pages that infants and toddlers can readily turn without tearing? Can toddlers easily grasp and pour from the pitchers you provide for milk and juice? Can they carry the box of farm animals from one part of the room to another, or is it too heavy for a toddler to handle? Are paintbrush handles thick enough for toddlers to control? Giving very young children opportunities to be successful as they handle objects helps them feel confident in their developing skills and abilities.

• **Squishy, messy materials.** Tactile experiences dominate children's exploration of the world in these early years. Infants and toddlers are fascinated, for example, as the water drips out of a plastic bottle when they hold it upside down and squeeze; when the mud in the sand table goes "splat" as they drop spoonfuls of it onto the table; when the gelatin breaks up into smaller pieces as they push it across a highchair tray with their fingers. As they explore materials that drip and ooze, children often seem to be pondering questions such as these: *What would it feel like if I put it in my mouth? What if I stick my hand in it? What will happen if I "smoosh" my fingers*

How Infants and Toddlers Manipulate Materials

In their sensory-motor approach to the world, infants and toddlers figure out what things are and how they work by **manipulating materials.** Some of the characteristic ways in which infants and toddlers manipulate materials are described below. As you read through this section, think about how adults can encourage the learning process in infants and toddlers by selecting and arranging appropriate materials and supporting children as they use them.

- **Children explore materials with their eyes, hands, feet, and mouths.** Infants and toddlers begin their explorations through direct, tactile contact with materials. Since very young children cannot ask questions about objects or hold mental images in mind, their "need to know" takes the form of direct exploration with the tools they currently possess—eyes, hands, feet, and mouth. Caregivers, therefore, expect infants and toddlers to grasp and hold things and put toys and playthings into their mouths. They are not put off by drool and stickiness. At the same time, they keep materials clean and provide playthings that are too large for children to swallow or choke on.

Since infants and toddlers regard other people as "objects," they use the same direct, exploratory approach to peers and caregivers that they use toward other objects. These very young children may lean against adults for balance as they cruise, push their fingers in adults' mouths, or pull on an adult's hair or earrings. In the spirit of exploration, caregivers tolerate a certain amount of having their own hair grasped and pulled. At the same time, caregivers protect children from one another's explorations when necessary.

- **Children experiment with materials to find out what these things do.** They bang, roll, shake, squeeze, and bite things to find out what will happen. They appear to be thinking such thoughts as: *What if I drop this spoon from up here in my highchair? What happens when I bang on my highchair tray with the spoon? What if I put the ball at the top of the slide?* Sometimes as they experiment with materials, children surprise, scare, or annoy themselves or others. At such times it is important for caregivers to approach children calmly, to acknowledge their feelings (comforting them if necessary), and to remember that very young children cannot yet predict or control the results of most of their actions.

- **Mobile children use their whole bodies to roll, sit, and climb on materials and carry them from place to place.** As children become more mobile, they discover challenging new ways to interact with materials. For example, when babies learn to sit with their hands free, they find that they have greater freedom to shake and bang things. Mobile infants climb into large, open boxes, experiencing with their whole bodies what it is like be in a small, enclosed space. Toddlers enjoy climbing up on large, adult-sized chairs, experiencing the sensation of moving to a higher level than they could before. These very young children also use their newly found powers of locomotion to move materials from place to place. They push and pull wheel toys and drag chairs across the classroom. In an active learning setting, **caregivers encourage children's whole-body mobility and respect their need to carry and move materials from place to place.**

- **Children use materials to imitate actions.** As young children explore materials, they also watch and imitate the way other people use them. Cleo, who has been eating with her fingers, watches another child eat with a spoon and then tries it herself. Jeremy puts a dress-up hat on his head. A caregiver rolls a rubber ball to Sidnee, and Sidnee sits down on the floor and uses both hands to roll it back. Imitation calls for the coordina-

tion of a set of actions. Since very young children are often several steps behind the person they are imitating, **caregivers are very patient with young imitators and adjust their pace to the pace of the child.**

- **Children use materials to do things for themselves.** Although newborns are dependent on others for their every need, they soon begin their quest for independence. Part of this journey is experimenting with materials that allow them to do things for themselves. Infants learn to comfort themselves by locating and sucking on their own thumbs and pacifiers. Later on, they learn to crawl to their favorite blankets or stuffed animals when they are tired and need a nap. Toddlers use sponges to wipe up spills at snack time, move child-sized chairs so they can sit near favorite people, and climb on couches or blocks to see better or to reach desired objects. As they observe infants and toddlers using objects as tools, **caregivers recognize the beginnings of problem solving.**

through it? Materials that are squishy and messy give children the chance to explore substances that change shape as they are handled, providing satisfying sensations to their hands and bodies.

   • **Materials that children can set in motion.** Young children are constantly trying to find out how things work. While they gather much of this information by watching what goes on around them and what others are doing, they themselves are also capable of causing things to happen and observing the effects of their own actions. Therefore, it is important that adults provide materials that allow cause-and-effect exploration. These might include balls and small vehicles that roll when pushed; balanced toys that sway when touched; toys that can be set in motion, such as wagons, riding toys, rocking toys, and push-and-pull toys; and suspended toys and sturdy mobiles that move when children reach out and touch them. These kinds of objects provide children with opportunities to try out an action and then observe the result.

• **Materials children can climb on and use to pull themselves up.** Infants and toddlers want to use materials to help them change positions and set themselves in motion. Therefore, caregivers provide them with sturdy tables, chairs, and couches to hold on to as they pull themselves upright, as well as things to climb on, such as sturdy low boxes, large hollow blocks, ramps, steps, and stairs.

• **Materials that children can use to make noise.** Caregivers provide materials that allow children to produce a range of sounds: wind chimes, shakers, stiff paper for crumpling, standard and unusual rhythm instruments, balls of all sizes, rattles, and wooden and metal spoons to bang on pots and pans. Infants and toddlers often are surprised by the sound an object makes when they strike it or drop it on different surfaces. In the course of their play, for example, they might find that dropping stones into a metal bowl produces one type of sound, while dropping the stones into a wooden bowl or into water produces another. Caregivers provide materials that allow infants and toddlers to experience and create sounds that vary in volume, pitch, quality, and duration.

In sum, interesting and varied everyday **materials** provide infants and toddlers with the key to understanding what things in their environment are and how they work. But materials alone are not enough to ensure learning. Young children also need to make **choices** about which materials they will use and how they will use them; they need to have time and freedom to **manipulate** the materials; they need to **communicate** about their efforts through language and action; and they need **adult support** for these explorations. When we offer all these **ingredients of active learning,** we are providing infants and toddlers with the tools they need to make sense of their world.

REFERENCES

Piaget, J. (1952). *The origins of intelligence in children.* New York: W. W. Norton.
Piaget, J. (1966). *Psychology of intelligence.* Totowa, NJ: Littlefield, Adams, and Co.
Post, J., & Hohmann, M. (2000). *Tender care and early learning: Supporting infants and toddlers in child care settings.* Ypsilanti, MI: High/Scope Press.

How Does Your Garden Grow?

By Ursula Ansbach, Rosie Lucier, and Suzanne Gainsley

• •

Last spring, teachers at High/Scope Demonstration Preschool decided to
try planting a garden with children. Our first step was to prepare children for the experience by discussing gardens at greeting circle and small-
group time, since we knew that our gardening would be more meaningful
to children if they participated in planning it. As we talked about gardening,
we provided children with books about gardens for them to look at and discuss. We encouraged them to describe the gardens they were familiar with,
the kinds of flowers and plants they enjoyed looking at, and the garden
vegetables they liked to eat.

We told parents about our garden plans, and encouraged them to get
involved. They responded by contributing seed packets, and later by volunteering to help with the digging and planting.

With our seed packets and garden books in hand, we
made more specific plans, asking children to choose things
they wanted to plant. Tomatoes, peppers, carrots, and
cucumbers were high on their list, along with a variety of
summer flowers. We explained to children that we would
be using both seeds and small starter plants.

After this preparatory phase, we took the children to
the spot we had chosen for our garden plot. The next step
was breaking up the turf so that what had been part of a
lawn could become a bed for plants. We gave children
small spades and trowels to dig with.

*Harvesting tomatoes is
a thrill.*

Digging was a total experience in itself, and one that some of the
children chose to stay with for the entire summer. Some children were so
interested in what they found in the soil that they simply had no interest in
planting. Worms, bugs, and roots were endlessly fascinating to them! Recognizing that some children were interested in digging for its own sake,
we soon marked off a separate area just for digging.

While the children did find the digging engrossing, the clay soil was
hard to work and the results of their digging were uneven. Luckily, one of

our fathers who had a rototiller volunteered to re-plow our not so consistently dug soil! The teachers then fine-raked the soil and marked it off in rows. Then we were ready for the seeds and starter plants, which we had purchased according to the children's choices.

As they planted, some children ignored the prepared rows. They loved scatter-planting the tiny seeds in a profusion no adult could have planned! Others were very interested in sowing their seeds in neat little rows, for a while anyhow. Later, beans came up alongside peppers, tomatoes, and marigolds in wild disarray, but nobody minded.

A separate digging area with no plants allows children to dig to their hearts' content.

The starter plants were the most fun for children to plant. The adults modeled the process of digging the hole to fit the size of the root system, filling the hole with water, putting the plant inside, and covering the roots with dirt. As they worked at this, some children became distracted by the wonderful mud-pie-making opportunities! We supported this exploratory play, recognizing that not all preschoolers would understand gardening as a purposeful sequence of events. Here again, some children simply loved the mud and stayed with it. Others became quite adept in placing the starter plants and patting down the dirt to anchor the plants in the hole.

Children had varied levels of interest in the garden. Our planting took place over about a week and a half. During this time, some children stayed with gardening for as long as 20–25 minutes at a time. Others would come and look, then run over to the swings and play. And there were many children in between these extremes who came and went at their own pace.

As adults who had many set ideas about gardening, it was important for us to keep in mind that this was the children's garden. Their learning needs were more important than developing prize-winning flowers or tomatoes. Like many adults who are gardening with children, we sometimes found it difficult to avoid taking over for them. The plants did need special care and protection from being trampled, over-watered, and so forth. But here we needed to ask ourselves the question: Which is more important, the quality of the plant or the experience for the child?

Ideally in such activities, we can reach a balance where children can experience gardening at their own levels while learning stewardship for living things. And this is indeed what happened at our preschool garden. On the one hand, we were supportive of children's need to explore the dirt and mud, and we understood that they would sometimes use the garden hose

Adult Strategies for Gardening With Preschoolers

Here are some strategies for gardening experiences that allow adults to support children without taking over for them.

1. Prepare children for gardening by discussing the garden beforehand, showing pictures or diagrams of other gardens, or visiting gardens nearby. Allow children to help choose what will be planted and where it will go.

2. Model appropriate techniques for planting, weeding, watering, and harvesting, explaining the reasons for these techniques in ways children can understand. Model an attitude of "stewardship" and respect for living things and the natural environment.

3. Allow preschoolers to play and explore as they work in the garden; set reasonable, age-appropriate expectations. Don't push them to be task-oriented. If they are more interested in exploring mud and worms than in weeding or getting things planted, find ways to support these interests.

4. Help children resolve any conflicts that occur as they garden.

5. Don't expect all children to understand that gardening is a series of connected events. Remember, the results of gardening efforts are often not immediately apparent; it may take days or weeks to "get results" and this extended time frame may be difficult for preschoolers to keep in mind. Therefore, support children as they experience gardening "in the moment," while providing opportunities for them to understand how each step in gardening leads to another.

to "water" one another rather than the garden. We accepted their lack of concern about having neat garden rows or keeping each type of plant in a separate space. At the same time we modeled appropriate practices, always explaining the reasons in ways that children could understand: For example, we explained that plants were living things that needed soil, water, and sunshine to grow and that walking on plants could break them and make them stop growing. As a result, children began to watch their feet and became more concerned about the plants. Once they understood that the plants were living things, they didn't want to hurt them.

We also realized that preschoolers, because they are present-oriented, have difficulty understanding the connections between planting, watering, weeding, and harvesting. Since the results of these activities were not immediately visible and changes in the plants took place over a long period of time, preschoolers often didn't see how one gardening activity led to another. We felt that by directly involving children in gardening we were providing them with an opportunity to understand and connect the events in this sequence. At the same time we realized that many children were not yet ready for this long-term perspective. For these children, experiencing gardening "in the moment" was enough. We accepted this and supported the many active learning opportunities that occurred as they enjoyed such thrills as digging up worms, being squirted with the hose, and tasting fresh tomatoes.

This year, as children played in the schoolyard, an incident gave us evidence that children had gained respect for nature through last year's gardening experience. We observed a child stop another child from stomping on a worm. (While working in the garden last year with children, we had emphasized that worms, bugs, and the plants themselves were all living things.) Repeating our language, the child said, "Don't do that—it's a living thing!"

A Garden Journal

By Linda Clegg Hawkins

• •

*O*ver the last 5 years, High/Scope UK, in partnership with public and private early childhood settings, has developed a number of High/Scope garden learning environments. Based on the work of Steen Esbensen (**The Early Childhood Playground: An Outdoor Classroom,** High/Scope Press, 1987, out of print) these "outdoor classrooms" embody the principles of the High/Scope approach and are used daily as part of the learning environment. They also give many children who live in areas of social distress and who do not have access to a natural outdoor environment the opportunity to experience planting and growing, to watch the life cycle of plants, and to see the changing seasons.

Children pitch in with wheelbarrows and shovels to help prepare the site for the sandpit.

The following are excerpts and photos from a garden journal written by Linda Clegg Hawkins, director of Clervaux Nursery, South Tyneside, England. With support from the South Tyneside Groundwork Trust, this center developed a large garden with several distinct play areas. The garden includes a wildlife area, marsh pond, sandpit, vegetable and flower plots, and covered areas for woodworking, crafts, and music explorations. (In an adjoining area, there is an enclosed paved space for other kinds of play.) The journal excerpts show how the garden developed and some of the learning experiences that resulted for children.

Spring

In March it all began—part of the tarmac was the first to go and our children were fascinated, watching large earth-moving machines, drills, and dumper trucks in action. . . . What a surprise we had when the workmen started to mark out the areas using paint spray on the grass! But now we could show the children where the areas illustrated on our garden plan were going to be. Each family was given a copy of the plan, and these are being updated as the work progresses.

Summer

We went on a sponsored walk (a fund-raising event) and brought back pieces of wood. These were made into a woodpile in the wildlife garden area. Soon we will be able to dig out a marsh area and a shallow pond. The funds raised on the walk will pay for a special sandpit liner that will let water through and keep soil out of the pond. Large rocks and seaside plants will be positioned around this area—there is still much to do and the children are enjoying the 'doing.'

A wide variety of herbs were placed between the stepping stones on one side of the pond. All our plants are growing now, and the pond has become a focal point for everyone entering and leaving the nursery. The learning that has grown from this work (science, math, geography, and so forth) is unbelievable. Children's listening skills have improved and their conversations—questioning and answering, describing, recalling, and reviewing—have been continuous. Children's satisfaction and enjoyment have been sustained throughout.

Autumn/Winter

Just before our Christmas activities began, the sandpit was finished. The special lining was fixed on the sandpit with wooden boards, so we all wanted to dig in it. We quickly pleaded for any surplus Wellington boots and after an immediate response we were off. Out came wheelbarrows, spades, rakes, buckets, brushes, and brooms.

Next we had a visit to the Tilcon quarry at Marsden. They donated large boulders and a quantity of smaller rocks and stones—of course, we had on our hard hats, and wheelbarrows were needed once again. The rocks were a source of great amazement as a fantastic variety of fossils were embedded in them.

A kind volunteer then offered to cement a post into the wildlife garden for a bird table. It was fun seeing how deep the hole was by lowering the children into it and comparing where the ground level was in relation to each child's body. We also watched while the cement was mixed and helped to hold the post in position as the cement was poured into the hole.

Early Spring

The garden looks lovely. Parents are amazed by the number and variety of birds we have in the garden. All the plants look healthy. The chimes ring in the wind on the music pergola and the children love the outdoor woodworking bench and tools we've placed under the other pergola. This really is an outdoor classroom—we have started having children do simple plans for outside time. This planning takes place at snack time once recall is finished.

What next? Probably seaside and rock garden plants, then a grand opening in May.

Late Spring

We have now started on another part of our High/Scope garden—our vegetable plots. We visited some plots near our nursery to see how they were set in rows and lines. An added bonus was that in one garden we saw a huge pond with newts and toads.

With help from some dads we dug up some beds (oblong strips). Then the children said we should

At right is a covered area for woodworking and crafts. Behind it and to the left is the sandpit. Digging tools are in buckets.

have some triangles, so we dug out some areas in triangle shapes (with two triangles making a square in the middle). Then one child said, 'We haven't got any circles'—how could we have forgotten! So we had to find something circular to dig around as we were a bit worried about making a really round shape. Someone suggested we use the barrel to cut out a circle in the grass—and so we did.

"Who wants to plant some potatoes?" we asked. "I do," said everyone. So in went the potatoes with their little mounds to keep them warm. "Who wants to sow some seeds?" we asked. "I do," said everyone, so we sowed lettuce, carrots, radishes in triangle beds, and on and on. We have broad beans, runner beans, sugar snap peas, carrots, lettuce, cabbage, and sprouts (a few flowers are planted as well in each area to attract bees for pollination). We also planted gooseberry bushes and raspberry canes, and we dug in a rhubarb crown.

We made a compost heap. . . . As we worked, we dug up all sorts of peculiar things—a door handle, a doll's head, a toy gun that was very old, a toy car, and some broken pottery.

A patio-stone path around a plot makes it easy for children to care for the plants.

Summer/Autumn

(This entry was written after the official opening.) We won't stop now—we have many ideas for the future and a few more things to do to our present garden. A wood sculptor is going to join us to make seats and a table. . . . The local college is interested in working with our children to make a garage, a market stall, and other items for our village, as well as extra bird tables and bird feeders. This will start in January but for the time being we will enjoy our garden as it is now, a little piece of paradise with so many learning areas available to us all.

REFERENCE

Theemes, T. (1999). *Let's go outside! Designing the early childhood playground.* Ypsilanti, MI: High/Scope Press.

Chapter Three

Learning and Exploring Throughout the Daily Routine

· ·

Comfortable Comings and Goings for Infants and Toddlers
Jacalyn Post and Mary Hohmann

Acknowledging Feelings at Arrival and Departure Times
Jacalyn Post and Mary Hohmann

Reading Throughout the Daily Routine
Betsy Evans

Active Small-Group Times
Michelle Graves

Dandelion Paintings: A Small-Group-Time Plan
Michelle Graves

Small-Group-Time Interaction Strategies
Michelle Graves

Movement All Day Long
Eileen Storer

Making Room for Make-Believe
Beth Marshall

Using Computers for Planning and Recall
Beth Marshall

*I*n High/Scope settings, the daily routine is consistent and includes a plan-
do-review process, small- and large-group times, outside time, transition
times, and times for eating and resting, if necessary. Throughout the day,
adults maintain a balance of child- and teacher-initiated activities and
provide variety and structure.

In the first article in this chapter, "Comfortable Comings and Goings for Infants and Toddlers," Jacalyn Post and Mary Hohmann emphasize the importance of separation and reunion rituals for infants and toddlers in child care settings, and provide strategies to help caregivers support both children and parents at these sometimes difficult times of the day. In the next article, "Acknowledging Feelings at Arrival and Departure Times," Post and Hohmann expand on this theme by showing caregivers how they can help reduce the emotional intensity of separations and reunions by gently and matter-of-factly describing the emotions they are witnessing in the children and parents in their centers.

In the third article, "Reading Throughout the Daily Routine," Betsy Evans provides examples of how adults in High/Scope programs find ways to incorporate books throughout the day when the story-reading experience can be personal and comforting to children—greeting time, work time, small-group time, and departure time.

Small-group time is a key component of the High/Scope daily routine. During small-group time, children freely explore and experiment with the materials provided by their teachers. The next series of articles provides examples of how teachers plan small-group activities and set them in motion. In "Active Small-Group Times," Michelle Graves provides the basic principles for planning stimulating and fun small-group times that focus on active learning. In "Dandelion Paintings: A Small-Group-Time Plan," Graves describes an actual small-group-time activity in detail, from the written plan to what actually happened during the activity. In the next article, "Small-Group-Time Interaction Strategies," Graves provides some basic interaction strategies for helping children make the most of their creations and explorations at small-group time.

The last three articles explain how movement, make-believe, and computers fit into the daily routine of a High/Scope setting. In "Movement All Day Long," Eileen Storer shows how teachers, by encouraging children's awareness, can help them build on their spontaneous movements throughout the day. Storer provides specific examples of how a teaching team at the High/Scope Demonstration Preschool included the exploration of purposeful movement throughout one day's routine. Each example is followed by a description of the movement strategies the teacher used. In "Making Room for Make-Believe," Beth Marshall illustrates some simple strategies for stimulating children's imaginations throughout the day. Finally, in "Using Computers for Planning and Recall," Marshall gives examples of how to use children's computer experiences as a source of ideas for planning and recall times.

Comfortable Comings and Goings for Infants and Toddlers

By Jacalyn Post and Mary Hohmann

. . . .

"Good morning, Martha and Monique," says Chantall, a caregiver, to Monique and her mom. Monique, a young nonmobile infant, has been coming to the child care center for 5 weeks. She arrives in her mother's arms and smiles at Chantall, who is her primary caregiver at the center. After her mom and Chantall chat for a bit about Monique's new interest in watching and laughing at the family cat, Monique's mom snuggles and kisses her, then gives her to Chantall, who hugs her, smiles, and says, "It's nice to see you, Monique!" Holding Monique, Chantall walks with Mom to the door. "Bye, bye, Monique," says her mom. "I'll be back this afternoon." "Bye, bye, Mommy—see you later," Chantall says for Monique.

§

At the end of the day, Monique lies on her back on a quilt next to Sasha, another infant. Monique holds and mouths a wooden ball. When she hears her mom arriving and greeting Chantall, Monique drops her ball, smiles, and wiggles all over in anticipation. Her mom sits down next to her, and after picking her up for a kiss, a hug, and a snuggle, she holds her close and says, "You've been playing next to Sasha again!" Monique smiles and coos in her mom's arms as her mom walks over to Chantall to catch up on the day's events and round up Monique's bottles and supplies. At the end of their chat, Chantall strokes Monique's arm and says, "Bye, Monique! See you tomorrow!" Monique and her mom depart.

§

For infants and toddlers in child care settings, their daily arrival at the care setting and their departure at the end of the day are momentous occasions that set the tone for their away-from-home experiences. For Monique, the infant in the above example, both arrival and departure times are relaxed transitions that strengthen her ties to her home and family and to people and places in the wider world. This article, based on excerpts from High/Scope's manual for infant and toddler caregivers, *Tender Care and Early Learning: Supporting Infants and Toddlers in Child Care Settings* (Post & Hohmann, 2000), presents ideas and strategies caregivers can use to encourage such comfortable, positive transitions.

In the block area, a dad prepares to say goodbye as his daughter makes a relaxed transition to her primary caregiver for the day.

Although this article focuses on infants and toddlers, preschool teachers and caregivers will find that the approach described offers many ideas that may also be used in working with older children.

What Do We Mean by Supportive Arrivals and Departures?

In High/Scope-oriented infant and toddler programs, respect and support for each child's way of separating or reuniting with the parent are the hallmarks of arrival and departure times.

At arrival time, warm, leisurely greetings from caregivers help to assure infants and toddlers that even though their parents must leave, they are in the hands of trustworthy people who will keep them safe until their parents return.

At departure time, the caregivers' pleasant, friendly goodbyes and warm wishes for return allow children to reunite with their parents, free of concerns about their sense of belonging at the center.

Where Do Arrivals and Departures Take Place?

Where arrivals (separation from parents) and departures (reunion with parents) occur depends on the needs and preferences of the child and parent. Even when a care setting has a reception area, there is no definite place in the center where greetings and goodbyes must take place. One mom may sit in a comfortable chair, nurse her infant, chat with the caregiver, and give her child to the caregiver without ever leaving the reception area. Other parents will come into the play space and say their goodbyes or hellos wherever their children are comfortable that day—at the sand table, on the mattress next to the books, or outside in the play yard.

At one center, Nolan (an older toddler who had been going to the center for 2 years) developed a fairly elaborate goodbye ritual that took him to the top of the indoor climber. He would first give his mom a goodbye kiss near the door, then hurry across the room and climb rapidly up to what everyone called the crow's-nest. When he got to the top, he would say "Okay, Mommy!" to signal that it was okay for his mom to go out the door. Once outside, she turned and waved at him, and from his high perch, he waved back at her through the window.

What to Expect From Children Who Are Arriving and Departing

As infants and toddlers separate from their parents to join the child care community at the beginning of the day, they typically engage in a variety of behaviors. These may range from crying, screaming, flailing, clinging, thumb sucking, avoiding eye contact, or simply ignoring the parent or caregiver involved, to smiling, cooing, picking up an interesting plaything, watching other children with interest, waving goodbye to their parents, or joining an activity in progress. Their responses to rejoining a parent at the end of the day may vary just as widely.

Nonmobile (very young) infants generally respond to separations and reunions with relative ease. At this age, an infant is apt to greet a familiar primary caregiver with a smile, settle peacefully into her arms, and gaze into her face. At the end of the day, the infant will often be alert to the sound and sight of a returning parent and begin to wiggle, smile, and vocalize with pleasure.

As they learn to creep and crawl, infants develop a sense of themselves as separate beings distinct from their parents. Realizing that parents can disappear, they fear their parents may not return! At arrival time, therefore, it is not uncommon for these **mobile infants** to cling to their parents, cry, avoid eye contact with the caregiver, and head for (maybe even try to open) the door through which their parents have just taken leave.

Young toddlers enjoy their newfound walking ability and the freedom it allows them to explore and carry all kinds of interesting objects. While they remain concerned about losing sight of their parents, they are usually irresistibly drawn to examine whatever they can get their hands on. They may still protest a parent's leave-taking, but they can also make connections with caregivers and peers

At the end of the day, father and son are happily reunited!

through objects and playthings of particular interest. At the end of the day, young toddlers may simply continue their explorations and play when their parents arrive, or they may throw themselves into their parents' arms and cry with relief!

Older toddlers are developing the ability to hold in mind mental images of absent people and past events. They remember their parents leaving them at the center on previous mornings and anticipate that it will happen again today. At the same time, they are developing a strong sense of independence and initiative and an increasing ability to communicate with such powerful phrases as "Mommy stay!" and "No!" At the beginning of the day, their objections to a parent's departure can be loud and physical. They need to assert some control over how they ease themselves into the setting and how long it takes to do so. Fortunately, they are usually increasingly interested in the people and materials in the child care setting and eager to make choices about what they are going to do after their parents leave. At the end of the day, older toddlers may resist leaving the center until they have finished a particular activity. They may be perfectly cheerful as they reunite with their parents, or they may be tearful, whiny, and demanding.

Arrival and Departure Strategies

During arrival and departure times, caregivers give children and parents warm welcomes and goodbyes and support their separation and reunion processes. The following strategies can help in carrying out this role:

✓ **Carry out your greetings and goodbyes calmly to reassure the children and parents.** Given the potential for family distress at the beginning and end of the day, it is important that caregivers approach these times calmly and optimistically, remaining attuned to, yet outside of, the emotional fray. The presence of a calm, friendly caregiver can help to reassure anxious children and their parents, while also reassuring other children who have already separated from their parents for the day.

✓ **Acknowledge children's and parents' feelings about separation and reunion.** Separating and reuniting can be difficult for children and their parents. The caregiver's job is not to minimize the emotions of parents or children nor to attempt to distract them from what they are feeling. Instead, the caregiver acknowledges the feelings of both children and parents by gently and matter-of-factly describing the emotions she is witnessing.

The caregiver also provides comfort and contact to children who are upset and provides parents with the time and space they need to comfortably separate from or reunite with their children.

✓ **Follow children's signals about entering and leaving the activities of the care setting.** Parents, of course, make the decision about placing their infants or toddlers in a particular care setting. However, when adults follow children's signals or cues about how they prefer to arrive or depart, children gain as much control as possible in the larger situation of having to be in that setting. Each child copes with making the transition from home to care setting and back again in a particular and personal way. Many infants and toddlers soothe themselves during this emotional time by clinging to some item that connects them in a tangible way to home—a special blanket, a dolly or stuffed animal, a pacifier, a photo of a family member. If a child hangs on to such a comfort item during arrival and departure, it is important for caregivers to respect this choice as an assertion of self and an important step in the development of self-help skills.

Even with another child in her arms, this caregiver takes plenty of time for a relaxed and playful hello. She knows Mom will pass her the baby when they are ready.

Older infants and toddlers who can move about on their own may cope with the transition from home to care setting in a variety of ways. For example, they may at first cling to their parents, then turn to a toy or select some plaything and come back to their parents, showing no desire for physical or eye contact with any caregiver. When ready, however, such children will gradually ease their way into caregiver contact in the presence of their parents, or after their parents depart. For example, when Evan (see next page) arrives with his mom for his third day at the center, Chantall (his caregiver) respects Evan's initial avoidance of her, knowing that he will make contact with her when he is ready. She also knows that if she imposes herself on him, she will only heighten his concerns about his new setting. Instead, she makes herself available for a more gradual approach.

Evan's Arrival and Departure

Arrival Time

Evan, a young toddler, arrives with Veana, his mom, for his third day at the center. "Good morning, Veana and Evan," says Chantall. Evan holds his mom's hand and watches another toddler, Athi, at the sand table while Mom and Chantall exchange information about the day. Observing Evan's tight grip on his mom and his focus on the sand play, Chantall joins Athi at the sand table with the thought that Evan might come there, enabling her to gradually make contact with him through a mutual interest in sand toys. She doesn't address or approach Evan at this point, because he is so clearly avoiding her.

Eventually, Evan and his mom make their way to the sand table. When his mom squats down by the table, Evan stands between her knees and scoops up sand with his hands. From her place on the other side of the sand table, next to Athi, Chantall moves a bucket and shovel within Evan's reach. He takes the shovel and begins to fill the bucket. Chantall, continuing to interact with Athi, says gently, "Athi, you're digging a pretty big hole!"—whereupon Athi gives her a spoon so she can dig a hole like his. Throughout this time, Chantall talks now and then with Evan's mom about how and why she is following Evan's cues in the getting-acquainted process. Eventually, when she sees Evan eyeing her spoon, she gives it to him, saying "Maybe you would like a spoon, too, Evan." He takes the spoon and begins to dig. As he enlarges his hole, he leaves the safety of his mom's knees and moves to the end of the sand table, between his mom and Chantall. When Athi begins to drive a dump truck around the sand table, Chantall backs away from the table so Athi and his truck can drive in front of her. When Athi gets to where Evan is playing in the sand, Evan puts his hand on the truck, and Athi stops. "Looks like Evan wants your truck to back up!" Chantall says. Athi laughs at this idea and begins backing his truck around the table. Looking up at Chantall briefly, Evan smiles and then returns to his play.

When it's time for Evan's mom to leave, she gives him a hug and tells him she'll be back after nap. He watches her sadly as she walks toward the door but remains at the sand table with Chantall and Athi. "Mommy go," he says to Chantall, pressing himself against her side. "It's sad for you to see Mommy go—she'll come back after nap," Chantall says, slipping her arm around his shoulders.

Departure Time

At the end of the day, Evan is just waking up from his nap when he sees his mom come through the door. He runs into her arms, and as she talks with Chantall, he strokes her face. After gathering Evan's things, his mom says goodbye to Chantall. Lightly touching Evan's back, Chantall tells him, "See you tomorrow!" He smiles at her from the safety of his mom's arms.

The Importance of Separation and Reunion Rituals

A 15-month-old in my center always has a difficult time saying goodbye to her dad at the beginning of the day. She often cries loudly and clings to her father, upsetting the other children and making it difficult for us to get on with our routine. Her father is usually in a hurry to get to work, and sometimes signals us to distract his daughter so he can leave quickly. Is this okay?

   —A caregiver in an infant and toddler center

Though occasionally a parent may wish to leave quickly and quietly while his or her child is engaged in play, we would discourage this practice. It is important for the child to know where the parent is, rather than to look up and discover that Daddy or Mommy has left without saying goodbye. In the long run, for the child, the pain of hearing a parent's "Goodbye, see you after nap" is less than the pain of actually feeling betrayed by a parent who leaves with no notice.

   One strategy that may be helpful to this father and his child is to encourage them to establish a ritual for their separation and reunion. Such rituals ensure that the parent's comings and goings are no mystery to the child, are usually fun for both parent and child, and provide both parties with the comfort of a predictable routine. In these rituals, each time parents say goodbye, they also let the children know when they will be coming back. Although very young children may not comprehend what such statements actually mean or precisely how long it will be until Mom or Dad returns, at some level they understand and are comforted by the parent's reassuring promise of reunion.

   Parent-child separations and reunions have a relationship to the endless games of peek-a-boo and hide-and-seek that caregivers play with infants and toddlers. Hiding behind the sofa and then popping out, or hiding the stuffed bunny under the blanket and then revealing the bunny with a flourish and an exclamation of "peek-a-boo," is a way for children to act out and begin to understand that people come and go, that parents leave in the morning and return at the end of the day.

✓ **Communicate openly with children about their parents' comings and goings.** To foster trust and communication, caregivers let children know when their parents leave and return to the center. They comment on parents' comings and goings ("I see your mom is waving goodbye") and participate as needed in the rituals parents and children establish for their separations and reunions.

✓ **Exchange information and child observations with parents.** Seeing parents at arrival and departure times provides an opportunity for caregivers to exchange information about their children's lives at the center and at home. Caregivers can fill parents in on their children's actions and communications at the center: "Today, Evan spent all of choice time with Emma at the sand table, digging holes and driving dump trucks." Similarly, parents can let caregivers know what their children did at home: "I couldn't believe my eyes this morning. Monique was standing up holding on to the side of her crib. She's never done that before!"

§

By patiently supporting children and family members through these transitions at the beginnings and end of the day, caregivers of infants and toddlers are nurturing abilities that are essential to children's development. In the short run, learning to deal with these daily greetings and goodbyes allows children to enlarge the scope of their trust from parents and family at home to caregivers and peers at the center. In the long run, coping successfully with these transitions gives children a solid basis for coping with the comings and goings of relatives and friends for the rest of their lives.

REFERENCE

Post, J., & Hohmann, M. (2000). *Tender care and early learning: Supporting infants and toddlers in child care settings.* Ypsilanti, MI: High/Scope Press.

Acknowledging Feelings at Arrival and Departure Times

By Jacalyn Post and Mary Hohmann

• •

One of the most important ways in which caregivers can support infants and toddlers and their family members at arrival and departure times is to acknowledge the wide range of feelings they may be having.

Acknowledging feelings is so important because these are often intense and emotional times for both parents and children. An infant or toddler may feel especially vulnerable when left by a parent in a place that is not home, with people who are not familiar. Having no conventional sense of time, the child cannot distinguish between being left for 6 hours and being left forever. Thus, young children's emotions at the beginning of the day in group care may range from discomfort, anxiety, fear, or terror to sorrow, loneliness, grief, or despair over abandonment.

At the end of the day, it is not unusual for children to express equally complicated and conflicting emotions—residual anger at being left by their parents, increasing fear that they may be abandoned by their parents as they watch other children being picked up before them, and finally, joy at their parents' return and relief that at last, in their parent's arms, they can safely fall apart from the stresses and strains of their day.

When parents leave their children at child care centers or child care homes, they may feel sad about missing their children, guilty about leaving them in someone else's care, and anxious about getting to work on time. Later, at the end of the day, they may look forward to reclaiming their children, feel hurt and perhaps jealous if their children ignore them or resist leaving the caregivers, and tense about fitting in all the household tasks that need doing before bedtime.

Caregivers can help reduce the emotional intensity of separations and reunions by gently and matter-of-factly describing the emotions they are witnessing. Here are several examples of ways in which you might describe a child's feelings at a parent's departure:

- "It's sad for you to see your mommy go, Terry."

- "You're crying so hard that your eyes are closed, Jamal. You don't like to see Mommy leave for work."

- "You're holding on to me so tightly, Angelina! It's scary for you to see Mommy go, isn't it? Let's sit in the cozy chair together."

You might also try to describe a parent's feelings. Here are some examples:

- "It looks like you want to stay with Verdell and leave in time for work, Ms. Smith. It's hard to be pulled in opposite directions."

- "It must be upsetting to have Mickey cry when you're so glad to see him, Ms. Greene. Maybe it's his way of telling you how relieved he is to see you at the end of the day. Now he really feels free to express himself."

Letting children and parents know that you recognize and are trying to understand their feelings actually helps them begin to regain emotional balance. By putting words to children's and parents' feelings, you help their emotions to recede, clearing the way for them to think about moving on to the next part of the day.

Occasionally a child may seem inconsolable when a parent leaves. The child may be new to the center, returning from a long absence, tired, coming down with an illness, or entering a new stage of self-awareness. At these times, it is important for the caregiver who always greets the child to remain calm, to describe the child's feelings, and to stay with the child to provide comfort and physical contact (holding, stroking, rocking, carrying) until the child recovers.

A Welcoming Space for Families

One way in which you can prepare the physical setting to support parents and children at arrival and departure times is to set up a family-oriented space or room somewhere between the center's entrance and the children's rooms. This space can be furnished comfortably (with chairs, tables, shelves, coat hooks, a telephone, a sink, a microwave, and access to a bathroom, for example).  This transitional area resembles a town square or café where parents can easily meet and mingle; sit down with their children, other parents, caregivers, and staff members; eat a sandwich; nurse an infant; make a list or a phone call; or simply collect themselves before leaving. Though parents and children are free to carry out their greetings and goodbyes elsewhere in the center, having a space like this encourages parents to take their time as they enter and leave and to look forward to the center as an enjoyable place for their children and themselves.

Sometimes, as they prepare to leave their children in a child care setting, parents have more difficulty with separation than their children have. Again, caregivers can support anxious parents by remaining calm, acknowledging their feelings, and encouraging them to take plenty of time and stay at the center as long as they are able to. Eventually, over time, with caregivers displaying patience and giving attention to the feelings involved, both children and parents will gain trust in the center staff and confidence in themselves. As their trust grows, they will enter and leave the center with an increasing sense of hope and ease.

Leaving a child in a center can be difficult for parents. Over time, as children and parents gain trust in center staff, they will settle into comfortable routines for these times.

Reading Throughout the Daily Routine

By Betsy Evans

• •

Perhaps no single activity is more important to children's emerging literacy than being read to by familiar adults and friends. As the process is repeated over and over again, children begin to make connections between the written and spoken word and to gain a sense of how to use language to tell stories. In High/Scope programs, reading and listening to stories is not confined to "story time." Adults read to children as they request throughout the day and look for ways to incorporate books into children's various activities. Here are some classroom scenarios illustrating the many different times adults read to children during a typical day in a High/Scope program.

Greeting Time

After Cody says goodbye to his mom, he walks over to the book area. Some of the children there are listening to one of the teachers read a story, while a few other children are exploring books on their own. Cody notices that a book about snakes has been added to the bookrack. (The children saw a snake on a walk to a pond the day before, and the teachers added this book to build on that experience.) Cody picks up the snake book and begins to look at the pictures. When the teacher is finished reading the story, Cody asks if she will read him the snake book. She says yes, and two other children join Cody and the teacher. The children are fascinated by the pictures of the poisonous snakes and notice with great interest the pictures of fangs dripping with poison. As the teacher reads, they interrupt her frequently to ask questions about poisonous snakes.

Work Time

It is the beginning of work time. Caitlin had cried when she said goodbye to her dad earlier, and she still doesn't seem to have completed the transition from home. Since planning time, she has been drifting about the classroom, clutching a story-

book in one hand and watching other children play in various parts of the room. Merrilee, one of the teachers, offers to read the book Caitlin is holding. Caitlin agrees. As Merrilee reads, Caitlin snuggles against her and listens quietly. When the story is finished, Caitlin gets another book for Merrilee to read.

ॐ

Denis is curled up on the floor, making soft humming noises. The teachers know that he is playing "kosh-ka," (kitty), a favorite fantasy game that he brought with him from Russia. Observing Denis and remembering that the school library has a National Geographic book on cats, Betsy, one of the teachers, goes to get it. She sits down on the floor near where Denis is "purring" and begins to leaf

through the book. Denis soon comes over, plants himself securely in her lap, and begins pointing to all the kittens in the book. On one page a kitten is pictured lapping milk. The kitten's tongue is photographed in sharp detail. Denis points to it and says "yaz-yk" (the Russian word for "tongue"). The teacher repeats the word, happy to have another Russian word to share with Denis.

These children are really enjoying their reading break!

Small-Group Time

The day after it has rained at outside time, the teacher holds small-group time outside (the day is sunny). The teacher begins by reading Rain (a wordless book by Julian Scheen) with the children. Then she sets out containers of water and paintbrushes in various sizes and encourages children to "paint" the building and various things on the playground. She observes whether children notice the effects of water on different materials, how things change as they dry, and which things dry faster.

Departure Time

Toddler Markie is being picked up by his mother at the end of the full-day program. Before leaving, Markie asks his mom for a story and chooses a favorite picture book about bunnies from the bookrack. As is their usual routine, Markie's

Snack time is a perfect opportunity for reading to a small group.

mom takes a juice box out of her purse and hands it to Markie, and Markie opens it and settles down on his mother's lap. When she has finished reading and Markie has finished his juice, they walk out of the center together, relaxed and ready for their drive home.

These are just a few of the many ways in which adults read to children throughout the day in High/Scope programs. As you read through these scenarios, you may have noticed that there were no examples of reading to children during large-group time. Though large-group story times are common in many early childhood programs, in the High/Scope approach we discourage story-reading to a large group of children because this setting lacks the intimacy that is so important to the telling or discussing of a story.

Most children's first reading experiences involve close physical contact with their parents and are thus associated with a warm parent-child bond. In the preschool setting, reading with children individually or in small groups enables the preschooler to continue to associate reading with warm and close relationships. Story-reading is often a time for giving "comfort and contact," a time to be close to an adult. Reading in small groups allows more one-to-one interaction with the adult, allowing children to ask occasional questions and to discuss the story as it is read.

This approach to story reading also provides more choices for children. When stories are read to the whole class, all the children have to sit quietly and remain still to enable everyone to hear the story and see the pictures. The fidgeting, frequent interruptions, and other behavior problems that often occur during large-group story time are evidence of the difficulty some children have with listening to stories in a large group. However, when adults read to children individually or in small groups, and whenever possible at children's requests, children can hear the stories they *want* to hear. In this setting children never have to struggle to stay quiet during the reading of a story that does not interest them.

Active Small-Group Times

By Michelle Graves

• •

For several days in a row, children have been spending part of their outside time peeking through the links of the playground fence, watching a house painter work on a nearby building. Inspired by the children's interest in the house painter, the teacher plans a related small-group time. She begins the small group by giving each child a plastic pail and an assortment of different-sized brushes. After she and the children briefly discuss the house painter's activities, the children leave the table and fill their own pails with water. Then they carry them outside and begin "painting" the school walls, the sidewalk, the chainlink fence, and the basketball hoop.

§

"I'm making science," Meghan says as she uses a plastic eyedropper to squeeze droplets of colored water into the tiny suction cups on a rubber soap dish. (The eyedroppers and soap dishes are new classroom materials that the teacher is introducing in this small-group time.) As Meghan continues with her "science experiment," Brittany and Cirra use their eyedroppers to create a "rainbow" on the soap dish they are sharing, making each stripe of the rainbow by filling an arch-

These children are using eyedroppers to create a "rainbow" by squeezing colored water droplets into the tiny suction cups on a rubber soap dish.

shaped row of suction cups with a different color of water. The girls work carefully, making one stripe at a time. Another child, Andrew, ignores his soap dish completely, instead choosing to use his eyedropper to mix colored-water droplets directly on a paper towel. "Look," he exclaims, "It's like magic."

§

"I learned a lot about the children in my small group today as they worked with the paper clips," a teacher says to her team member after children have left for the day. *"I was expecting to see the classification and space key experiences, and I did observe those happening with the children. But what I didn't expect to see was the number of different ways they used what seemed like such a simple material."* She then explains that Vivian made a long chain of paper clips, calling it a *"fishing pole,"* while Elyse sorted her metal and plastic clips into separate piles and then separated out the single butterfly clip because it was *"not the same as the others."* Andrew, on the other hand, experimented with shaking and stirring the clips in a bowl. He repeatedly dumped his clips on the table, refilled his bowl, and dumped them again, saying he was *"making music."*

§

Children's interest in a recent Fourth of July community fireworks display has led the teachers to plan a small-group time around making paintings that resemble fireworks. Teachers have provided squeeze bottles of brightly colored paint, soda straws, and paper. The children squeeze dollops of paint onto the paper, then scatter the paint by blowing at it through the straws. The opportunity to make the paint *"dance"* and to create interesting effects by mixing the colors are the highlights of this small-group time for children. In addition, as they work children discuss the excitement and fears they experienced while attending the real fireworks display.

§

These examples illustrate the variety of engaging learning experiences that can take place during High/Scope small-group times. This article describes the **planning process** for small-group experiences and how adults interact with children during this time.

Basic Principles for Successful Small Groups

In the High/Scope Curriculum, small-group time is a segment of the daily routine in which a group of five to ten children meet with an adult at a consistent time and place to work with materials selected by the adult. While this general statement could describe small-group experiences in many early childhood programs, **what really defines a High/Scope small-group time is its focus on active learning.** Here are some basic principles for planning small-group-time experiences that promote active learning:

Do Children Learn Anything From Open-Ended Small-Group Times?

I've been trying to move away from having specific objectives for small-group time. Instead, I've tried to conduct small groups in which I simply provide materials and let children explore them in individual ways. My biggest concern about making this shift is that the children will not learn anything if I don't plan with particular results in mind. How can I overcome this roadblock?

—An early childhood teacher

Planning open-ended small-group times is a stumbling block for many teachers; your concern that this type of experience will reduce learning opportunities is a common one. Teachers working in the field have shared the following ideas for identifying children's learning opportunities at small-group time.

Start by first planning simple small-group times around those everyday materials you see children choosing regularly at work time. Some examples include modeling compound (such as Play Doh®) markers and paper, or plastic construction sets (such as Duplo® or LEGO®). Keep the introduction of the materials to a minimum by simply saying as you pass them out, "These are some things I noticed you playing with during work time." Then sit down with the children and watch and listen closely to what they say and do, playing quietly with the materials yourself in ways that imitate their actions. If possible, set up a tape recorder so that after the group is over you can listen to children's conversations or comments you may have missed.

A similar technique is to enlist the help of a volunteer parent or a student teacher to sit nearby and objectively record children's actions and comments. When the small group is over and children are napping or gone for the day, review the recordings, notes, or your own recollections of the small-group happenings. Ask yourself what the notes tell you about individual children's interests (for example, putting things together and taking them apart), how they interact with others (playing alone with materials, interacting with adults only, or joining other children in cooperative efforts), or how they solve problems (leaving the problem behind, trying different approaches until the problem is solved, asking for help from others). On another day, look at a list of the key experiences or selected High/Scope Child Observation Record (COR) items to categorize your observations. As you go through this process, you will begin to see that children's actions fall into categories that give you lots of information about their social, emotional, physical, and cognitive skills.

REFERENCE
High/Scope Educational Research Foundation. (1992). *High/Scope child observation record for ages 2½–6*. Ypsilanti, MI: High/Scope Press.

• **Start by examining your beliefs about the goals of small-group time.** In the High/Scope approach, small-group time is an opportunity for children to experiment, explore, create, and solve problems. Have you ever been frustrated because children weren't using small-group-time materials in the ways you intended? When you adopt an active learning perspective you are freed from the frustration of trying to control what they do. Instead, you can concentrate on supporting children by observing, listening to, and participating with them in the personally meaningful experiences they have chosen. For example, in the paper clip activity described above, Vivian, Elyse, and Andrew had very different approaches to working with the paper clips. Observing the children with an open mind, the teacher was able to see that Vivian had the manual dexterity to link the clips together and the imagination to label her creation. She also learned about Elyse's ability to notice similarities and differences, an important pre-reading skill. Plus, she was available to share in Andrew's excitement that paper clips, when shaken in a bowl, make "music." Had the teacher planned this small-group time with a specific objective in mind—for example, that all the children should sort the clips—it would have been difficult for her to notice and support the children's individual interests.

In open-ended small-group times, teachers provide materials—in this case, paintbrushes and water—which children use in a variety of ways!

• **Feel free to gather ideas for small-group time from a variety of sources: children's interests; new materials; the High/Scope key experiences; and community experiences.** You'll note how these idea sources are illustrated, respectively, by the four scenarios that open this article. Whatever the source of small-group-time ideas, the true test of their value is how well they inspire and spark ideas in children.

• **Choose materials with children's interests in mind.** Watch how children work with classroom materials, observe their actions at outside time, and listen "to how they describe things or converse with others throughout the day. Use that information to guide you in selecting materials for small-group times. For example, the small-group-time activity "Painting With Dandelions" (see p. 122) grew out of an outdoor experience in which adults took children to an open field filled with dandelions. Observing the children's curiosity about dandelions, the adults planned an activity for the next day's small-group time that included children exploring watercolor paints and dandelions.

Different children will use similar materials in different ways.

Likewise, in planning the fireworks painting activity, teachers built on the children's interest in a recent community fireworks display. Many of the children in the classroom had attended and talked about the display; they also acted out their interest in fireworks in a classroom incident in which they threw large quantities of toys into a pile on the floor, calling it a "fireworks explosion." This made it very difficult for children to sort through the toys at cleanup time and created problems for other children who needed the space for their own work time pursuits. The fireworks small-group activity was intended in part to give children an opportunity to find a more constructive way to express their interest in fireworks.

• **Make certain that the materials you provide can be used in a variety of ways.** Since the goal of small-group times is to provide children with materials they can use to pursue their own ideas and creations, it is important to stay away from games with rules (for example, a store-bought game) or projects that require children to assemble pre-cut pieces (giving children three white paper circles and asking them to make a snowman). Replace such materials with open-ended manipulatives such as Duplo® blocks, markers, paper, pebbles, acorns, paper clips, modeling compound (Play Doh®), and water. In the outdoor water-painting activity described earlier, the teacher was careful not to instruct the children where or how to "paint" with their buckets of water. Instead she gave them the freedom to paint in a variety of places. This led to many discoveries—the sighting of a spider web, the observation that water dries up faster in the sun than in the shade, and the realization that "painting is hard work, 'cause your arms get tired and it's hot outside."

• **Think about the individual children in your group—their developing abilities, personality traits, and the various ways in which they may use the materials provided.** When planning the dandelion experience, the adults thought about the differences between the children in the group. They knew that some children were still mostly interested in sensory exploration of materials, while others enjoyed using materials to create representations with a fair amount of detail. Understanding this, they were not surprised when some children ignored the dandelions they were given and instead dipped their fingers into the watercolor paints to make fingerprints on the paper. Nor were the teachers surprised when other children used their dandelions as paintbrushes to create representations of specific things and people.

• **Prepare your materials before the group begins.** Having materials ready in individual baskets or bags near the small-group meeting place helps adults make the transition into small-group time go quickly and smoothly.

• **Keep any introduction of the materials brief.** Beginnings can be as simple as "Here are some soap dishes for you to use with the eyedroppers and colored water." Remember, your goal is to let children decide on the direction of the activity; if lengthy instructions are necessary for children to understand

Prepare your materials before the group begins and keep any introduction to the materials brief so children can get started on their explorations.

what to do, you may want to evaluate whether the activity really is appropriate. Eliminating detailed explanations enables children to get started on their explorations right away and prevents the management problems that often occur when children are kept inactive too long. Occasionally it may be necessary to make the introductory part of the activity longer. For example, if the activity is intended to build on a previous experience (such as a field trip), you may want to conduct a discussion of the experience to refresh children's memories, or you may want to tell or read a story that relates to the activity you have planned. In general, though, try to avoid lengthy introductions, and keep the ingredients of active learning in mind as you begin the activity.

• **Plan and prepare backup materials** that complement or support those originally selected. It often happens that some children finish with the materials early while others are just beginning to form their ideas. Having related backup materials on hand will help keep the early finishers interested in the small-group activity, while other children who are still engrossed with the original materials continue their explorations. For example, for the dandelion small-group time the teacher set aside traditional paintbrushes and magnifying glasses as back-up materials; for the fireworks painting activity, she prepared cotton swabs and paintbrushes. On some days the backup materials will be used, and on others they may not be needed.

The teacher works alongside children at small-group time, imitating their actions with materials and looking for ways to support each child's learning.

• **Always begin small-group time by gathering at a consistent time and place,** for example, at a table in the house or art areas. Occasionally, the actual activity may take place in some location other than the usual small-group space (outdoors, for example), but in these cases it is still important to **meet first at your usual small-group location.** In the water-painting activity, for example, the small group met at their usual table in the art area before the children went outdoors to paint with water. This gave the teacher a chance to pass out the empty pails and to talk to the group about the house painter, his tools, and how the children would use materials similar to his but in a different place than their usual small-group area. Starting small group at the same time and place each day helps children inter-

Gather your small group in a consistent place and time to help children internalize the sequence of the daily routine.

nalize the sequence of the daily routine as well as understand the general kinds of activities that take place during this part of the routine. Children will come to understand that small group is a time when an adult chooses the materials but children are free to use them in creative ways.

   • **Plan a cleanup strategy as part of the small-group-time process.** To help bring closure to the small group, and to offer another option to children who may finish sooner than others, plan for a novel way to return materials to their original places and their regular storage containers. Turning cleanup into a game or a thinking challenge makes it a more interesting and appealing activity for children. For example, in the dandelion activity, the teacher encouraged children to blot the wet watercolor paints with paper towels before putting them away. As they did this, she helped them notice the interesting designs they were creating on the towels with the colored water.

   Following these principles will help make your small-group times stimulating and fun for both children and adults.

Children learn that small group is a time when an adult chooses the materials but children are free to use them in creative ways.

Dandelion Paintings:
A Small-Group-Time Plan

By Michelle Graves

• •

In the previous article in this chapter, I discussed how teachers plan for successful small-group times. Here, I describe one small-group-time activity in detail, from the written plan to what actually happened during the activity.

The Small-Group-Time Plan

Originating Idea

For several days children have been running through the grass, picking up dandelions and examining their characteristics (floppy stems, bright yellow color).

Materials

- Enough **dandelions** so each child in the group has at least four

- **Construction paper**

- **Watercolor paints** and **water**

- For backup: **paintbrushes** and **magnifying glasses**

Possible Key Experiences

Creative representation: *Drawing and painting*
Classification: *Using and describing something in several ways*

Beginning

Play a guessing game with children by telling them you brought watercolor paints for small-group time, but not paintbrushes. Give them clues about what they could use to paint in place of a paintbrush ("It's something I picked from the grass outside," "It has a floppy stem"). Wait for the right guess, then give each child a piece of paper and some dandelions.

Middle

Observe how children use the materials. Some may examine the dandelions by twisting their stems together, pulling the flowers away from the stems, or rubbing them under their chins and checking in a mirror for a yellow spot. Others will use them as paintbrushes, dipping them in the water and making splashes of color on their sheets of paper. Some of their paintings may include recognizable representations of people or objects.

End

Let children know that the small-group time is about to end. Have paper towels available so children can dry off the table and blot the watercolors before putting them back on the shelf. Ask children to store their art work in the usual place where children's projects are left to dry.

Follow-up

1. *Bring a large sheet of paper and brightly colored tempera paints outdoors for children to use with dandelions to make a group mural.*

2. *Bring a dandelion to the next planning time. Ask the child holding it to describe his or her plan and then to pass it so the next child can plan.*

Painting With Dandelions: What Actually Happened

Following is the teacher's account of how the dandelion small-group time unfolded:

I started by passing a watercolor box to each child. Tanuka was the first to comment on the fact that there were no paintbrushes inside, saying "Hey, my box does not have a brush inside." I acknowledged her discovery, then asked children to guess what material might be used to paint instead of paintbrushes. I began to give clues that pointed to dandelions. After the first clue ("It's something I picked from the grass outside"), Sue shouted, "I know." However, instead of making a guess, she gave her own clue: "People let you pull these, but not their flowers." Later I recorded Tanuka's observation as an example of using the word "not" in conversation correctly (High/Scope COR* item X), and Sue's clue as an example of a sentence that included two or more

---

*The High/Scope Child Observation Record (COR) for Ages 2½–6 is High/Scope's child assessment instrument. Teachers record everyday observations of children's behaviors, like the ones I've described here. Later they evaluate and interpret the observational notes they've collected, using items from the COR instrument to assess the significance of children's behaviors as indicators of developmental progress. In this instance, the teacher later coded Tanuka's comment as an example of COR item X, level 3: "Child correctly uses the words not, some, or all in conversation."

separate ideas (High/Scope COR item R). It took one more clue ("They're yellow and have floppy stems") before Michael said, "Dandelions!"

After I passed around the dandelions and set out the paper and water, children began combining the materials in a variety of interesting ways. Using her dandelion as a paintbrush, Sue made two pictures, one with splashes of color (at right) and one of a person with a head, arms, legs, and body (p. 124). I sat next to Rachel and imitated the way she twisted the stems of her dandelions together to make a chain. Finally she asked me if she could have my chain, too, so hers could be longer. I gave it to her and watched her twist it on to her chain, then asked her to hold it up so I could see how much longer she had made her chain. Michael went straight for the watercolors, pouring a little water in each color. He then stuck his thumbs and fingers into the paint and made fin-

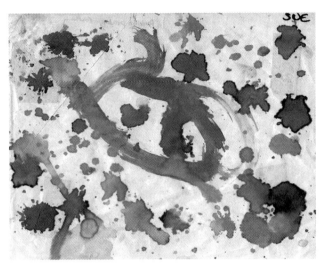

Sue used her dandelion as a paintbrush and made two pictures. In her first picture, above, she experimented with the effects she could create by making splashes of color all over the paper.

gerprints directly on the table. When I wondered out loud if he might want to take those prints home at the end of the day, he paused for a moment, got up, helped himself to a piece of white paper, and sat down to continue his work. Later he asked me to write his name on the top of his paper so no one would think the prints belonged to someone else.

Only Tara and Jason chose to use the prepared backup materials. After several attempts to make a dandelion function as a paintbrush, Tara threw it on the table. I commented that she seemed frustrated, and she said the dandelion didn't work and she wanted a real paintbrush. After I got her a watercolor brush, she painted three pictures. Jason was hunching over his crushed-up dandelions to look more closely at them, so I offered him a magnifying glass. Much like what I did when I got my first pair of glasses, Jason lifted the magnifying glass away from the dandelions every so often to compare how things looked with it and without it. I joined him in his observations and we played a game of "bigger, smaller" as we moved the magnifying glass back and forth.

The second picture Sue painted using the dandelion as a paintbrush is a representation of a person showing the arms, legs, body, head, and face.

In thinking back on this small-group time after children had left for the day, I recorded my observations on the COR and also thought of ways to build on the children's actions and reactions in upcoming classroom activities. I decided to capitalize on the "bigger, smaller" game by bringing a block to the next planning time. I would ask children to choose a material that was included in their work time plans and then to tell the others whether it was bigger or smaller than the block. I also decided to plan a small-group time in which children would use magnifying glasses to explore the outdoor environment. When that small-group time took place, children enjoyed using the new tool to examine tree trunks, blades of grass, particles of sand, and insects crawling on the ground.

Small-Group-Time Interaction Strategies

By Michelle Graves

• •

At small-group time, children need **adult support** to help them make the most of their creations and explorations. Here are some basic interaction strategies for working with children at small-group time (many of the examples refer to the dandelion small-group time described earlier in this chapter):

- **Put yourself at eye level with children.** Sitting down at the table with children or lying on the sidewalk outdoors will enable you to share the children's work from their own perspective. This sends the message that you are ready and available to share in their excitement and enthusiasm.

- **Watch what children do with materials, resisting the urge to give them directions about how to use a material.** For example, rather than saying "First, take the dandelion and dip it in the water then rub it in the color and make splash marks all over your paper," **give children the materials and observe the many different ways the same set of materials will inspire individual children.** Attend to all of their efforts, not just those that result in a recognizable product. For example, caution yourself about valuing the actions of a child who uses his dandelion to make a painting of a person more than those of the child who explores the dandelion by pulling it apart and crushing it.

- **Give attention to each child, knowing that acknowledgment can take many forms.** Simply sitting next to a child who is quietly exploring materials and imitating that child's actions is one form of acknowledgment, one which is often appropriate because it does not disturb a child's work. During the dandelion small-group time, a teacher joined a child who had momentarily left the table and was lying quietly on the floor. She learned that he was "lying in the warm sun" after pretending he had picked a handful of dandelions, and that he "had to rest before making a painting."

Matching a child's level of enthusiasm with your own actions and words is another strategy for acknowledging children's actions. For example, a child who was examining pieces of his dandelion with a magnifying glass excitedly said, "It's bigger!" His teacher responded by raising her voice a bit and saying, "It *is* bigger."

• **Listen to what children are saying, acknowledge their comments, and wait until they invite you to converse with them further.** As children work, they occasionally talk to themselves about what they are doing, giving you valuable insights about their interests. When a child exploring a dandelion says, "Soft on my fingers," the teacher might simply repeat, "Soft on your fingers." This gives the child the opportunity to decide whether to take the conversation to the next level, yet does not disrupt the flow of his or her ideas. If the child then says again, "Soft on my fingers," the teacher might say, as a way to extend the child's discovery, "Soft on my fingers (pausing for a moment), soft on my cheek," and rub the dandelion on her own cheek. Then she would wait to see if the child continues this turn-taking game.

• **Accept children's explanations of what they are doing, resisting the urge to correct their mistaken perceptions.** For example, Vivian (who had made a "fishing pole" out of a chain of paper clips) told her teacher, "Next week when I went fishing I caught two big fish!" The teacher focused on Vivian's excitement rather than on her inaccurate time language, responding "Two big fish! You caught two big fish when you went fishing last week!"

Listen to what children are saying and accept their explanations of what they are doing.

• **Look for opportunities to stimulate children's thinking throughout the small-group experience.** As children were cleaning up after the fireworks painting activity mentioned earlier, Alex commented, referring to the "fireworks explosion" the children had made by dumping and throwing toys at work time, "This is easier to clean up than those toys were." This sparked a lengthy discussion (gently guided by an occasional comment from the teacher) in which children talked about their discomfort with the mess

Adults look for natural opportunities to stimulate children's thinking. At small-group time, children brought up the mess they had made by scattering toys the previous day (above), and the adult encouraged a thoughtful discussion.

that had been created with the toys. The result was that the children made a rule that throwing and dumping that many toys should be replaced with other, less messy ways to create fireworks.

• **Offer backup materials to children whose interest in the activity seems to be dwindling, but be sure the new materials connect to their original ideas.** For example, in the dandelion activity the teacher had set aside paintbrushes and magnifying glasses as backup materials. When the teacher saw Tara throw her dandelion down after several attempts to get the color she wanted on the paper, and after Tara talked about her frustrations, the teacher offered the more familiar tool, a paintbrush. Likewise, when Jason pulled apart his dandelions and looked at them closely, the teacher offered him a magnifying glass as a way to "get a different look." Sometimes, as in this example, teachers will be able to anticipate the additional materials needed to enhance children's work. On other occasions, they can suggest to children that they look for the additional materials they need: "The glue doesn't seem to be working for you. Is there something else in the art area you could use on your picture?"

These strategies illustrate a framework, rather than a set formula, for interacting with children at small-group time. Closely observing children in their classroom will help teachers decide how to adapt the general teaching strategies given here to support each child's active learning.

There is no set formula for interacting with children at small-group time. Base your interactions on your careful observations of what children say and do.

Movement
All Day Long

By Eileen Storer

• •

Many teachers think that movement activities occur only at large-group time or during outdoor play. However, children in early childhood settings explore and initiate movement throughout the day. Whether children are scooping sand in the sand table or pretending to be kitties in the house area, they are trying out new ways of using their bodies to manipulate objects and express themselves. This process of experimenting with new movements is similar to what children do when they explore the uses of a new material, like paper towel tubes or colored water. Once explored, the material becomes a resource children can use in future play activities. In much the same way, movements children have explored become a resource they can draw upon in the future, to include in their plans, experience, share, alter, and review.

When children are aware of their movement explorations, these movements become purposeful. Throughout the day, teachers can help children build on the spontaneous movements they are exploring by **encouraging movement awareness.** Here are some examples of how a teaching team at the High/Scope Demonstration Preschool included the exploration of purposeful movement throughout one day's routine. After each example, we describe the movement strategies the teacher used.

Greeting time. After children and teachers had greeted each other and reviewed the message board, one teacher asked the children, "I wonder how we could move to our planning tables? " Will said, "I'm flapping my arms like a flying dinosaur." Tara said, "I'm crawling like a crocodile. Grrrr," and crawled to the table with her body low to the ground. The teacher said, "You're crawling like a crocodile," and crawled alongside her, saying "Grrrr."

Strategies: The teacher encouraged children to initiate their own movement ideas and to describe how they were choosing to move. She imitated their movements as a way of acknowledging their choices.

Planning time. At planning time, the teacher introduced a long scarf that children could use as a "planning train" to take them to the different interest areas. (As the "train" reached each area, children who planned to work there were to "get off" the train and describe their play plans.) To get the activity started, she asked the children, "How should we move with our planning train to the areas?" Brian said, "March." The teacher said, "March? Okay, to what area shall we march?" Brian said, "Block area." The children took hold of the scarf and sang, "We're all marching to the block area, just like Brian."

Strategies: The teacher encouraged Brian to plan a movement that could be tried and shared by the other children, and she supported his use of language to label the movement.

Adult Support Strategies

- Encourage children to describe their movements.
- Label children's movements.
- Establish the beat. Then reinforce it by repeating a single word.
- Imitate children's movements.
- Sing songs while keeping a steady beat. (Beat begins before the song is added.)
- Use children's names when exploring steady beat. (Use one beat for the entire name.)
- Listen for movement directions that children generate during their play, and incorporate them in movement experiences.

Work time. During work time in the house area, Jasmine and Andrea put on dress-up clothes. Jasmine handed Andrea some plastic bracelets, and Andrea put them on. Andrea said, "Let's jump." The two girls held hands and jumped up and down. The teacher, who had been sitting nearby observing the children's play, chanted, "Jump, jump, jump, jump" in time with the girls' movements.

Strategies: Here, the children planned a movement. The teacher helped them develop an awareness of their movement by using one word, "jump," to describe it. In addition, she encouraged their attention to the inherent beat in their movements by repeating the word in time with their movements.

Recall time. To get recall time started, the teacher patted his hands lightly on the table and chanted to the beat, "Watch and copy. Luke, Luke, Luke, Luke." Then he began to sing, "I wonder what Luke did at work time today. Won't he tell us now." The other children sang with him. When they stopped, Luke said, "I played with horses in the water table."

Strategies: The teacher initiated a steady beat and used a child's name to anchor the beat of the movement and later, the song. The children then took turns setting a beat with their names and telling their plans.

Plan movement experiences around the new movements you see children exploring.

Large-group time. The teacher put on some music and told the children, "Watch and copy." He patted his stomach to the steady beat. At the end of the musical phrase, he said, "Watch the change" and patted his toes to the steady beat. The children watched and then imitated the teacher's movements. As Terrell patted his toes he said, "Toes, toes, toes, toes." Other children suggested various other movements for the group to follow. Fol-

Active Play—It's Not Just for Outdoors

Recently I observed at the High/Scope Demonstration Preschool. I noticed that at work time, children sometimes took part in activities that were very active and physical, like pretending to play hockey, jumping off large blocks, or putting on music tapes and dancing to the music. I've always felt that most activities like these are too disruptive to permit indoors. We do have some music and movement activities during circle time, but there the children are closely supervised and everyone is participating and learning something. How can you allow such boisterous activities?

—A preschool teacher

We believe that spontaneous movement activities like these are just as important to children's development as traditional indoor activities like painting, working at the sand table, or building with LEGO's®. Through such active physical play, children develop physical coordination and learn to connect patterns of movement with thinking and language.

Some kinds of movement experiences (for example, riding wheeled toys or playing ball games) are probably not appropriate indoors, but many other kinds of active play can work well—with thoughtful adult support. Try the following suggestions for dealing with active physical play indoors:

- **Instead of policing such activities, observe children closely so you can see what kinds of support they need to keep the activity safe and focused.** Be where the action is—get involved as a play partner when you can (but don't try to direct the play). To join the movement play, imitate it nearby and see what happens. Wait for children to comment on what they are doing, and use this as an opportunity to comment on your own move-

ments ("I wonder if I can twist while I jump") or theirs ("You jumped pretty far"). Solicit children's ideas for play variations ("Are there some other ways we can move our scarves to the music?").

- **As children play, assess whether there is adequate space for them to move actively.** If there isn't, plan to change your room arrangement to provide space for vigorous movement in one or more classroom areas (the block area, for example). Also, think about materials you can provide to encourage *focused* movement (large, soft blocks; cardboard bricks; beanbags; scarves; simple musical instruments).

- **Make comments that encourage children to use the plan-do-review process with movement,** that is, to plan what they are going to do beforehand, to be aware of their movements as they are moving, and then to describe their movements afterwards. For example, say to a child who has been jumping, "I wonder how you're going to jump off the block next time."

- **If disruptions arise from movement activities, use a problem-solving approach** to help children become aware of the impact of their actions on others and to resolve any conflicts. If you see a safety hazard developing, engage children in finding a solution. For example, one teacher made the following comment to children who were playing "hockey" with beanbags and sticks: "I'm worried because the beanbags are going high in the air when you push them with your sticks, and one of them might hit someone." This encouraged a discussion of the activity; the children decided to use a basket to make a goal, and the play became much safer.

Encourage movement choices at transition times: "How can we move to the coat rack?"

lowing this experience, the children chose several action songs and finger plays they were familiar with. At the end of large-group time, the teacher said, "How should we move to our small-group tables?" Linda said, "Crawl like a bug." The teachers and children crawled to their tables, singing "We're crawling like a bug to small group."

Strategies: The teacher initiated movement to a steady beat for children to imitate. Later, children initiated their own movements to the beat for the other children to follow. At the end of this segment, the teacher again encouraged children to plan and describe their movements as a way of transitioning to the next part of the day. This provided opportunities for children to build upon and explore other children's ideas.

Small-group time. During small-group time, Alicia explored play dough and sticks. The teacher sat beside her, watching and copying Alicia's movements. As Alicia pounded the play dough with her fists, she said, "I'm pounding my play dough." The teacher imitated her movements and said, "Pound, pound, pound, pound."

Strategies: The teacher helped the child become aware of her movements by using a word to label the movement and echoing the pace the child had set. This strategy often becomes a springboard for conversation, encouraging the child to begin to talk about what he or she is doing.

Outside time. At outside time, Michael asked the teacher to push him on the swings. The teacher pushed him high in the air. As Michael moved his legs in and out, the teacher said, "In, out, in, out." Michael said, "I'm moving my legs in and out to make me go higher."

Strategies: As in many of the above examples, the teacher here labeled a child's movements with a simple phrase. This strategy encouraged Michael to link language with movement patterns and reflect on his movements, as exhibited by his statement.

Making Room for Make-Believe

By Beth Marshall

• •

Children, like adults, enjoy illusion and fantasy, and this enjoyment is part of the fun of superhero play. Superheroes are appealing because their super powers allow them to do things that aren't possible in everyday life. You can stimulate children's imaginations and build on their interest in the imaginary aspects of superheroes by encouraging other kinds of experiences with illusion, mystery, and fantasy throughout the daily routine. Here are some ideas.

Greeting Time

• **Solve the mystery.** Introduce new materials and build children's excitement about them by creating a mystery message on your message board. For example, when our teachers replaced the sand in the sand table with pea gravel, on the message board they drew a simple line drawing of the table with a large question mark next to it. Children quickly figured out that the question mark meant "It's a mystery," and they set about trying to guess what might be in the table instead of sand.

• **Fantasy-oriented books and computer programs.** Introduce books and software that have themes of fantasy and mystery. Examples of good books with fantasy characters are *The Hungry Thing* by Jan Slepian and Ann Seidler, *Sleeping Dragons All Around* by Sheree Fitch, and *Where the Wild Things Are* by Maurice Sendak. Computer activities that tap into children's interest in mystery and fantasy include the software program *Harry and the Haunted House* by Mark Schlichting (a talking storybook from Broderbund's Living Books CD-ROM Series), and the castle scene from the "Create a Scene" activity on Broderbund's *The Playroom* software program.

You can stimulate children's imaginations and build on their interests by encouraging other kinds of experiences with illusion, mystery, and fantasy throughout the daily routine.

Planning or Recall Time

• **Magic wand.** Before the children arrive, make a simple wand using a stick and some narrow ribbon. At planning or recall time, ask the child who is sharing ideas to use the wand to point to something he or she will use (or did use) at work time. Another idea is to ask children to share their work time plans or experiences, and then use the magic wand to point to the next child who will share.

• **Treasure map.** Draw a simple map of your classroom. Give children a dot sticker with an X drawn on it. Ask children to place the X on the map in an area where they are going to play (or where they did play) and then to share their plans or experiences.

• **Mystery bag.** Collect some materials you saw children using at work time and put them in a bag. One by one, pull the items out of the bag, asking who used them and what they did with the materials.

• **Buried treasure.** Gather up a few materials that you saw children using at work time, and bury them in the sand in your sand table. Hold recall time at the sand table and ask children to help you find the buried treasure. When they find the hidden toys, encourage children to talk about who used them at work time and what they did. Be sure you have enough buried treasure so that each child in your group has something to find!

Small-Group Time

• **Magic paper.** For this strategy, find some gold-colored *Astro Brites* copy paper at an office store. (When you add plain water to the gold-colored paper, it turns bright red.) For small-group time, give children cups of water and paintbrushes and invite them to see what happens when they paint with water on this "magic paper." When small-group time is over, be sure to add this paper to your art area so children can continue to experiment with it at work time.

Large-Group Time or Outside Time

• **The Woman in the Woods.** Children in our preschool love to play this game. It starts with someone telling a short, simple story that goes like this: "Once upon a time, there was a woman (or man) who lived in the woods. One day some children knocked on her door. She answered the door and waved her wand. POOF!—she changed them all into kittens!" After the story, ask the children if they would like to knock on the woman's door. Children delight in sneaking up to the "door" (the back of a shelf or the fence outside) and knocking. The adult (or one of the children, after they have played the game and understand how it works) then says something like "Who's knocking on my door? I'll change you into kittens! POOF!" The children crawl back across the room meowing like kittens. Repeat the game for as long as children are interested, asking them what they would like to be turned into.

Using Computers for Planning and Recall

By Beth Marshall

· ·

Children's day-to-day interests are an important factor to consider as you develop teaching ideas for planning and recall times. As you formulate planning or recall strategies, don't forget to consider the strong interest children have in computers. Your strategies could relate to the computer equipment itself or could build on images or activities from the software children have used. Here are some favorite "'puter planning" and "'puter recall" ideas from the High/Scope Demonstration Preschool (most suggestions can be adapted for either planning or recall times):

- **Computer drawings of area signs.** Use a drawing program to draw or re-create the area signs from your classroom. We used Broderbund's *KidPix,* a program our children are familiar with, to make a sign for each interest area: art, block, house, book, toy, and (of course) computer. We left the computer paper tractor holes on the sides of each sign to help children see that it was printed on the computer. Then we covered each sign with clear adhesive shelf paper to make it more durable (you can also purchase large sheets of laminating paper at an office supply store). We then asked children to use the signs as area cards for planning. Children were asked to point to (or place a marker on) the sign for the area in which they were going to start their plan.

- **Computer-mouse recall.** This strategy requires an old computer mouse with a shortened cord (stores that sell used computer equipment are often happy to donate these) and a large map that you have drawn showing the areas of your classroom. Children click on the map locations that designate where they played, then share what they did in those areas.

- **Keyboard planning.** On small stickers or labels, draw the area symbols for your classroom and stick them to the keys on an old computer keyboard (again, you can often get donations from computer stores or businesses). For planning time, ask the children to "type" the area they are going to work in and tell you what they are going to do there.

• **Treasure hunt.** The inspiration for this strategy is the software program *The Backyard* (Broderbund), which includes the "Sandbox Treasure" game. In this game children use a map to find a buried treasure in the sand-

box. Since this was a popular program with our group of children, we devised a related planning/recall strategy that you could use with your group as well. For planning time, draw a simple map of your classroom and give a copy to each child in your planning group. Also, give each child a sticker with an **X** on it. Ask the children to paste the stickers on their maps to mark an area where they plan to play during work time. Then have each child talk about what he or she is going to do in that area. For recall time, bury items in your sand table that were used during work time. Ask the children to dig in the sand and find the items. As

Taking advantage of the children's interest in computers, the teacher employs the computer-mouse strategy to guide this planning time.

each "treasure" is found, ask who used it. Then have that child describe how he or she used the item and share other work time experiences.

• **Character partners.** We noticed that children enjoyed using the "Mixed-up Toy" activity from *The Playroom* software program (Broderbund) to create silly-looking characters that matched those their friends had created. To build on this interest, we devised a matching game for planning time. We printed out some matching pairs of silly characters, mixed them up, then asked each child to choose a character and find the other child in the group who had the same character. These partners then told each other their plans.

• **Bucket recall.** The program *Katie's Farm* (Lawrence Productions) features Katie and McGee picking berries and putting them into a bucket (with McGee always eating more berries than he puts into the bucket). Our children loved this part of the program and returned to this screen over and over again, never failing to giggle over McGee's behavior. To build on this interest, at recall time we gave a bucket to each child. Then we asked children to put something they had used at work time in their bucket and talk about what they had done during work time.

These are just a few of the many ways you can use children's computer experiences as a source of ideas for planning and recall times. Your own observations in the computer area should yield many more ideas.

Chapter Four

Key Experiences in the Preschool Classroom

· ·

*Children in High/Scope settings are encouraged to make choices about materials and activities throughout the day. As they pursue their choices and plans, children explore, ask and answer questions, solve problems, and interact with classmates and adults. In this kind of environment, children naturally engage in "key experiences"—activities that foster developmentally important skills and abilities. High/Scope has identified **58 preschool key experiences** and grouped them into 10 categories: creative representation,* language and literacy, initiative and social relations, movement, music, classification, seriation, number, space, and time. The articles in this chapter focus on the key experiences in the preschool classroom.

In the first article, "All the Ways Preschoolers Read," Betsy Evans explains that preschoolers learn to read by actually reading, but in their own way—picture reading, pretend reading, reading games, signs and symbols, their own writing—long before they are formally instructed in the mechanics of reading in elementary school.

In the second article, "Message Board: A Preschool Communication Center," Suzanne Gainsley and Rosie Lucier tell about their experiences using a daily message board at the High/Scope Demonstration Preschool and illustrate how you can incorporate one in your early childhood program. Message boards use symbols, pictures, and objects to "write" messages children can "read" and understand. These messages help them prepare for their day, give them a better understanding of the activities that will occur, and alert them to special events and changes in their surroundings (for example, an absent classmate or visitor to the classroom).

In the next selection, "Beyond the Blue Horizon—Promoting Outdoor Experiences," Ursula Ansbach describes how the natural outdoor environment adds a special dimension to the High/Scope preschool key experiences and the learning that results from them. Ansbach also provides ideas that staff in early childhood settings can use to bring experiences with nature to children in their care.

"Supporting Children's Development in Drawing and Painting," by Mary Hohmann, provides several basic strategies for supporting and encouraging young children's adventures in painting and drawing. These strategies range from providing an art area and sufficient time for the activity to quietly watching in a way that lets children know that drawing and painting are valuable and important things to do.

In the next article, "Thinking About Art With Young Children," Ann Epstein makes a convincing argument that by using active learning strategies such as those in the High/Scope approach, we can encourage young children to appreciate art and other aesthetic aspects of their world. In "Walking and Talking About Art," Epstein relates a charming account of how a preschool walking tour to look at the architectural features of houses in the neighborhood allowed children to make a number of interesting observations about shape, size, and color.

"Master Pretenders: Dramatic Arts in the Preschool Classroom," by Ursula Ansbach, shows adults how to support children's dramatic play by becoming involved as observers, "stage managers," co-players, facilitators *and troubleshooters, and occasionally as dramatists. Ansbach also provides an example of one plan she created for a large-group experience that incorporated these five supportive adult roles.*

In the final article, "Moving With Purpose: Rhymes, Action Songs, and Singing Games," Phyllis S. Weikart illustrates how the High/Scope preschool key experiences in movement provide the basis for planning movement-based activities in High/Scope classrooms. In addition to providing this framework, Weikart presents a teaching model and movement and music strategies to make experiences with rhymes, action songs, and singing games successful for children.

All the Ways Preschoolers Read

By Betsy Evans

• •

One year, a new child entered our preschool program and reminded us of the importance of the universal language of symbols. Four-year-old Denis was adopted by his parents from an orphanage in Siberia. Upon learning of his enrollment, our preschool staff began to learn some key Russian phrases. While these phrases did help us communicate with Denis (and also appeared to amuse him as we struggled with pronunciation), the extensive use of labels and symbols in our classroom proved to be most helpful.

We realized that although children from all over the world speak diverse languages, they nevertheless share a common understanding of symbols and pictures. When Denis entered our High/Scope-oriented classroom, he quickly understood the signs and labels used to identify toy shelves, interest areas, the parts of the daily routine, and each of his classmates. Although Denis couldn't speak English or write in a conventional way, like most other preschool children he could "read" pictures and symbols. Because of our emphasis on child-friendly signs and symbols, in our classroom Denis was already a "reader" who was confidently continuing to develop his literacy skills.

Denis's use of signs and symbols to "navigate" in our classroom is typical of the literacy experiences that abound in High/Scope programs. In the High/Scope approach the development of reading and writing skills—*emergent literacy*—is seen as an outgrowth of children's maturation and their active involvement with materials and people. High/Scope environments are designed to support and encourage this natural process.

Language and Literacy Key Experiences

- Talking with others about personally meaningful experiences
- Describing objects, events, and relations
- Having fun with language: listening to stories and poems, making up stories and rhymes
- Writing in various ways: drawing, scribbling, letterlike forms, invented spelling, conventional forms
- Reading in various ways: reading storybooks, signs and symbols, one's own writing
- Dictating stories

In the High/Scope approach, emerging literacy is supported by the six language and literacy key experiences (p. 147). These key experiences illustrate the wide range of activities and interactions that contribute to children's literacy development.

This article focuses specifically on children's **reading experiences,** which are included in the key experience *reading in various ways: reading storybooks, signs and symbols, one's own writing.* For adults who work with young children, the significance of this key experience is the understanding that **children learn to read, literally, by reading.** The phrase *in various ways* is an important part of this message. It tells us that as educators we must become familiar with the many ways in which preschoolers read, in order to encourage the development of their literacy skills. The rest of this article will provide guidelines and strategies for recognizing and supporting preschoolers' reading experiences.

Emergent Reading

Note: *the steps below reflect a general sequence of reading development. However, all children will not pass through these steps in the same order; children's behavior at any given time often reflects a mixture of emergent reading forms.*

1. **Exposure:** early contact with pictures and print and with reading (being read to; seeing adults read for pleasure and purpose)

2. **Exploring picture books, both with and without print** (learning how to handle books; reading-like play)

3. **"Reading" picture books:** relating pictures to real things (labeling objects; following the action; storytelling from pictures)

4. **Identifying symbols, signs, labels and logos:** relating symbols to real things (classroom labels, stop sign, commercial logos)

5. **Being aware that print (rather than the picture) carries the message** (sometimes refusing to read at this stage—"I don't know what the marks say.")

6. **Reading one's own "writing"** (whether at the drawing, scribbling, letterlike-forms, or real-letters stage)

7. **Identifying letter names, sounds** ("*D* is for me and Daddy and my uncle David!")

8. **Recognizing one's own name,** a few other words (classmates' names, Mom, other important or frequently seen words)

9. **Understanding print conventions** (left to right, top to bottom, word spacing, simple punctuation)

10. **Reading independently:** words, phrases, sentences, books (includes sounding-out, known words, comprehension of what is read)

Reading Storybooks and Other Forms of Print

Children build the foundation for actual reading by **reading storybooks and other forms of print, in their own ways.** To encourage this kind of reading, High/Scope teachers **create a print-rich environment.** This means providing easy access to books and print materials, not only on the classroom bookrack but also in all the interest areas—for example, catalogs and magazines in the art area; cookbooks, empty food boxes, and phone books in the house area; letter blocks and puzzles in the toy area; story and writing programs in the computer area.

In such a print-rich environment, children will "read" spontaneously. Here are some examples of how children use print materials:

• **Picture-reading.** Hannah frequently goes to the book area and "reads" stories she knows well to others by paging through the books and talking about the pictures. Sam also likes to "read" to others, reciting stories he has memorized word for word as he points to the pictures. Ramon likes to turn the pages of a book and make up a story, talking to himself as he "reads."

• **Pretend reading.** Erica pretends to look up a number in the phone book, then calls the hospital about her sick baby doll. Dan "reads" the recipe on the back of an empty brownie box as he makes a pretend treat for his friends.

• **Reading games.** Victor works at the computer playing the *Word Rescue* game (Pembroke). As new words appear on the screen, Victor looks them up in the on-screen picture dictionary. Sam enjoys going on "word hunts" at work time. In this game (introduced by teachers one day at small-group time) children hunt for words on classroom signs, figure out the words by looking at the symbols and nearby materials, and then "write" the words in their own way in blank workbooks.

Children use storybook pictures as clues to the story's meaning.

It is important for teachers to **enthusiastically support all these forms of reading as they occur.** Teachers should not push for conventional reading when children picture-read or engage in reading-like play.

Reading Signs and Symbols

Interpreting signs and symbols is an important step in the continuum of emerging literacy. For most preschool children, pictures and symbols are more easily understood than words or letters. As Denis used the symbols in our classroom to help him understand his new environment, he was exhibiting typical preschool-age reading behavior. By supporting Denis in using symbols, we were not only helping him adjust to a new language and culture but were also supporting his development as a reader and writer.

Large wooden letters are part of a print-rich environment.

You can provide similar "reading" experiences for the preschoolers in your program with the following strategies. First, **provide an environment that is rich in signs and symbols.** You can **start by labeling the physical environment—for example, adding signs and labels to the interest areas and labeling the shelves and containers where materials are stored.** Consider the developmental levels of your program's children as you go through the labeling process. If your setting serves toddlers, you might make labels consisting of simple pictures or real objects (a picture of a dinosaur or a single toy dinosaur to stand for the box of small dinosaurs). For preschoolers, create a variety of labels, including some that combine words with appropriate symbols, pictures, or real objects. This will help children begin to associate the printed word with the object.

The next step to creating a sign-and-symbol-rich environment is to **help each child choose a personal symbol,** usually a simplified drawing of a well-known object such as a small fish or a triangle. Next to the picture symbol, print the child's first name. Some programs use stickers or stamps as personal symbols, but these have disadvantages: They are hard for both children and teachers to reproduce freehand and they must be purchased.

The process of assigning a personal symbol to each child should take place early in the school year, either during home visits before school begins, on the first day of school, or during the first week. If possible, **let children choose their own symbols.** For example, teachers may have children choose a personal symbol they like from a set of pre-cut shapes the adults have prepared beforehand. Or, children may suggest particular objects based on their interests, and teachers may create the symbols based on the children's suggestions. In one classroom, children suggested objects that had personal meaning for them. Oliver, who was very fearful about his first preschool experience, asked to have a bunny like the one on the blanket he took to bed each night; Eliza wanted a fish like her goldfish at home; and Trevor chose a ladder, having just learned to climb to the top of his jungle gym.

Julia's artwork is hanging directly above her name, and she knows just where to place her personal symbol to further identify her creation!

Whatever process you use to give children their personal symbols, understand that children will quickly form a strong attachment to *their* symbols. Due to their keen interest in "reading" the symbols, children also will quickly learn to identify the symbols of their classmates, as well as those of classroom adults. (Yes, adults in the classroom need symbols too!)

Symbols can be used in a variety of ways in the preschool classroom. In addition to the labels for the interest areas, toy shelves, and containers, symbols can be used to label children's personal cubbies, their hooks on the coat racks, lunch boxes, artwork, and other personal items. A daily routine chart with symbols for each time period helps children learn the routine. You can also use a combination of personal symbols and other small pictures on a daily message board to give children messages such as "Beth will be the substitute teacher today for Carol, who is traveling," or "Field trip today to Riverside Park." These picture messages can be "read" and discussed at daily greeting time. Interest area symbols can also be incorporated into the day's planning strategies, and symbols can be used on an attendance board to identify which children have arrived or gone home.

Examples of Emergent Reading

"I can write my cat's name. Watch," Lia tells you. Then she prints BRND. *"Brandy,"* she reads.

§

"Here's the list," Jezra says, handing you a sheet of paper covered with scribbles. *"Now you go to the store and get all those things for the camping trip. It says meat, pop, flashlights, and a new tent."*

§

Gena is reading to her stuffed monkey from a picture book version of Hansel and Gretel. *"Stay away from that house!"* she reads, pointing to the illustration of the gingerbread house. *"There might be bad poison candy that makes you sick and knives and stuff."*

§

At planning time the teacher asks children to look at cards marked with both the interest area name and symbol, and to choose the card that represents the area where they want to play. Trevor chooses the toy area card and points to the *T* on the card. *"I have one of those in my name!"* he exclaims. The adult says, *"I wonder what area starts with a T."* Trevor makes a few *T* sounds, then guesses, *"Toy space!"*

§

Several children have been working in the playhouse, creating a pretend pizza parlor. They decide to close the restaurant so they can go grocery shopping. They go to the art area and draw a big circle with a pizza inside it, draw a line across the circle, and write KOSD underneath. They show it around the classroom, saying *"See, it's closed!"* Then they tape the sign to the playhouse.

§

It's time for lunch and the children go to the coat room to get their lunch boxes. There is a moment of confusion as Sam and Hannah both reach for a Power Ranger lunch box. They tug on it for a few seconds. Then Hannah lets go. *"This has my symbol, Sam. See? A princess. Yours is over there."* She points to an identical lunch box with Sam's dog symbol on the side.

§

Sara is pretending to put Casey to bed. She gets the book Goodnight, Moon by Margaret Wise Brown from the bookrack and *"reads"* it to Casey, reciting every word from memory.

Many uses for children's symbols also arise in response to children's individual needs. For example, David, whose divorced parents shared custody, was having trouble predicting which parent would be picking him up at the end of the day. After conferring with his parents, the teachers and David made a chart together to show his daily household schedule. David chose to use a bunk bed picture to symbolize "Daddy days" and a picture of a single bed to symbolize his "Mommy days." When David became confused, he would go to his chart. "Oh, a bunk bed—it's a Daddy day."

Reading One's Own Writing

The last type of children's reading that you will commonly observe in the preschool classroom illustrates the connection between reading and writing skills. Historically, educators believed that reading and writing developed in an orderly sequence, with speaking and listening skills developing first, followed by reading and finally writing. It was commonly thought that most children did not begin to acquire reading skills until kindergarten or first grade and that children were not ready to learn to write until they had begun to read. The modern "whole language" view, however, is that speaking, listening, reading, and writing abilities are interrelated and develop side by side, starting in infancy. Thus, one important way that preschool children "read" is by reading their own attempts at writing.

To encourage children to read their own writing, High/Scope teachers **stock the classroom with a wide range of writing tools and materials** and then **encourage children to read the "writing" they produce.** Preschool-age children write in a variety of forms, including drawing, scribbling, letterlike forms, and conventional letters and words, often mixing two or more of these conventional and nonconventional forms. Teachers recognize and support all these ways of writing. When teachers use these strategies, they will often observe children eagerly reading their own writing in the classroom. For example:

• Emlyn brings a piece of paper to Tara with some squiggly lines on it, saying "This says come to my dolly's birthday." When Tara asks, "Does it say when I should come?" Emlyn answers, "Yeah, right here. It says twenty o'clock."

• David shows his dad the "book" (drawings on a folded piece of paper) he made at small-group time. "It's a book about an alien. See all the arms it has—eight. Those are for fighting Robbie (his brother)."

• Caitlin proudly displays the valentine she has made for her mom, explaining "It says 'I love you, Mommy.'" The message Caitlin has written on the cutout heart includes an *I*, a *U*, the letter combination *NA*, a small heart, and her personal symbol.

Experiences like those of Emlyn, David, and Caitlin illustrate the fact that reading and writing start long before grade school. For many adults who associate learning to read and write with phonics and letter drills, flash cards, and "Dick-and-Jane"-style readers, the realization that **preschoolers are already reading and writing, in their own ways,** may come as a surprise. By encouraging these early literacy efforts, however, we let children know that it's okay to draw, write, and read in any forms they choose. As supportive adults, we know this will lay the foundation for writing and reading conventionally in the future.

At greeting time, adults and children "read" picture messages about the day's activities.

Message Board: A Preschool Communication Center

By Suzanne Gainsley and Rosie Lucier

• •

Teachers at the High/Scope Demonstration Preschool are continually working to support the development of language and literacy by encouraging children to use all forms of language in purposeful ways. One way that we encourage children's emerging reading and writing skills is by using a daily **message board.** This article shares some of our experiences with the message board and illustrates how you can incorporate one in your early childhood program.

The message board in our demonstration preschool is a large dry-erase board that is hung on the wall in the book area. Before children arrive each day, teachers write two or three new messages on the board to provide the children with information about daily events, materials added to the classroom, staff or child absences, and other news that affects the children's daily routine. Once most of the children have arrived, children and teachers gather around the message board for greeting time, the first event of the daily routine. Together they read, interpret, and discuss the day's messages.

"Reading" the messages on the board helps the children prepare for their day. It gives them a better understanding of the activities that will occur and alerts them to special events and changes in their surroundings. For example, if Ben ordinarily plans to play with the same friend, he will notice right away a message that his friend is absent, and he will begin thinking of a new plan even before planning time.

We have found that the children look forward to reading the messages each morning. When children have to figure out the content of a message, they seem to recall it better than if adults simply tell them the same information.

The board stays up throughout the daily routine so children and adults can refer to it throughout the day. Children often check the message board to remind them what will happen next. For example, one day as the chil-

These are the symbols used in the High/Scope® Demonstration Preschool for the interest areas and segments of the daily routine.

dren were cleaning up their snack and getting ready for large-group time, Kamari looked across the room at the message board and said, "Oh yeah, we're using the feather dusters at large group." Children who arrive late can also use the board to orient themselves to the day's events. Reading over the messages with a teacher or another child helps the latecomer make a smooth transition into planning, since children are used to giving their plans shortly after messages are read.

Symbols, Pictures, Objects: How Messages Are "Written"

Our messages are written on the board using pictures, simple symbols, and real objects, sometimes with accompanying words. For children, reading the message board is like "picture-reading" a story book. Just as children derive meaning from the illustrations in a book, they can "read" and understand the pictures and symbols drawn on the message board.

Our message-board language consists of stick-figure people and other simple line drawings, symbols that are familiar to the children, a few small Polaroid photos, and other easily understood images. For example, small photos are used to represent each of the teachers, and a half-moon stands for a planning table of that shape. Because we often have visitors to the Demonstration Preschool, we've developed a symbol—stick figures holding clipboards and pens—to stand for our "writing visitors." Occasionally, color is used to add meaning to these pictures and symbols—for example, we draw a blue oval to represent a rug of that color and shape. This is used as a symbol for large-group time, because the class gathers around a blue oval rug during that segment in the daily routine.

To help children recognize the symbols on the message board, the preschool teachers take care to draw them consistently each time. Through repeated experiences with the same pictures and symbols, the children become aware that these images have consistent meanings. For example, the High/Scope Demonstration Preschool is always drawn as a rectangle with two large windows and a door, a symbol that is readily recognized by children.

Children quickly learn what the symbols mean because the same set of symbols is used not only on the message board but also throughout the preschool setting. There are several types of symbols. **Personal symbols** are used to identify each person's coat hook, cubbie, and any artwork he or she has made. Simple shapes that are easily reproduced by the teachers—for example, a heart, star, or triangle—are used for personal symbols. Adults and children choose their personal symbols from a set provided by teachers at the beginning of the school year. These personal symbols are used in combination with other symbols to convey messages about specific children, for example, that the child is absent that day or that a child has a special experience to share.

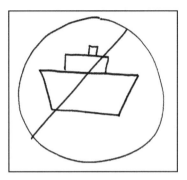

A "no/not" symbol drawn over Brian's symbol, a boat, indicates he is absent.

Area symbols identify the different areas of the room—a crayon for the art area, a hammer for the woodworking area. One way to inform the children that new materials have been added to the classroom is to tape the actual item to the message board and draw the corresponding area symbol next to it. **Daily routine symbols** are another kind of symbol we often use. Each daily routine event has its own symbol, for example, a swing set for outside time. These symbols are used on a picture chart of the daily routine, which is posted on the wall. Teachers use the daily routine symbols on the message board to announce the rare occasions when there are changes in the daily routine, for example, when the order of large- and small-group times is changed because of a field trip or visitors to the classroom. Symbols for the daily routine are posted below the message board so children can refer to them as they read the messages. (The picture on p. 156 shows the daily routine and area symbols used at the Demonstration Preschool.)

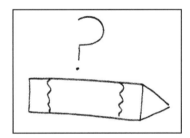

A question mark over the symbol for the art area conveys this message, "Guess what's new in the art area!"

Another common symbol—a "no" or "not" symbol—consists of a red circle with a line through it. Each Friday, the teachers draw two school symbols with a red circle around them and a line through the circle. Children announce in unison, "Two no-school days!" This is a way of preparing children for the upcoming weekend. Occasionally, the teachers must explain their drawings, and the children become "art critics" ("That doesn't look like the tape player!"). But once everyone agrees that the black rectangle with knobs on top *is* the tape player, it is recognized right away if it appears again.

Question mark symbols are also used often. These mystery messages, like "something new in the block area," are always well received. (This message would be drawn with a question mark over a block, the symbol for the block area.) Such messages often prompt children to start thinking about their work time plans.

As the children develop an awareness about and interest in print, teachers add a few words or numbers to the messages as well. For example, we add the names to the area symbols, and we write children's names next to their symbols.

What Do Children Gain From the Message Board?

Whether messages are all in pictures, or contain words as well, interpreting them is seen as a reading experience for children in our classroom. This reflects the High/Scope approach to literacy, in which teachers promote reading and writing experiences that grow naturally out of the needs for communication in the classroom. To encourage children's reading and writing, adults provide them with opportunities for all forms of verbal communication and surround them with language in all its forms, both spoken and written.

The message board is well suited to this approach to language and literacy because it supports many different kinds of communication experiences. All the **key experiences in language and literacy** (see list on p. 147) occur around the message board.

First, the messages on the board provide a shared **reading** experience. Since reading symbols is an important pre-reading skill, it is one of the activities included in *reading in various ways,* one of the language and literacy key experiences. This kind of "reading" about daily events is a far more natural and meaningful reading experience than the rote phonics exercises or reading drills provided in some preschools. Since children usually have strong curiosity about the upcoming events of the day, the motivation to "read" takes care of itself.

The daily reading of the messages also presents a great opportunity for **conversation,** as children exchange ideas about what the messages mean, and children and teachers make comments about the day's news (key experiences: *talking with others about personally meaningful experiences; describing objects, events, and relations*).

The message board also provides **dictation** and **writing** experiences for children, since the children themselves often initiate messages. When

I Can't Draw!

I'm really interested in getting started with a message board in my classroom, but I'm not much of an artist. How can I possibly do a message board when I can only draw stick figures?

—*A Preschool Teacher*

Stick figures are fine, as the illustrations throughout this chapter show. Even very simple drawings can be understandable to children. Remember, too, that you don't have to draw everything in a message—you can also include photos and real objects to illustrate certain words or ideas.

If you do decide to get started with a message board, don't be disappointed if children don't "get" every drawing right away. You can expect that the first time you draw a symbol, many children will not understand it. After the symbol has been used and discussed several times, children will recognize it right away.

Remember, too, that it's not the end of the world if children can't recognize one of your drawings. The value of the process is in the discussions that occur at the message board; there is no need for every picture to be perfect.

Those times when a drawing is unclear to children present valuable learning experiences in themselves. For example, one morning High/Scope Demonstration Preschool teachers Rosie and Sue drew on the message board some cross-hatched lines with a building next to it. The message they intended was that the class would be taking a walking field trip to the local farmer's market, which is located right next to some railroad tracks. However, the class read the message as "We're going to the fire station! Yahoo!" Though the children were disappointed to find out that the fire station was not their destination that day, a good discussion followed. The children talked about other field trips they might want to take, and the group planned a trip to the fire station that took place several weeks later.

Keep in mind that when children are open in their criticism of a drawing, it's a sign that you are doing a good job of encouraging honest discussion in your classroom. For example, a message-board drawing may elicit child comments like these: "Your picture is wrong." "It doesn't look like that." These can be valuable occasions for the teacher to respond with thought-provoking questions (Why doesn't it look like...? What does it need? What else can I add to make this look more like...?).

Children enjoy these discussions of adult "mistakes," and you'll enjoy them too, once you realize how much children learn from their experiences at the message board, even if you are not an accomplished artist.

Ben arrived one morning upset that he had lost one of his toy cars, he asked the teacher to write a message on the message board to let children know about his predicament. Ben suggested that the teacher draw his picture (a stick figure with Ben's symbol underneath) with a frown and tears under his eyes (key experiences: *dictating stories; writing in various ways*). While reading the message board, Ben's classmate Loryn noticed Ben's symbol and the expression on the figure's face. She said, "Ben's symbol! He's sad." Ben then had the opportunity to explain that he had lost his car and to ask children to help him look for it during work time (key experiences: *reading in various ways; talking with others about personally meaningful experiences*).

Some of the most meaningful of messages on the board are those generated by children after group discussions of classroom issues. After work time one morning, the class had a discussion about the consequences of putting water in the Play Doh® container. Becca, one of the children, was upset that it had turned to mush. After the class had finished its discussion, Becca decided to put a message on the container as a reminder not to put water in the Play Doh®. Her message consisted of some pink squiggles (to stand for the Play Doh®) next to droplets surrounded by a "no" symbol. The teacher posted this drawing on the message board the next morning and asked Becca to explain it. Becca beamed as she reminded the class about their group decision to keep water out of the Play Doh® (key experiences: *writing in various ways; talking with others about personally meaningful experiences*).

One reason we posted Becca's message was to let her know how much we valued her attempts at writing. High/Scope teachers support the development of children's writing by encouraging them to "write in their own way" and by valuing all their writing efforts, no matter what form the "writing" takes. So when children expressed an interest in writing their own messages on the message board, the teachers supported this interest by adding smaller wipe-off boards and dry-erase markers to the greeting area, along with other writing materials, such as note pads, Post-it® notes, envelopes, pens, pencils, and clipboards.

Knowing that children's "writing" comes in all different forms (lines, scribbles, mis-made letters, conventional letters, words with invented spelling, and words spelled conventionally), the teachers were not surprised that children chose their own special ways to write on their personal message boards. They were also not surprised that children used their boards to communicate about things that were important and meaningful to them. As children created their own messages and then "read" them to the class, they were engaging in two key experiences, *writing in various ways* and *reading in various ways.*

For example, Jessie arrived one morning, announcing that she had a new kitten at home and wanted to bring it to school. She drew a picture of a cat on her small message board and then asked how to spell "Luke," which she wrote underneath her drawing. She propped her message board next to the big board and told the class about Luke the cat's upcoming visit. Kamari's writing took a different form. He drew spirals of blue over his message board and, pretending to read, said, "I went to the movies . . . ."

In using the class message board and their smaller personal message boards, children begin to see that writing and reading are tools for communicating about things that are meaningful and important in their daily lives. For both children and adults, the message board provides a handy summary of information relevant to the day. Many children find the message board so useful that they look at it even before they hang up their coats in the morning. Because children are familiar with the message board's format and symbols, they are confident in their ability to decode the messages, and they are eager to be the first to "read" what the day's messages mean.

Through these cooperative experiences in reading, interpreting, and writing messages, children are developing beginning reading and writing abilities. They are also learning, in ways that are personally meaningful to them, about the usefulness of written communication and its contribution to the well-being of the community.

This sign with children's personal symbols is posted in the house area. It lists the children who have small-group experiences at the house area table. The same symbols are used whenever anyone needs to "write" a child's name.

A Message Board Diary

Here's how we used the message board during the first seven days of school one year. Most of the children were already familiar with the message board, having been in the summer program. Below we describe (and when possible, illustrate) each day's messages as well as some of the children's responses to these messages.

Thursday (first day of school)

• It was preschooler Michael's birthday. Our first message (at top of p. 162) showed a picture of a boy in a baseball cap with a birthday cake. We drew Michael's symbol (a fish) on the boy's shirt. Ben read our message about Michael's birthday with no difficulty. When Sue asked Ben what gave him the clue that it was Michael's birthday, Ben said, "Because I saw his symbol on the shirt." Ben then tried to put his own baseball cap on Michael so he would look like the boy in the drawing (Michael wasn't wearing a cap that day).

- To let individual children know which group and teacher they would be with for small-group activities (planning, recall, snack, and small-group time), the board also listed children's symbols in two separate groupings. Each set of symbols was drawn in a different color and one of the teacher's pictures appeared above each set. A picture of Polly, a visitor, was posted between the two groups—this let children know she would be traveling between groups. At the end of greeting circle, we told the children, "If your symbol is red, go to Rosie's table. If your symbol is blue, go to Sue's table."

Friday (second day)

- We taped colored strips of paper (used in small-group time the day before) on the board next to the art area symbol so children would know the strips were available to play with and where they could find them.

- To prepare children for the upcoming weekend, we drew two symbols of the preschool with the "no" symbol (a red circle with slash through it) drawn over them.

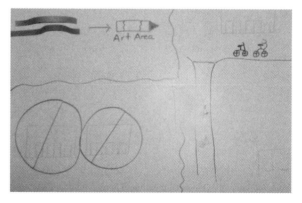

- We also included drawings of two kinds of bikes and the playground's inclined walkway to remind children of a previous discussion about riding the bikes safely. This message about the bike policy was instantly recognized by some of the returning children. They explained the message to the newcomers: The tall bikes should stay at the top of the hill, while low bikes could go down it. When Joshua arrived late, Ben helped him read the messages before he made a plan to play.

Monday (third day)

• We posted Rosie's picture inside the "no" symbol to indicate she wouldn't be in school that day because of a medical appointment. The small picture of a foot represented the cast on Rosie's broken foot, which she had to have changed that morning. Also included was a drawing of Mary, the substitute teacher.

• We taped up a red scarf tacked onto the oval rug symbol to tell children that the class would be using silky scarves at large-group time.

Tuesday (fourth day)

• We posted a work-in-progress sign next to one of Erika's Play Doh® cupcakes. (These signs warn children not to disturb a project—such as a block structure—that a child is still working on.) The day before, Erika had used a sign like this to let others know not to touch her cupcakes. Our message had two goals: First, we wanted the new children in the class to know how the work-in-progress sign is used. More important, we hoped to encourage a discussion about how the Play Doh® changes when it is left out. As we had hoped, the children did discuss these changes. "It gets crumby," Lauren said. Erika decided right away to put away the dough so it would not "get hard." Joshua added "Put the lid on tight."

• We drew Ellie's symbol over a picture of a frog to let the class know it was Ellie's turn to feed the frogs. We repeated this message, with a new child's symbol, on each subsequent day.

Wednesday (fifth day)

- Humza was absent. We drew his symbol, a car, with a "no" sign over it.

- We taped a few of the jungle blocks from the previous day's small-group time onto the board, with an arrow pointing to the toy area symbol. This told children that the set was now available in the toy area at work time. Tristin and his mom arrived after the message board had been read. They stopped at the board first, before finding Rosie for Tristin's planning.

Thursday (sixth day)

- Rosie wanted to make sure that the children in her small group knew where to find the magnet fish and poles used during the previous day's small-group time. She attached a rod and a fish to the board, along with a drawing of the block area symbol.

- We drew a car in distress (indicated by some red lines), next to a clock and Robin's symbol (a mitten). At greeting circle, we explained this message: Robin was going to be late because her mother's car was in an accident on the way to school. This discussion sparked quite a bit of concern among the children. They had lots of questions to ask Robin as soon as she arrived at school.

Friday (seventh day)

- We used Ellie's symbol inside the "no" symbol, plus a picture of a nose with a facial tissue attached. Translation: Ellie would be absent that day because of a runny nose.

- We drew stick figures of a woman and a man next to two children sitting on the floor playing. This was to inform children that Michelle (the visitor coordinator) was hosting observers at the preschool that day. Just before greeting time, Michelle read the message board with her own child as she dropped him off for preschool. The children noticed right away that Michelle had on a black and white dress, just like the woman in the picture. Michelle then explained a little more about the visitors she would be hosting.

- Finally, we again displayed two school symbols with "no" symbols over them to reveal that the weekend was coming up.

As these examples demonstrate, the message board is easy to work into a program's daily routine. It provides a vehicle for reminding returning students about classroom routines and events, as well as a structure for introducing the classroom and routine to preschoolers entering for the first time. Children are eager to read the messages because they always convey important information—they are never make-work for children. Because the messages present such valuable "real-life" information, children quickly realize that the message board is a useful form of classroom communication.

Beyond the Blue Horizon—
Promoting Outdoor Experiences

By Ursula Ansbach

· ·

While driving through a suburban neighborhood recently on a beautiful spring Saturday, I noticed that there were no children playing outside. In fact, there was no sign of anyone. I was stunned. Where were the children? Were they watching cartoons? Playing video games? Taking karate classes? I thought back to my own childhood: on a day like this, the neighborhood would have been filled with the sounds of children playing outside.

Most of us have childhood memories of favorite outdoor places—a creek near our neighborhood where we could play alone or with friends, a park near our apartment building where we didn't have to worry that our loud voices would bother the neighbors upstairs, a grandparent's farm where we actually helped to bring in the cattle, a country house where we could explore the fields and woodlands on our own. Many of us also remember how comfortable the adults in our lives felt about our being outdoors without them—they would pack us a snack and send us off for the morning with only the reminder "Be back in time for lunch!"

The Outdoors—A Boost for the Key Experiences

Think back to a favorite outdoor place from your own childhood. Using a copy of the High/Scope preschool key experiences, make a list of everything you learned in this setting. As you look over your list, you'll probably notice experiences in **number, seriation, classification, creative representation, movement,** and more—most likely, all the categories are included abundantly. Now imagine the impact of all these key experiences. Add to this the peace of mind and pure joy that children exhibit as they play outdoors, and we can begin to understand the value of these outdoor experiences for children!

The natural environment adds a special dimension to the key experiences and the learning that results from them. For example, consider how the **creative representation** key experiences are enhanced by outdoor play. The first key experience in this category, *recognizing objects by sight, sound, touch, taste, and smell,* is intensified in outdoor settings. When children are standing under a crab apple tree in full bloom on a playground in early spring, this key experience comes alive in moments. The richness of sensory stimulation we experience in nature can't be duplicated in an indoor classroom. For example, consider the profusion of smells we experience outdoors after a rainstorm and compare this with what happens when the teacher brings in a few "smelly jars" or "smelly bags" and asks children to guess the smells.

The pure joy of exploring the outdoors in springtime is evident in these children's faces.

The vivid, multi-sensory experiences children have when outdoors inevitably lead to other kinds of learning experiences. For example, children who are watching and listening to a seagull (*recognizing objects by sight, sound, touch, taste, and smell*) soon begin imitating its call, thus engaging in another **creative representation** key experience, *imitating actions and sounds.* When they make a clay model of that seagull later in the day (or even right then, if an adult has brought art materials outside) they're participating in another key experience, *making models out of clay, blocks, and other materials.* Thus we move down the list of **creative representation** key experiences.

Similarly, key experiences in **language and literacy** flourish when children go outside. How eagerly and naturally children describe the activity of the ants they discover while planting in the soil (*describing objects, events, and relations*)! Children acquire a unique vocabulary outdoors. Without planting a garden, how will children learn such words and phrases as *trowel, rototiller, preparing the soil, scatter planting?* The concept of growing food in itself is a revelation to city children, many of whom reply "the supermarket" when asked where food comes from. Exciting discoveries like this one about the origins of food naturally lead to conversation, and in the process children expand their use of descriptive language.

Now let's consider the key experiences in **space.** Children are developing their understanding of spatial relations as they watch ants crawl around, up, over, and under branches, soil, and blades of grass *(experiencing and describing positions, directions, and distances).* To get a closer look at the ants, the children assume various viewpoints and positions *(observing people, places, and things from different spatial viewpoints).* Planting a garden offers multiple opportunities for spatial learning. As they help to decide where to plant the tomatoes and peppers in the garden, they again make judgments about positions, directions, and distances. Later, when tiny shoots emerge from the ground, the children *fill and empty* the containers needed to water the new plants. Other **space** key experiences emerge when the children make a drawing of the garden at recall time to show where and how they planted the marigold seeds *(interpreting spatial relations in drawings, pictures, and photographs).*

Planting a garden also involves a wide range of **social relations and initiative** key experiences. *Making choices, plans, and decisions* comes into play as we plan the garden. The children weigh all kinds of choices—what flowers to plant, which vegetables go where, who wants to water the garden, who wants to plant each day. Later, caring for the garden becomes a group routine that children can choose to take part in *(participating in group routines).* If some children would prefer to go to the swings for a while or sit under a tree, they do so, *taking care of their own needs* for a different kind of play. Children learn social skills by *dealing with social conflicts* that arise when everyone wants to water the garden at once. They have another opportunity to negotiate solutions when some children find they enjoy squirting one another with the garden hose while others think this isn't fun at all.

Key experiences in **movement** and **music** occur naturally and spontaneously outdoors as well. We typically think of children outdoors as *moving in locomotor ways*—they run, jump, hop, climb, and twirl. They also *move in nonlocomotor ways*—bending to examine insects, standing on tiptoe to smell flowering shrubs, twisting to see who is yelling behind them. Children outdoors *move with objects,* whether pedaling a tricycle or carrying pails to the sandbox. With the freedom to use the full range of their voices, children sing loudly as they run and play outdoors. As they *explore their singing voices,* children *move to music* and *express creativity in movement* invented to accompany songs and chants. Children *explore and identify sounds* with the objects they discover in nature—banging two sticks together, tapping a stone on different surfaces, listening to the whoosh of the wind or the patter of the rain.

The rest of the key experience categories are equally represented in children's outdoor play. All of these learning experiences occur effortlessly as children explore the outdoors, work in the school garden, and experience nature firsthand!

Other Benefits of Outdoor Experiences

Besides encouraging the key experiences, some other benefits of outdoor experiences are the following:

✓ **Children respond favorably and immediately to nature.** A group of preschoolers I worked with were living in a homeless shelter. Most of these children had very little exposure to natural settings. Some had not even had the opportunity to play in an outdoor playground before they came to us. I remember one little boy who expressed his fear of trees by kicking and hitting them with sticks the first time he went outdoors with us. Other children were so frightened of the full-grown tomato plants that were thriving in our container garden that they would cry and run from them. We responded to this with gentle encouraging statements: "This garden is available to you—you do not have to come out here, but it is here if you decide you want to." With no more prompting than this, in a very short time children began coming into the garden. Within a week or two children were not only comfortable, but joyful and eager as they participated in the outdoor activities provided. I recall being greeted by a smiling child picking a tomato and saying "See, Ms. Ursula! I'm not afraid of the 'matoes any more!" Thus, we don't have to show children how to accept nature. We simply have to provide them with the opportunity to interact with it.

✓ **Children with special needs may benefit from outdoor experiences in surprising ways as well.** Children who are easily distracted or upset often appear more calm, secure, and focused in a natural environment than when they are indoors. This may be because there is less pressure outdoors for children to restrain their movements or voices, and/or because they experience more sensory stimulation outdoors. The greater variety of smells and textures that are available outdoors can be valuable for children with visual impairments as well. By carefully choosing and arranging scented plants in a garden, we can help such children orient themselves. A soft carpet of sand can provide a wide range of interesting play possibilities and safety for children who are prone to falling. Thus the natural environment provides interesting activities and opportunities for success for children of varying needs and abilities.

✓ **Outdoor experiences are also a natural way to introduce environmental education.** Abstract exhortations to "save the environment" do not mean anything to young children. Rather, the environment will become interesting and valuable to them through their direct and concrete interactions with nature. Young children who have opportunities to connect with nature can understand why it is so important to care for and nurture the environment. As older children and adults, they will better appreciate the lessons of environmental science because they've had healthy outdoor experiences.

✓ **Finally, nature is healthy for children.** Simply being outdoors in the open air is necessary for young bodies to grow strong. This simple truth seems obvious, yet so many educators forget it when they cancel recess and outdoor activities. Outdoor activities should not be thought of as a frill but as a basic part of the curriculum. Children need to experience nature in all its variety every day, not just when it's 70 degrees and sunny.

If the benefits of the outdoors are so obvious, why are we often so hesitant to provide these experiences? A normal aspect of outdoor play used to be that this was often unsupervised time for children. As they played independently, children felt empowered—a feeling of "I can do it by myself!" arose. Children flourished when they could explore and make their own mistakes, and amazingly, accidents were few. Today, the fear of accidents is one reason we do not allow children to be outdoors without adult supervision. The dangers of our society are another. The press constantly informs us of child molestations, kidnappings, accidental deaths, and injuries suffered by children who are left unsupervised. Yet is it wise to restrict all children because of the sadness of such isolated incidents?

Safety considerations *are* important, and leaving children unsupervised is clearly not an option for preschool teachers. However, we can keep in mind children's need for independence as we plan for experiences outdoors. Included in the suggestions below are ways that adults can be less intrusive outdoors while still providing for children's safety and meeting their needs for support.

Ideas for Outdoor Experiences

Once we are convinced that outdoor experiences are important, the next step to consider is how to provide such experiences for our children, who no longer have vacant lots readily available in the city nor meadows and streams behind their suburban homes. Here are some ideas that staff of early childhood settings can use to bring experiences with nature to children in their care.

Children explore the soil as they plant spring bulbs.

✓ **Plant container gardens or regular gardens.** Gardening can work well with young children if we consider their developmental needs.

✓ **Take field trips to parks,** where the goal is simply to give children time to explore and enjoy. (By contrast, an activity like visiting a petting zoo, while fun and exciting, does not provide the same opportunity for open-ended exploration). At one urban child care setting I was involved with, we took our children to a nearby park where we roped off an area that was easy to supervise. We divided the children into small groups, each of which was assigned to two adults. The adults supervised the children for safety while being as unobtrusive as possible. In other words, we were available for interaction when desired and necessary. However, we made it a priority to "take a back seat" when possible. This did not mean that we spent time talking with other teachers or having a coffee break. Our focus was the children, and that meant giving them private time when possible. This private time was also an opportunity for the adults to silently observe children and possibly take anecdotes from a safe distance. This approach can also work well on the playground *with certain children at certain times;* it is not intended to be used at all times. As an example of its benefits, however, consider how important having time alone in an open space can be for a child growing up in an over-crowded apartment.

✓ **Plan ways to make your preschool playground more "natural."** For example, incorporate stones, sand, weathered wood, or tree stump slices in the outdoor setting; set up bird feeders in your playground so children can observe birds in their natural setting as opposed to indoor cages.

✓ **Plan ways to make the outdoor play area more supportive of children's privacy and independence.** Plant trees and shrubs that provide natural hiding places where children have privacy but can still be supervised

Outdoor Time in All Kinds of Weather

The teachers in our preschool believe children should have a wide variety of outdoor experiences, so we have our outdoor time in all but the most extreme weather conditions. Some parents object if children go outdoors in drizzly or snowy weather because they are afraid their children will get dirty, cold, or sick. How can we respond to this?
— *A preschool teacher*

Parents give many reasons for resisting outdoor experiences in the preschool — dirt, disease, kidnapping, encounters with strangers, exposure to crime and drugs, insects, asthma, allergies, cars, sun, animals, as well as the weather. To arrive at a policy for outdoor play, staff must consider which concerns are realistic and how to deal with each one. Here are some suggestions for educating parents about the importance of outdoor learning:

- **Explain your all-weather policy to parents when children enter the program.** Follow up by discussing this further in a parent newsletter or at a parent meeting. Collect a back-up supply of boots, slickers, umbrellas, jackets, mittens, hats, and so forth, and reassure parents that you are well-prepared for all weather conditions because of the extra clothes you have on hand. Some parents who may be especially concerned about their children being well-dressed at school may want to send in extra sets of clothes for muddy or wet days.

- **Point out to parents that active learning doesn't stop at the preschool door; in fact, it continues in full force outdoors.** Explain that you don't consider outdoor time to be "break time" for you or the children; in fact, you are just as busy supporting learning outdoors as you are indoors. Give parents specific examples of what children are learning through outdoor play, referring to the High/Scope preschool key experiences to illustrate the learning value of these play incidents. Be sure to include anecdotes of quiet play as well as active physical play, and include some that show how children's thinking and language skills expand outdoors.

- **Remember that some parents may be uncomfortable with outdoor experiences for their children because they've had few outdoor experiences themselves.** Provide opportunities for parents to enjoy the outdoors by planning some parent-child activities. For example:

  - Ask parents to help in the school garden.

  - Invite parents to come along on a field trip to a park that will focus on exploring nature.

  - Plan a collecting walk. Have each parent and child collect leaves, stones, shells, acorns, burrs, seeds, etc., and bring them back in a paper bag to explore further.

  - Plan a parent-child nighttime nature walk during which you encourage everyone to notice smells and sounds.

  - In winter, plan a family sledding excursion.

  - Plan an outdoor potluck or cook-out in the spring or fall, during cool weather. Encourage everyone to dress warmly. Offer plenty of hot beverages.

Solitary experiences with nature are empowering for children. They learn to set their own limits and rarely have accidents.

by nearby adults. Some outdoor playground equipment provides such private hiding places as well. At the child care setting described earlier, our playground had a "tree house" that was only accessible by the steps to the sliding board. The space felt completely private to children, although we could supervise every corner of this little house. Children rarely invited adults into this special place, and we respected this desire by staying away.

✓ **Encourage children to contribute to the natural environment of their community** by planting trees in your playground area and in local parks. Nursery trees are readily available from the National Audubon Society for very little money. In our child care setting, we planted these small trees first in our playground garden and then transferred them to a nearby park. (If you try this, be sure to get the park's permission first.)

❦

As I drive through the countryside and see woodland after woodland being torn up without much forethought, I wonder why we have so little concern about what is precious and irreplaceable. I place my hope in a future generation of children who will be so connected to nature that they will not allow such a ravaging of the earth to happen so easily.

Supporting Children's Development in Drawing and Painting

By Mary Hohmann

• •

As toddlers become preschoolers they gain the capacity to form and hold mental images, and thus are able to talk about and represent their experiences through a variety of media. In this article we examine **young children's creative representation** as it emerges through **drawing and painting experiences.** We also highlight some important ways in which adults can support these experiences.

Young children are intrinsically motivated to draw and paint. They are usually eager to explore drawing and painting materials, discover how it feels to use the materials, and see what effects they can create with them. Once young children learn they can literally "make their mark" with felt-tipped markers, chalk, crayons, and paint, they begin to use these tools to express their feelings, give form to mental images, and consolidate and communicate what they know about their world.

Phases in Drawing and Painting

Drawing and painting abilities develop gradually. Children begin very simply, by making marks and scribbles, but eventually discover lines, shapes, and colors. They learn to combine all these elements to make designs, simple figures, and other images. With time and experience, they add distinctive detail to these images.

Create an atmosphere that encourages children to converse about their drawing and painting experiences.

Development in Painting and Drawing

In *Art and Experience* (1993, pp. 6–9), artist and art educator Nancy Smith and her colleagues define the following phases in the development of children's painting and drawing .

"Learning the Elements"

"Motions and the Marks They Make" (ages 1½–3). For beginners, drawing and painting are mainly physical experiences; they are occupied with the feelings of making large arm and body movements and the sensations of touching the paints, brushes or drawing tools, and painting surfaces. Eventually children discover that they are creating interesting marks—visual effects—through the actions of their bodies, arms, hands, and fingertips.

"Finding Out About Lines, Shapes, and Colors" (ages 3–5). As children gain control of their bodies and motions, they become increasingly aware of the visual elements of their artwork. They notice that they can create lines of various lengths and configurations, distinct shapes (especially rounded shapes), and patches of color. They notice the boundaries of shapes and the sections and boundaries of the paper surface. They often keep colors separate and may mix them deliberately to create new colors.

"Designing" (ages 4–6). Children begin to combine lines, shapes, and colors to create visually interesting nonrepresentational patterns and designs.

"First Representations"

"Names for Configurations and Symbols from Designs" (ages 2–5). At ages 2 and 3, children occasionally discover that something they have drawn or painted resembles an actual object in the world, and they attach names to these creations to identify the objects they see. Gradually, children begin to modify their creations to look more like the objects they've discovered in them. Finally they select a subject to represent before starting a drawing or painting, often using simple graphic symbols (such as a circle and two lines to represent a person) as stock elements in their creations.

"Picturing Experience"

Children make deliberate efforts to represent objects and experiences. They add increasing amounts of detail as their understanding of the world becomes more complex. This phase contains the three levels described next.

Simple Images: People, Houses, Animals" (ages 5–7). Children typically depict the most personal and familiar aspects of their lives.

"Richer Symbols: Friends, Workers, City Streets" (ages 7–9). The subject matter of children's art expands to include the broader social world they are now familiar with, including events and people they have personally experienced and those they know indirectly through books, television, and other media.

"Metaphors and Styles: The Den of a Wolf, A Cat on a Cushion" (ages 9–11). Children gain the ability to express emotions and concepts symbolically through art.

Artist and art educator Nancy Smith describes the development of painting and drawing in three overlapping phases: "learning the elements," "first representations," and "picturing experience" (see sidebar on p. 176). "As their painting evolves," Smith reports, "children use three distinctly different modes of thought. After the first [phase], in which the characteristics of the visual-graphic elements—line, shape, color, and paper space— are learned, there is a second period in which children encounter the possibility of graphic representation using emotional and expressive modes of thought. In the third phase children . . . create increasingly more complex images of their experiences in the world. Thus, children's concepts about paint, design, and representation build on one another" (Smith et al., 1993, p. 6).

Allow children the time they need to do artwork.

Adults working with young artists understand that young children *want* to paint and draw but that painting and drawing abilities evolve at individual rates over a long period of time. So it's important to identify specific ways in which we can nurture and encourage all children in their creative growth as art explorers and creators of symbols and images. Following are some strategies for supporting this process.

Support Strategies for Drawing and Painting

Set up an attractive art area. An inviting and well-stocked art area, with materials on hand to initiate painting and drawing experiences at small-group times, is an essential element of every High/Scope classroom. With an art area in place, children can choose to paint and draw as part of their daily plan-work-recall sequence.

Provide enough time for drawing and painting. As with any endeavor, children who are painting and drawing need time to explore and try out their ideas. "Children must be allowed time," says Nancy Smith, "to move through all the necessary processes: getting materials, thinking over ideas, carrying out paintings, and finally, cleaning up. Children also need ample time over the course of the year to learn routines, to explore and gain confidence in their use of materials, and to develop meaningful ideas" (1993, p. 104).

Allowing children the time they need to do artwork may require a flexible approach to your schedule. For example, one teaching team discovered that when children finger-painted at small-group time, this period lasted longer than when they drew with markers. So, on finger-paint days they planned for longer small-group times and shorter large-group times.

Create a playful atmosphere for children's art. "A playful atmosphere is essential for the experimentation of young drawers and painters," says Greek artist and art educator Eli Trimis in the High/Scope videotape *Drawing and Painting: Ways to Support Young Artists.* Painting and drawing are enjoyable undertakings, full of action and surprises. It is important for adults to relax and enjoy the creative process of children's painting and drawing rather than worrying too much about possible spills, wasted materials, or how long cleanup might take.

Begin with primary colors (red, yellow, and blue) and white paper. When children have had little or no experience with painting and drawing, their initial experiences are primarily physical, often consisting of simple rhythmic motions, for example, moving a marker or paintbrush back and forth across a piece of paper. Nancy Smith describes this kind of activity: "They continue this for so long sometimes that the paper is worn through from the vigor and repetition of strokes. They have no idea that paint colors can mix or be guided to make lines and shapes. They experience the kinesthetic sensation of their arm movement, the tactile sensation of the paintbrush (or finger paint), and then discover marks produced on the paper" (1993, p. 17).

To support children in this early stage of development, begin by offering a single primary color of finger paint on paper plates during small-group time, along with individual pieces of white paper. Presenting finger paints on paper plates allows children to dip and paint with the whole surface of their palms and fingers, using large arm movements. Fairly thick paint will be easier to control than thin paint.

You might next offer small-group times using brushes, large sheets of white butcher paper, and one primary color of paint on a paper plate. Have another primary color of paint ready for those who wish to add another color.

Later, you might offer a finger-painting small-group time in which you provide large sheets of white butcher paper and paper plates of red, yellow, or blue finger paint. You might, for example, gather the children into groups of three around three lengths of butcher paper—with one group using red finger paint, one using yellow paint, and the third group using blue paint. You may find that some children are happy working with one color for some

Children's Drawings: A Way to Recall

Drawing and painting experiences needn't be confined to small-group or work times. Here's how one High/Scope teacher planned recall time around a drawing activity.

At recall time in the High/Scope Demonstration Preschool, Beth, a teacher, and the children in her recall group meet on the floor around a large sheet of butcher paper. Several containers of colored markers are positioned on the paper so children can reach them easily. To get recall time started, Beth makes this suggestion: "Today at recall time we have paper and markers. You might want to go get something you used at work time and then try drawing around it. Or you might just draw a picture of something you did or something you used at work time."

The children quickly become engaged in making drawings of their experiences. Jack uses a brown marker to draw the ladder he used in the block area and then draws a large dinosaur with spines (stegosaurus) that figured in his work time role play. Brendan, who made a structure from interlocking blocks, traces around the structure and then stops drawing to transform the structure into a "guy" he also played with. Carleen traces around a rubber stamp she used at work time and then fills in the details, using many colors. Frances draws the envelope and sticky-back picture stamps she used at work time. Her drawing includes a colorful design decorating the envelope. Rachel traces around the basket of markers using lots of different colors and then draws a few economical lines to depict what she calls a "swing set" right in the middle of her multicolored circles. Beth moves from child to child and converses with children about their work as they pause to look at their drawings.

---

length of time, while others are ready and eager to try out and combine a second and third color almost immediately.

Encourage children's discoveries about lines, shapes, and colors. As you observe children painting and drawing, you will gradually begin to see some of them moving from rhythmic motor actions to the more controlled motions that allow them to explore lines, shapes, and colors. At this point you can encourage them by introducing new painting and drawing materials in the art area or as part of the materials you provide at small-group time—for example, paper in different sizes and shapes and brushes of different thicknesses.

One teaching team planned several small-group times for children who were becoming aware of the kinds of lines and shapes they could create in painting. In a particular small-group time, the teacher gave children round white pieces of paper; brushes; and red, yellow, blue, black, and white paints. She said, "Maybe you would like to pretend that your round white papers are plates that need to be decorated." The children took up her chal-

Labeling Children's Artwork

I have always been interested in children's art. My children paint and draw on a regular basis, and when they show me a painting or drawing, I encourage them to talk about it. Then, writing directly on the child's painting or drawing, I usually transcribe a few of their words about what they have done. This way, I can remember the children's ideas about their creations, and their family members can tell what they are looking at when the children take their artwork home. Recently, however, I heard from another early childhood teacher in my community (who had attended a High/Scope workshop) that writing children's words on their pictures is not a good idea! What are your thoughts on this issue?

—A preschool teacher

For many years we did encourage teachers to take dictation from children whenever they had the opportunity, because we wanted to help children see the connection between spoken and written language. While we still encourage teachers to take dictation from children, we urge them to do so only *at the children's request*. We suggest that they refrain from writing on children's paintings and drawings unless children ask them to do so, which usually doesn't happen.

We have arrived at these recommendations based on our growing knowledge about the development of language and literacy as it relates to children's drawing and painting experiences. We now understand that children's writing begins with drawing and scribbling and evolves into letterlike forms, invented spelling, and finally, into conventional letters and spelling. Most 3- and 4-year-olds are at the stage of producing drawings, scribbles, and letterlike forms. Further, we also know that many 3- and 4-year-old children are "reading" picture books by interpreting the pictures. These children often believe that when adults read stories to them, adults are "reading" the pictures as well. Therefore, when preschoolers show us their paintings and drawings, they may well see them as complete statements that already say what they mean through their forms and images. Since drawing *is* a form of preschool writing, it is important that we "read" what we see and that we treat and value drawing as legitimate preschool writing rather than completing or interpreting it with our own adult form of writing. When the child's piece goes home as is, without adult writing, the child has another opportunity to look at it and discuss it with other interested people.

As you move away from taking dictation from children about their artwork, keep in mind that it's still important to converse with children about their creations. If you want to remember what a child says about a drawing or painting, write down the child's words on a separate piece of paper or a sticky note, as you would in gathering any other kind of anecdote about what a child does and says. Share this anecdote at daily team planning and enter it on the child's Key Experience Note Form. Not writing on the child's painting or drawing respects the child's work as complete and valuable in itself.

lenge with interest, often following the round shape of their paper as they painted. One child completed his decorated circle while the others were still working, so the teacher provided him with a round, blue piece of paper. "I wonder what will happen if you decorate a blue plate," she said.

At another small-group time, the teacher had the children work outside, sitting and kneeling on the ground around a long piece of butcher paper. She provided paints in an array of colors as well as big brushes in three sizes for making thin, medium-wide, and thick lines. "See what kinds of lines you can make with these brushes," the teacher suggested.

In a third small-group time the teacher provided children with nontraditional drawing materials to continue their explorations with lines. She encouraged children to "draw" with stones by arranging them to make lines, shapes, and patterns. She first presented plain stones for this activity; and on another day she provided colored stones the children had painted. The children worked in pairs and threesomes. One group was especially pleased with a design they made by laying out blue stones on a red tabletop.

Watch and converse with children as they draw and paint. Quietly watching a child who is painting or drawing is a way to let children know that these activities are valuable and important things to do. Also, such careful observation can help adults understand and appreciate where children are in their personal development in painting and drawing, how their work emerges, and what their particular interests are. One teacher, for example, quietly watched Nicolas as he worked at a large easel. Nicolas held his brush in his hand, watched a child who was painting next to him for a while, and then slowly painted a web of black lines. Nicolas then carefully filled in the spaces of his web with red, orange, and finally a square of yellow paint. Seeing that Nicolas had stopped painting and seemed to be studying his piece, his teacher joined him in his study. After looking for a while with Nicolas, she commented on what she saw: "I see curved lines and straight lines."

"Uh-huh," Nicolas agreed.

"I saw you make the lines first," she commented.

"Then I put in the colors," he said.

"Then you put in the colors," she affirmed, adding, "I see you put in a lot of red."

"And just this one of yellow," he said, pointing.

"A lot of red shapes, and just one shape of yellow," his teacher affirmed.

Nicolas's teacher used several important strategies in her conversation with Nicolas. First, she waited until he had come to a stopping point in his work before approaching him for conversation. Most people, young children

Helping Parents Value Children's Art

A child in my classroom spends a great deal of time in the art area. His mother often resists when he asks to bring home all of his artwork, much of which she considers "fit for the trash." How can I tactfully explain to her how important it is to value her son's artwork?

—A preschool teacher

Dealing with parents when you don't approve of something they are doing with their child can be touchy. It is best to deal with these situations in positive and non-threatening ways.

In your situation, it seems that the parent may not be aware of the importance of the *process* of her son's work versus the final product. Rather than focusing on the child's experience of creating art, she is judging his artwork by adult standards. In situations like these, you will want to find ways to communicate your beliefs about child development in ways the parent can understand. In this case, this may mean that instead of giving an explanation of High/Scope's process-oriented approach to art, you would attempt to provide the same information in an indirect way. For example, as you hand the parent the child's artwork at departure time, talk about the actual things the child was doing when he made the item, about any companions he may have had in his efforts, and about how much he seemed to enjoy the experience. Your description might sound something like this:

"Today at small-group time the children worked with some 'bubble stuff' in different colors that we made with bubble liquid and food coloring. We also gave them straws to use as bubble-blowers. Jarred and Corey spent all of small-group time working together—with lots of talking and laughing. They had a great time experimenting with the different ways to blow bubbles. They tried blowing fast and slow into the cups of soap and there was a lot of talk about the sizes of the bubbles, the number of bubbles, and about who had made the taller 'bubble tower.' After they did all these things with the bubbles, Jarred took this paper and pressed it on the top of his bubbles to make this print."

This kind of indirect communication is often the best way to help parents be more effective in supporting their child.

included, focus a lot of energy in the act of creation and construction and find it distracting, if not annoying, to be interrupted. Second, she joined Nicolas. She took the time to really *see* his work. This gave him the opportunity to start a conversation if he so desired. After a companionable silence, she initiated conversation with a comment that conveyed information about what she saw in his drawing. She didn't make a judgment about his work, or pressure him with a question. Had the conversation continued, she might have asked him something about his painting that she herself wanted to know, such as "I'm wondering, how did you decide which colors to put in which shapes?"

When talking with children about their paintings and drawings, remember to share your observations about what Smith calls the **visual-graphic elements** you see (descriptive comments about the colors, lines, shapes, and so forth), rather than comment on what you perceive as the **subject matter** of the drawing or painting. This helps you avoid making judgments about children's work, and it also gives children the idea that there is a lot to see and contemplate in drawings and paintings. Smith observes, "While there is a temptation to look for subject matter in paintings by young children, it is wise to resist this temptation and to focus instead on the child's use of visual-graphic elements. When children are involved in organizing lines, shapes, and colors, it is confusing and even deflating to them to suggest that they might or should be making representational paintings" (1993, p. 38).

In High/Scope active learning settings, children quickly learn the joy and value of painting and drawing!

Even for children who intend their art to be representational, a descriptive comment about such visual elements is still appropriate because, Smith points out, "A descriptive comment draws the child's attention to the process used and thus encourages growth" (1993, p. 52): "Look," said Ben, "I made a whale." Yes," his teacher replied, "You used an oval for his body that is wide on the end with his eye and gets narrower on the end with his tail."

Not all conversations about children's painting and drawing activities take place at the point of completion. After each small-group art experience, it's important to hang up children's paintings and drawings and talk with the small group about what they see in their collective works. This can occur at the end of small-group time, at recall, or at snack time.

Visit visually interesting places with children. Stimulate children's desire to paint and draw by providing visual experiences. Visit artists in their studios, look at paintings and drawings in galleries and museums, point out stained glass windows in neighborhood churches, watch boats in the harbor, look at a garden of flowers in bloom, watch ducks swim on the river, or visit an apple orchard. Find an interesting place close to your center that children can visit on a regular basis. Back at the center, provide paper and drawing and painting materials so children can represent what they remember about the special place they visited.

These, then, are some basic strategies for supporting and encouraging young children's adventures in painting and drawing. For further ideas, see the references listed below. By enjoying and valuing the painting and drawing process, providing the time and place for it to unfold, and paying close attention to each child's efforts, adults can have an important impact on the growth of children and their understanding of themselves as creative agents.

REFERENCES

Hohmann, M., & Weikart, D. P. (1995). *Educating young children: Active learning practices for preschool and child care programs.* Ypsilanti, MI: High/Scope Press.

Smith, N. R., with Fucigna, C., Kennedy, M., & Lord, L. (1993). *Experience and art: Teaching children to paint* (2nd ed.). New York: Teachers College Press.

Trimis, E. (1996). *Drawing and painting: Ways to support young artists* [Color slides transferred to videotape, 34 min.]. Ypsilanti: High/Scope Press.

Thinking About Art With Young Children

By Ann S. Epstein

• •

Although few early childhood teachers would dispute that young children enjoy and benefit from making art, *appreciating art*—thinking about art and developing an awareness of its meaning and aesthetics—is often seen as an activity far too abstract and academic for early childhood programs. Yet, who is better equipped to appreciate art than young children, whose senses and perceptions are so open and finely attuned to the world around them? Appreciating art is a natural extension of what they already do.

At High/Scope, we believe that children in preschools and early elementary programs can think about, talk about, and learn about the art of others. We know this not only from research but also from the classroom experiences of early childhood educators (including teachers in High/Scope's Demonstration Preschool). This article presents a rationale and guidelines for providing art appreciation activities to young children. As we describe this approach, we'll discuss some of the research studies and accounts of classroom experience that lend support to our pro-art-appreciation position.

Children's keen senses and original perceptions come to play in "art talk."

Why Provide Art Appreciation?

The goal of art education is "to help children increase their capacity to create meaning and make sense of themselves and the world around them" (Smith et al., 1993, p. 3). Producing their own artwork—exploring materials and representing ideas and experiences—is one way children create meaning in their lives. But they can also discover meaning in the artwork created by others and in the natural aesthetics of their environment. This discovery, and its infusion into daily life, is what art appreciation is all about. Art becomes a way of perceiving and thinking about the world, a sensibility that enriches human experience.

Using active learning strategies such as those in the High/Scope approach, we can and should encourage children to perceive these aesthetic aspects of their world. As early childhood educators, we naturally emphasize the importance of language development in preschool and the early elementary grades. To this end, we provide activities that help children not only express themselves but also reflect on the words and meanings of others. We encourage children to have fun with language, to appreciate its variety and its multiple shades of meaning. Similarly, we should do the same for visual imagery—that is, encourage children to go beyond its purely functional aspects and lay the foundation for finding lifelong satisfaction in the aesthetic possibilities that surround them.

Art Appreciation—an Appropriate Activity for Young Children

Schiller (1995), an early childhood practitioner, prides herself on implementing a developmentally appropriate classroom in which art appreciation is a natural part of classroom activities. In her experience, children enjoy talking about art and identifying the aesthetic, personal, and social dimensions of artists and their work. For example, she posted reproductions of fine artworks and made art books available to her preschool students. After giving the children time to explore these additions to the classroom, she engaged them in a discussion of what they saw and thought about the paintings. The children were fascinated with the story of Michelangelo painting on the ceiling; they noticed the "cracks" in the reproductions of old paintings, and they were surprised to find out that the names of Ninja Turtles characters were once the names of real artists. "What was interesting was that the children instantly recognized that Matisse had a very different style than the realism of Michelangelo and da Vinci" (p. 37).

Recent research in developmental psychology (summarized in Gardner, 1990) supports Schiller's observations, indicating that young children are capable of more art appreciation than we give them credit for. These studies reveal that very young children do not show a natural tendency to focus on the aesthetics of art. They are more likely to focus on its subject matter. However, they can display a sensitivity to the quality and styles of artwork if engaged in meaningful conversation about it. If adults ask children open-ended questions (rather than teach them directly) children can discuss what they think the artist is trying to say or how the artwork makes them feel.

Guidelines: Art Appreciation in Early Childhood Programs

If, as these researchers and art educators suggest, young children *can* engage in the activities we call art appreciation, we must ask ourselves: **How do we create the kind of learning environment and provide the kind of adult support that encourages such experiences in thinking about art?**

Below are some ideas for supporting young children's appreciation of art. These guidelines are founded on child development principles and reflect the experimental efforts of adventurous educators. As with any activities planned for young children, however, be prepared to adapt and change our suggestions as you follow where the children's interests lead.

1. *Use children's own interests and projects as the starting point for experiences in art appreciation.* According to Schiller (1995, p. 34), "Talking about art should spring from the interests of the children and be initiated, for the most part, by them." Similarly, Gardner (1990) states that art education should be based on student-initiated projects. These views, of course, are also compatible with High/Scope's approach, which emphasizes that children's personal interests and goals should be a central part of all learning experiences.

All three viewpoints point to the same conclusion: **to involve children in noticing and talking about art, relate the art discussion to children's ongoing interests,**

To introduce experiences in art appreciation, observe children's own creative activities, then plan around the interests they express through their own projects.

projects, and experiences. For example, Schiller gave her children the opportunity to notice and explore the art she had added to the classroom—to experience it on their own terms—*before* she attempted to engage them in a discussion about it.

Similarly, teachers at High/Scope Demonstration Preschool recently planned an art appreciation experience that they saw as a natural outgrowth of interests children had already expressed. Noticing that children had been very active making houses and other buildings in the construction and block areas (their constructions often had features like windows, porches, and doors), they wondered whether it might be possible to extend this interest to the "architectural" features of real houses. They planned an "architectural walk" in which they hoped to encourage children to notice and describe the architectural features of homes in the neighborhood. This experiment was successful: the teachers found that children could indeed appreciate and discuss these visual features, perhaps because of their original strong interest in building their own structures. (For a full discussion of this activity and its follow-up experiences, see "Walking and Talking About Art," p. 195.)

2. *Help children develop a language for talking about art.* Assuming that you've found a way to include art in a context that interests children, what kind of language should you use to encourage art-related discussion? Will you need to teach children a special art vocabulary?

Actually, no—the language of art is not so different from the language we normally encourage in early childhood programs. Common terms like *color, shape, line,* and *size* can be used to describe what Smith (1993) refers to as the "visual-graphic elements" of art. Ordinary descriptive words, such as *empty* and *full,* and comparison words, such as *lighter* and *darker,* also come into play in art discussions. To encourage art appreciation, teachers can help children expand the ways in which such common terms are used. Instead of focusing only on their *functional* aspects, such as clarifying that one wants the **red** cup, make observations about how features such as color evoke *aesthetic* responses—"The bright red dresses in that painting give the dancers a lively look." When possible, encourage a meaningful dialogue about the aesthetic aspects of classroom activities. For example:

- **Engage children in reflecting about the artwork they and their peers have created.** Use *descriptive* rather than judgmental terms: "I see . . ." or "It makes me think of . . ." rather than "I like it" or "It's pretty."

- **After a small-group art activity, encourage children to look at one another's productions,** and pose this question: "Why do you think they look so different from one another even though you all made them out of the same paper and markers?" Introduce language that goes beyond "This is a picture of . . ." to talk about the *emotional tone* and *aesthetics* of the artwork. For example, "These look like sad colors to me" or "This big, bright circle makes my eye keep coming back to look at it."

- **Ask questions that encourage children to reflect on the intentions and feelings of artists.** For example, "Why do you think this artist makes little pictures but that artist makes big pictures?" is a question that art critics studying the minimalist and abstract expressionist movements might debate. It is also a question that young children can ponder, based on their interests and preferences.

A final and very important point about any art-related discussions you have with children: **Accept and encourage whatever statements children make about art.** To feel comfortable in sharing thoughts about art with others, children must know that what they have to say will be respected and accepted. "It is important to accept a child's interpretation of what he or she sees, even if it is not the conventional view" (Hohmann & Weikart, 1995, p. 322).

3. *Help children observe with an artist's eye by pointing out the art in their environments, both man-made and natural.* Try the following suggestions:

- **Bring reproductions and illustrations of fine art into the classroom.** Add prints, posters, photographs, models, magazine clippings, and postcard reproductions of fine artwork to your classroom. Place these reproductions of works of art in places that will relate to the children's interests and activities (Schiller, 1995). For example, place reproductions of Mary Cassatt's paintings of mothers and children in the house area, pictures or models of junk auto sculptures in the block area, prints of Jackson Pollack drip paintings in the art area. Observe and listen for children's

Encourage children to observe nature with an artist's eye, noticing patterns, textures, color.

responses. Make comments that relate what children are doing to the art reproductions; for example, "The artist painted a picture of a mother giving her baby a bath, just like you are doing." This invites the child to comment on what they see in the pictures.

- **As you read familiar storybooks with children, encourage them to notice the artistic elements of the illustrations.** (The sidebar on the next page describes an art appreciation experience planned by High/Scope teachers around illustrations in a favorite storybook.)

- **Take advantage of nature's aesthetic qualities.** Talk to children about how changes in natural lighting (sun, clouds) affect the color of objects. Observe and comment on the shapes, textures, and patterns in plants, rocks, and wildlife. Look at how nature is depicted in fine works of art, and see if children can compare how the artist's conception matches or differs from what they see.

4. *Use art to establish a connection between the home, the community, and the school.*

- **Begin by learning about the art forms and art materials found in children's homes** (see Hohmann & Weikart, 1995, p. 75). Are there family members who create art? Incorporate these forms and materials in the classroom, for example, calligraphy brushes, yarns, feathers, weaving looms, quilting materials, cameras. Invite family members to visit the classroom and share their creative activities and materials with the children.

- **Find out about artists and art organizations in your community.** Invite local artists in to demonstrate their art in your setting, or visit artists in their studios. Provide children with materials and tools similar to those used by the artists they've seen. Organize field trips to museums, art galleries, and art fairs, especially to see works that use materials and techniques similar

An Art-Oriented Small-Group Time

Encouraging children to notice and discuss the artistic aspects of illustrations in favorite storybooks is one kind of art appreciation experience that grows naturally from preschoolers' interests. Teachers at the High/Scope Demonstration Preschool experimented with this approach, using one of the children's favorite books, *Snowballs* by Lois Ehlert. This book's illustrations have a distinctive artistic style featuring colorful paper cutouts decorated with many real-looking objects. Because the children were already very familiar with the book, it seemed a good starting point for small-group experience.

Snowballs is a story about a family who waits for the first snow, and saves "good stuff" to make and add to the snow people they build. The story shows a snow man, a snow woman, a snow baby, and a snow boy and girl. Each snow person is decorated with a variety of gathered materials, including both natural materials and everyday household items.

For the *Snowballs* small-group time, the teachers brought in the following items, sorted in muffin tins: sunflower seeds, nutshells, buttons, tiny pine cones, pine boughs, sticks, black walnuts, pieces of gravel, small square tiles, golf tees, fabric pieces, tissue paper, and ribbons. Each teacher began the experi-

ence with a discussion of the book. The children looked at several of the pages, noticing and talking about details in the illustrations. Next, the teacher gave each child a large piece of construction paper, paper plates, and glue, and pointed out the materials in the muffin tins. Using the words from the book, the teacher wondered what they might do with the "good stuff we saved to use."

The children proceeded according to their own developmental levels and particular interests, choosing materials from the muffin tins to make unique creations. Becca made a face, including many layers of fabric pieces for hair. Her project was very elaborate, including many items all carefully glued on one by one. Tristin, on the other hand, spent small-group time choosing materials and repeatedly sorting and dumping them. Other children used the items to pretend with, for example, using the golf tees as rocket ships blasting off into space. It was clear that some children, such as Becca, made a connection between the illustrator's technique in *Snowballs* and the process of creating their own artwork. As for the others, they enjoyed exploring the many different textures and colors of their own materials and artwork.

Are Art Museums Appropriate for Preschooler Visits?

I'd like to take my preschoolers on a field trip to an art museum or art fair. Given the "Don't touch" rules in these types of places, is this a reasonable idea for active preschoolers?

—A preschool teacher

Young children do explore things with their hands, so it may not be a good idea to take a group of 20 preschoolers and 2 adults to a museum or exhibit where fragile items are in easy touching range. Here are some alternative ideas for community art excursions, as well as some suggestions in case you still want to try an art museum trip.

- Instead of visiting a museum, take children to visit a studio where the artist feels comfortable having the children use some of the materials. The artist may have some of his or her own work on display. Another idea is to visit a small art fair or a place like a farmer's market where artisans have set up booths and encourage people to touch as well as look. In either case, talk with the artist or craftsperson beforehand about children's need to explore, and arrange to have some nonbreakable objects and materials available for children to touch.

- If you do want to visit an art museum with children, try planning this event as an optional "family field trip." This would be scheduled on a Saturday so children could attend with their parents. This way parents can decide whether their child is interested in (and ready for) this kind of experience, and parents can go through the museum with their child. With each family taking responsibility for their own children, adults can give children the support they need. Also, be sure to contact the museum staff beforehand to see if there are particular exhibits or special activities they would recommend for preschoolers.

- Another idea some groups have tried is to give children something to hold as they go through the museum. In one program, teachers visited the museum before the trip and got four or five postcards showing art that children would see. They made duplicates so that each child had a small reproduction to hold and compare with the works hanging on the walls. This helped meet the children's need to touch things, and the children had fun finding the matches for their postcards.

In any of these cases, plan the field trip around materials and techniques that the children have been working with in the classroom, and plan related follow-up experiences for after your excursion. Remember, too, that it is always a good idea to visit these places yourself first, so you know what is available, what to anticipate, and how you can provide materials and activities related to what the children will experience in these settings.

to those children have been using in the classroom (see the sidebar at left for suggestions for developmentally appropriate art excursions). After these trips, encourage children to mount their own classroom exhibits to showcase artwork made in school or by their family members.

By following the above suggestions, you will be creating an environment that encourages children to be art appreciators as well as art producers. In doing so, you can deepen their understanding of the aesthetic aspects of their world and enrich their lives immeasurably. You can also help them develop perceptual, cognitive, language, and social skills. The truth is that beyond childhood, at least in this culture, few of us will continue to be art producers. But being an art appreciator is a skill and a pleasure that can last a lifetime.

Invite parents into the classroom to share their creative activities. This mother shares her hobby of spinning wool, letting the children explore the materials.

REFERENCES

Gardner, H. (1990). *Art education and human development.* Los Angeles, CA: The Getty Center for Education in the Arts.

Hohmann, M., & Weikart, D. P. (1995). *Educating young children: Active learning practices for preschool and child care programs.* Ypsilanti, MI: High/Scope Press.

Schiller, M. (1995, March). An emergent art curriculum that fosters understanding. *Young Children, 50*(3), 33–38.

Smith, N. R., with Fucigna, C., Kennedy, M., and Lord, L. (1993). *Experience and art: Teaching children to paint* (2nd edition). New York: Teachers College Press.

Walking and Talking
About Art

By Ann S. Epstein, Beth Marshall, Rosie Lucier,
Mary Delcamp, and Sue Gainsley

• •

Starting Out

One morning at the High/Scope Demonstration Preschool, children took part in a specially planned "art appreciation" experience—a neighborhood walking tour in which they looked at the architectural features of the houses. This "architectural walk" grew out of a recent team planning session in which teachers brainstormed ways to create art appreciation experiences related to children's interests.

The class had recently been very interested in building things in the construction and block areas. They frequently made models of buildings, often including such features as windows, doors, and porches. So planning a walk to look at the architectural features of neighborhood houses seemed like a logical extension of their interest in buildings.

The area around the school has many old residences with a wide array of styles, materials, and ornamentation. The teachers wondered whether the preschoolers, with encouragement, would take an interest in noticing and discussing any of these features.

To prepare them beforehand, the teachers told the children that on the walk they were going to look at all the different doors and windows in the houses. As the group started out, the children first stopped in front of a garage door in an alley near the school. As they crowded around it, a child shouted, "Look—A garage door!" The garage door was a grid of square panels surrounded by raised moldings. The children all wanted to touch the door. One child ran his hands along the lines of the molding. Another marveled, "It has squares!" while another observed, "Lots and lots of squares." Yet another child noticed that in addition to the square shapes, there were round screws in each square. Others noticed and commented on nearby objects—a garbage can, squirrels, and cars going past on the street. But the

These children are eager to start their "architectural walk." This class has been building things in the construction and block areas, frequently making models of buildings. Taking a walk to look at interesting features of houses is one strategy their teachers use to create art appreciation experiences based on children's interests.

square design clearly made an impression. The next day, the children had pretzel squares at snack time. One of the children observed, "These pretzels look just like the garage door!"

As the group continued on its walk, the children also commented on many architectural features in the houses they passed, including doors, windows, roofs, porch railings, columns, "gingerbread" (ornate wooden trim), and other decorative elements. It was a warm winter day, and naturally the children noticed many things in addition to the structural features on the houses—small animals, ice crunching underfoot, and oozy mud. Despite these competing interests, the children remained surprisingly focused on the houses. They commented on what they saw and added their thoughts to observations initiated by the teachers. Here are some of the things the children noticed:

- **Shape**—Children noticed the shapes of the windows, including square, rectangular, round, oval, and pointed windows as well as a few in odd geometrical shapes. Looking closely at the gingerbread trim on some of the houses, they noticed diamonds, triangles, circles, and scalloped patterns. One child noticed a half-circle design with rays emanating from it and said, "It looks like a sun." She spotted the same motif on several other houses during the walk and commented on seeing the "sun" each time.

- **Size**—The children noticed windows of all different sizes. There were big picture windows and tiny attic windows. In addition, the houses themselves varied enormously in scale. Some children liked the big houses; others responded to the small, cozy, one-story structures. For children cued into size, here's a thought for future art discussions: Using child-level language, point out that some artists like to work on a large scale while others prefer working in miniature. Then pose the question "Why do you think this happens?"

• **Color**—The children noticed colors ranging from the natural red of brick houses to an elaborate salmon-and-turquoise color scheme on a painted wooden house. Some children recognized when the trim colors differed from the base colors of the houses. One child discerned the use of color to create pattern. She observed that the corner diamond at each peak was painted a color that contrasted with the rest of the surface of the roof. This demonstrated her awareness of the elements of color and design, since this detail was not obvious from a casual look at the roof. At another point on the walk, the children passed a house that was painted gray with a thin red stripe around the door and window frames. The teacher asked, "Why do you think the owner painted a colored stripe around the door and windows?" Replied one child, "Because he wanted to." This may seem like an obvious answer but, in fact, that is often why artists choose to do things—simply because they want to or think it will create a nice visual effect!

Following Up

The teachers planned several related experiences to follow up the architectural walk. They compiled an architectural features notebook using scanned photos from a home design book, as well as a notebook with photos of children's own homes. One child, who rarely sat looking at *any* book, looked at the photos for an extended period of time with one of the teachers, and talked about how the doors and windows in the photos compared to those in her own house.

The teachers also planned a small-group time in which children discussed the walk and represented what they did. One small group worked with crayons and paper, the other with Cuisenaire rods and blocks. In the crayon group, one child drew doorknobs and doors; another drew the garage door grid. In the other group, one child used the rods and blocks to build a house, while another used the materials to make patterns reminiscent of the grids and geometrical shapes seen on the walk.

The architectural walk and the follow-up activities illustrate the wide variety of ways in which children respond when they are encouraged to notice and appreciate the visual elements of an experience.

Master Pretenders: Dramatic Arts in the Preschool Classroom

By Ursula Ansbach

· ·

Children are master pretenders. They move in and out of their play dramas with the finesse of Shakespearean actors who have trained for years to refine their skills. If we're willing, they will draw us into this delightful, imaginative world. How can children and adults benefit from this experience?

Let's consider the environment that our children will enter: highly complex, fast-moving, global, a world of constant changes and unpredictability. This is an environment that demands a quick mind, concentration, creativity, a grasp of the big picture, attention to detail, teamwork, and the ability to appreciate and distinguish quality. To this list we can add self-confidence, discipline, and problem-solving abilities.

The arts are ideally suited for developing these qualities. In particular, research studies have documented the educational impact of **dramatic arts experiences** for children. Research summarized by Nancy Hensel (1977) suggests that experiences in creative dramatics help to develop children's language skills, creative thinking, problem-solving abilities, capacity for self-expression, and ability to work cooperatively. More recently, Victoria

Children are master pretenders!

Brown and Sara Pleydell (1999) have argued that dramatic play in early childhood is essential to creating the "base patterns of memory" that brain researchers have described as a template for all future learning.

Through dramatic arts, children learn to use their minds and bodies in creative ways. They learn to communicate both verbally and nonverbally, to present complex ideas in a variety of forms, and to understand what others are communicating through words, sounds, and images. Through these experiences, children imagine new possibilities and follow through on making them happen.

What comprises dramatic arts for preschoolers? At the preschool level, the term "creative dramatics" simply refers to the pretend play we observe every day in the preschool center or home. In this play, children take on make-believe roles ("I'm the mommy"), cast others in roles ("I'm the mommy, you're the baby"), create make-believe situations ("We're going to the hospital"), use objects as props in their dramas (an appliance box becomes a subway station), and communicate about their characters and situations, using both language and pantomime. Preschoolers may pretend individually or in small groups, and their play scenarios may be simple or complex. Play incidents may be short-lived, or they may be repeated and developed over a period of days or weeks. All the High/Scope key experiences come into play in dramatic arts, especially those in *creative representation.*

In preschool children's dramatic play we can often see almost all the qualities of drama as an art form—plot, characterization, setting and scenery, story, intensity, and themes that are a reflection of society and self. The only exception is the element of performance. Standardized performances with memorized lines and gestures, repeated for the benefit of an audience, are not an appropriate activity for preschoolers. And while preschoolers may pretend to be performers in a movie or play—and may even request an audience for their pretend shows—their focus is not on creating something for others to enjoy. They are pretending for themselves and for the enjoyment of the experience. This is as it should be, and as adults we should respect and support their dramas.

What do we gain as teachers by involving ourselves in dramatic play? Vivian Gussin Paley, in an anecdotal account of her classroom experiences (1990), concludes that adults who participate in children's pretend play observe children more closely, understand children better, and communicate with them more effectively. When we skillfully enter the pretend world of children, we build trust and understanding. Dramatic play offers an opportunity for us to establish a partnership with them. As we take on roles in children's play, we have a chance to observe children firsthand and to relate to them on a deeper level, communicating through our actions and shared imaginings, as well as with words.

Support Roles for Adults

When working with children who are pretending, it is important for adults to act as **supporting players** who facilitate children's play rather than control it. Here are some guidelines we can follow to keep us in this supporting role.

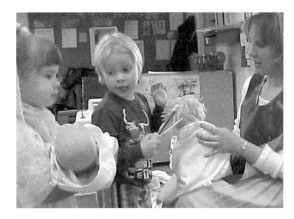

By assuming pretend roles assigned to them by children, and by joining—not redirecting—the flow of children's play, adults develop a deeper understanding of children.

1) *We become observers. We silently approach children who are pretending, watch and listen to what is happening, and gain some understanding of the activity, waiting to see if the children invite us into their play.*

2) *We are "stage managers." We support the play by providing props and costume materials and space to play in, and by keeping the play area safe and uncluttered. As stage managers, we stay "backstage." We do not attempt to change the story or redirect the players.*

3) *We may become co-players who participate by taking on roles in children's play scenes. The roles we assume are supporting ones; we leave the "leading roles" to the children. For example, Jane Davidson (1995) suggests that adults involve themselves by enacting subordinate roles like these: a person who doesn't know what is happening and needs to find out, a person who needs to be looked after due to infirmity or age, a visitor from another place, a special messenger.*

4) *We are facilitators and troubleshooters. We use our High/Scope adult-child interaction strategies to help children communicate and solve problems, just as we would do during any other kind of play. Therefore, as children pretend, we acknowledge their efforts, encourage conversation, support them in talking through issues that arise, assist them when they get frustrated or encounter problems, and mediate conflicts if necessary.*

5) *We occasionally take the role of dramatists. To help children expand on their favorite play themes, we make up a story based on the play we have observed and then give that story back to the children for them to add on to, embellish, and act out.*

To Do or Not to Do: Performances for Parents

In our preschool, children put on a special play every year for parents. It's a real play with costumes, props, and memorized songs and speeches. I recently learned that High/Scope doesn't recommend these kinds of performance experiences for preschoolers. But the parents really enjoy these plays—the children are just so cute, even when they forget their lines. So what's wrong with putting on a show like this once in a while?

—A preschool teacher

To understand High/Scope's position, try to see such performances from the young child's point of view. What do children gain by performing for adults in scripted plays? Do the words they are reciting make sense to them or are they simply memorizing meaningless words? What does their body language tell us as they stand before us, stammering, shifting from one foot to the other, or dashing offstage? How do they feel when they forget their lines or actions? Is this an experience in which they are likely to feel successful and competent?

Consider the alternative to such stage performances—dramatic play that is facilitated by adults and is not performance based. Children may either develop the story themselves or base their pretending on familiar stories and characters. The language is entirely the children's own so there are no lines to forget; and since it expresses the rich and varied experiences the children are involved in, it is always based on their interests. As we observe children's body language as they act out their play roles, we often see that children are so immersed in their play that they "become" the characters. Doggies crawl and bark joyfully. Mommies rock, feed, and wash their babies, in such a flurry of activity that an adult visitor is barely noticed. If this visitor wishes to take a part in the play as a subordinate player, however, the children may or may not extend an invitation to join in. Either decision should be respected.

Encourage parents to look for opportunities to take part in children's pretending as supporting co-players. By becoming a subtle, supportive character in children's dramas, the parent will not only enjoy the child at play but will learn about him or her in surprising and wonderful ways!

In addition, you can also plan some other special events to take the place of child performances. Some fun ideas include a family sing-along, family potluck, or a family reading night in which children are welcome to come in their pajamas to read a variety of storybooks with their family members.

We've just outlined **five roles** adults play as they support and participate in children's dramatic play. Since children in High/Scope programs pretend throughout the daily routine, adults may find themselves assuming any of the first four roles at any time they are working with children. The fifth role, in which the adult initiates dramatic play by telling a story, is used during adult-planned parts of the day, such as large-group and small-group time (the resulting play may also spill over into outside time or work time). Later in this article, we'll describe this fifth role in more detail. (For detailed information on the first four *support* roles, see High/Scope curriculum materials on adult-child interaction and pretend play; for example, see Hohmann and Weikart, 1995, pp. 29–41, 43–67, and 323–330).

Extended Dramatic Play

When children are particularly interested in a certain dramatic play theme, they will want to repeat it frequently until they have gained all the benefits possible from that play. Over time, more children will become involved, adding characters and detail to the play scenes. Using the support roles described above, adults can tune in to this process and encourage children to extend their play further.

One such example of this expanded play occurred at a child care program serving preschoolers and kindergartners. The children's pretend topic was a hospital emergency room. Adults used the **five roles** described above to encourage children to expand the complexity of their play. The rich and detailed play that resulted from this approach is described in the sidebar on page 204.

One of the techniques the teachers used to support the emergency-room play was to occasionally plan a large-group experience that would build on what children had been doing. The new play ideas children developed during these group experiences encouraged further expansion of the emergency room play in the days that followed. Following are suggestions for adults who wish to plan similar group experiences around their observations of children's pretending.

Drama-Based Group Times

To become a dramatist at large-group time, start by telling a story you've made up based on some of the pretend play you've observed in the classroom. For example, suppose three children have been playing doctor for several days and you've noticed that other children around them are becoming involved in this play. Because the play is expanding, you can assume that children's interest in this topic is high. So start out the large-group time by making up the beginning of a short story about doctoring that the children could then add on to and act out.

The beginning of your story might go something like this: "Once upon a time there was a little girl who was coughing so hard that her daddy took her to the doctor. So they got in his car and drove to the doctor's office. What do you think happened once they got there?" Then let children propose ideas of their own to continue the story, with the whole group acting out the ideas as they are offered. For example, a child may suggest that the doctor gave the little girl a shot or told the dad to take the little girl home and put her to bed. With each suggestion, the teacher encourages role play by asking questions or making comments: "What would that look like?" "Can we pretend to be daddies and put our sick babies to bed?" "I wonder what the doctor said to the daddy and the little girl."

As the children's enactments become more and more involved, you can shift away from the role of initiator and begin to follow the children's lead in any of the supportive adult roles mentioned above. Often, children will add many variations in response to your starter idea. Another possibility is that children may choose not to respond to the open-ended questions or comments you have prepared, or they may decide to develop their pretending in a completely unexpected direction. In either event, respectfully follow their lead.

Extended Dramatic Play: An Emergency Room

A hospital emergency room was the topic of extended dramatic play in a child care program serving preschoolers and kindergartners together. The play began with four or five children and deepened and expanded over 4 weeks, as more and more children from the classroom joined in.

The initial characters were simple: a doctor and a few mommies bringing in their babies. Props were simple, too: a pair of crutches, a stethoscope, and some scattered chairs. By the end of a month (with the help of teachers who had made many more materials available), the children had developed an elaborate emergency room setting. This included a waiting room with tables and chairs neatly lined up, a receptionist's area, and an inner office for the doctor who came only after the nurse had done her preliminary checks. Doctors and nurses carried around "doctor books," in which they wrote notes

A "doctor" bandages a "patient."

(scribbles mixed with symbols and a few numbers) about their patients' temperatures, appointment times, and "medicines" (prescriptions). The older children had taken the lead in suggesting many of these realistic details.

Over the weeks of this play, the characters in the waiting room took on personalities, too. Some waited patiently, some impatiently; some were very ill, while others were only in need of "medicines." Some would chat with each other while waiting, others would moan and groan in discomfort. At the end of the 4 weeks, the group's interest in emergency room pretending began to wane. Children gradually dropped out of the play as they became interested in other pretend play themes. By the time 5 weeks had passed, the play had died down, the emergency room was dismantled, and the objects and props had been channeled into other uses.

Another possibility is that a few of the children may lose interest in pretending and may need another play option. When this happens at the High/Scope Demonstration Preschool, we have agreed that children may always explore a book quietly in the book area. This is our solution, but each teaching team must resolve the issue in their own way.

Using a Dramatic Arts Planning Sheet

One tool teachers can use when they are planning to initiate dramatic play at small- or large-group times like these is to write a plan similar to our small- and large-group-time lesson plans. Having a written plan helps teachers stay focused during the activity and expand on the children's ideas. The plan should list materials to bring in, a few comments and open-ended questions the teacher may use as prompts to begin the activity and keep it moving along, and ideas that may be fun and interesting expansions of the children's ideas. The plan may include ideas for "scenes" that you expect may occur based on your observations of children's play, and ideas for supporting children as these scenes unfold.

Dramatic Arts Team Issues

Even when you have prepared for the large-group experience by writing a plan, it's important to remember that a multitude of teaching issues can arise when an entire class and two teachers are involved together in active and animated dramatic play. As a result, teamwork skills are critical. Both teachers need to be aware of the plan and have their eye signals and verbal signals well developed! They will need to make quick and creative decisions: Who will move to the child who has left the group and is looking for another activity? Should we allow large-group time to go on for 10 more minutes, continue it into outdoor time, or bring it to a close? If the activity is getting too rambunctious, how can we gently focus it in a calmer direction? These are the kind of issues that team members must be prepared to deal with on the spot. Thus, dramatic arts with children requires strong improvisational skills from both the players and those guiding them.

Sailing to Atlantica: A Large-Group Drama Experience

One particular plan I created for a large-group experience was based on observations I had made as the children at the High/Scope Demonstration Preschool played during several work times. Four children had been pre-

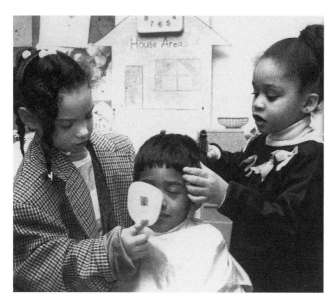
Using props added to the classroom after a field trip to a barber-shop, these children enacted a play "drama" about haircuts.

tending with boats made of large blocks. They used the boats to sail to a place they called "Atlantica." Another group of children were pretending with a real camping tent the teachers had set up in the classroom. In the children's pretending, the tent was pitched on a mysterious island. A third group had been playing mermaids.

My plan incorporated these ideas and listed related props and materials I had seen children using, plus additional materials I intended to make available. Each of the play activities I had observed was included on the plan as a possible "scene." Possible props and materials for each scene were listed on the plan: fabric pieces for the mermaids to dress up with, a large sheet for a sail, a broomstick for a mast, and hats children might use to pretend to be sailors.

I started large-group time by inviting the children to "sail to Atlantica" with me. While building the "boat" (a platform of large blocks), I said to the children, "I thought I'd sail to Atlantica, and I'm making the boat to take me there. Would anyone like to help me?" To help me focus, I had written a similar beginning statement directly on the plan. This didn't mean, of course, that I had to use that exact language, but I had expected to use some version of it as a beginning.

The children immediately responded to my opening by helping to build the boat and finding related props. Then we set out for Atlantica (scene one). As we sailed, some children used long blocks for oars to row the boat, others found cardboard wrapping paper rolls to use for spyglasses, and the mermaids dressed up and began swimming in the water around the boat (scene two). As they swam around, the mermaids found their own treasures of seaweed (cellophane strips) and jewels (buttons).

The first pretend scene that I had imagined, rowing the boat and getting there, unfolded at a leisurely pace. I had written the questions "Are we in Atlantica yet? Are we close? Are we there?" on the planning sheet

Planning Sheet: Sailing to Atlantica

Originating Idea: Some children were building boats out of wooden blocks and "sailing to Atlantica." Other children were dressing up and pretending to be mermaids. Yet another group was camping out in a tent that was set up in the classroom.

Materials: Props—sheet and broomstick for sail and mast, cardboard wrapping paper rolls, green streamers, tent. Costumes—fabric pieces and hats.

Beginning: Start building boat. "I'm making a boat to sail to Atlantica. Anyone want to help out?"

Scene 1: Sailing to Atlantica on the boat. "Are we in Atlantica yet?" "Are we close?" "Are we there?"

Scene 2: Mermaids swimming.

Scene 3: Arriving in Atlantica and seeing it together. "What do we see?" Take cues from the children as well as contribute our own view of Atlantica.

Scene 4: Discovering the tent and other things children invent.

Scene 5: Extending the island to the playground for outside time. "Let's explore some more of this island outside."

as possible prompts to use to help children move into the third "scene" in the story, arriving on the island. When I asked the children these questions, however, they said no several times and continued to enjoy the boat ride!

By this point, I had turned the direction of the play over to the children—I had become the stage manager who was following the children's lead. The children found lots to do on the way to Atlantica—they discovered whales, sharks, and turtles in the water and, of course, the mermaids! Finally, after looking through their "binoculars" for a while, they spied land and decided we had arrived. This initiated scene three: arriving in Atlantica. I then referred to my plan for this scene and used the prompt I had written, "What do we see?" The children replied by describing real and imagined parts of the island. They discovered the tent and entered on tiptoe, being careful not to disturb a variety of monsters they pretended to see inside. They pointed out golden snakes and pirates, gardens with exotic plants, and mountain-sized treasure chests filled with toys!

Since outdoor time came after our large-group time, some of the children took their play outdoors and discovered more of Atlantica outside. Some children took their spyglasses outside and continued watching for pirates. Others unrolled balls of yarn to mark the way back to the boat so we wouldn't get lost! Some of the mermaids stayed inside to find more treasures, while some children ran off to the swings and slides and quickly became themselves again.

In the case of this large-group time, the children acted out the basic "scenes" I had expected, adding many variations of their own creation. However, teacher-initiated dramas often stray far from the teacher's original plans. In this case, be prepared to follow children in whatever direction they choose to go.

§

While it takes time and energy to plan creative ways to support children's play dramas, teachers who make the effort to involve themselves in pretend play are usually pleased by the results. Dramatic play is where preschool children "live." In fact, children become our teachers when we allow ourselves to participate in their dramas as co-players who follow their leads. As adults gain more skill at entering children's pretend worlds, both children and adults will experience increased growth and learning.

REFERENCES

Brown, V., & Pleydell, S. (1999). *The dramatic difference.* Portsmouth, NH: Heinemann Press.

Davidson, J. (1996). *Emergent literacy and dramatic play in early education.* Albany, NY: Delmar Publishers.

Hensel, N. H. (1977). *Evaluating children's development in creativity and creative drama.* San Francisco: R and E Research Associates.

Hohmann, M., & Weikart, D. P. (1995). *Educating young children: Active learning practices for preschool and child care programs.* Ypsilanti, MI: High/Scope Press.

Paley, V. G. (1990). *The boy who would be a helicopter.* Cambridge, MA: Harvard University Press.

Moving With Purpose: Rhymes, Action Songs, and Singing Games

By Phyllis S. Weikart

• •

Rhymes, action songs, and singing games are popular activities in early childhood settings everywhere. While most preschool teachers include such group movement and music activities in their programs (usually at circle or large-group time), they may not understand why such activities are important for all aspects of children's development or how to make the most of their intrinsic learning opportunities.

Group Movement Experiences: What Do Children Learn?

If you ask preschool teachers for a rationale for introducing rhymes, action songs, and singing games, they will often give answers like these: "Children enjoy them so much." "Children need to get up and be active." "It's something that the whole group can do together." While these are all good reasons, the value of such group movement experiences extends beyond these justifications. In High/Scope programs, such activities are seen as an opportunity to support children's **purposeful movement.**

Purposeful Movement—A Definition

When a child thinks about a movement beforehand or while moving, he or she is engaging in **purposeful movement.** While preschool children are moving all the time, purposeful movement is especially important for learning because it requires **conscious thought.** These kinds of movements are carried out with self-awareness and can be recalled and talked about later. A child hurrying down the driveway to catch the school bus is focused on reaching the bus. If the same child deliberately chooses to skip down the driveway, he or she is still concerned about meeting the bus, but has consciously included a purposeful movement as well.

When children are engaged in making and carrying out a movement plan—by choosing a specific movement, thinking about the movement while doing it, and recalling and talking about the movement afterward—they are making connections between thought and movement that provide a base for all kinds of learning. Examples of purposeful movement occur all the time in a preschool center. For example, suppose that during work time in the music area a child picks up a drum and says he is going to march in a parade around the room. Then he carries out this plan. Another child, swinging on a swing at outside time, says to her teacher as she stretches out her leg to

With adult support, children become more aware of their movements.

pump, "My feet are going out." Experiences like these—in which children combine action, thought, and language—build the foundation for later experiences with coordinated movement, such as learning to drive or learning a sport. These early movement-based experiences are also an important foundation for development in other areas, such as learning to read aloud or to play a musical instrument.

In the past, opportunities for purposeful movement abounded in children's everyday lives. Children learned basic movement patterns through active neighborhood games and physical chores like pumping water, vacuuming, or hoeing the garden. Today, however, we often rely on appliances to take care of everyday chores, and experiences with watching television and playing video games have replaced active physical outdoor play for many children. As a result, children often do not have simple patterns of movement in place before advanced physical skills are taught and competitive sports begin.

As preschool teachers, we can make a conscious effort to incorporate such experiences in our centers and classrooms. The rhymes, songs, and singing games we provide are some of the many natural ways we have to help children connect movement and music with language and thought.

Key Experiences Involved in Movement Activities

High/Scope's **preschool key experiences in movement** (see list at right) provide the basis for planning movement-based experiences in High/Scope classrooms. Some additional "learning ingredients" that adults may think about as they plan singing and movement games and activities are three of the **music key experiences**—*moving to music, exploring the singing voice, and singing songs*—and the **language and literacy key experience** *having fun with language: listening to stories and poems, and making up stories and rhymes.* In addition to the **movement, music** and **language and literacy** key experiences, learning in many other curriculum areas occurs during rhymes, songs, and singing games. For example, **time** key experiences occur as children become aware of stopping and starting their movements on particular signals and as children become aware of speeding up and slowing down their movements; **space** key experiences occur as children develop awareness of their body positions; and **social relations and initiative** key experiences occur as children plan movements and choose movements for the rest of the group to follow.

The Teaching Model

In addition to the framework of the key experiences, High/Scope teachers use the following **teaching model** and **movement and music strategies** to make experiences with rhymes, action songs, and singing games successful for their children.

The three basic components of the teaching model are **separate, simplify,** and **facilitate.** Use them as follows:

• *Separate.* When presenting a movement or music activity, use only one "presentation modality" at a time. In other words, **separate** the *verbal directions* from *physical demonstrations* or *hands-on guidance.* If you are *demonstrating* an action for children, avoid *describing* the action at the same time. Similarly, avoid showing children the action while describing it verbally. For example, suppose a teacher is demonstrating the "arms in" movement in the first verse of the "Hokey Pokey." She might first get the children's attention with a statement such as "Watch and copy what my arms are going to do." Then the children would follow the teacher, moving the arms together to the inside of the circle (the teacher does not talk while moving her arms). Then the children would watch and copy the teacher again as she moves

Key Experiences In Movement

- Moving in nonlocomotor ways (anchored movement: bending, twisting, rocking, swinging one's arms)
- Moving in locomotor ways (nonanchored movement: running, jumping, hopping, skipping, marching, climbing)
- Moving with objects
- Expressing creativity in movement
- Describing movement
- Acting upon movement directions
- Feeling and expressing steady beat
- Moving in sequences to a common beat

As they play "follow me" games, children connect movement patterns with thought and language.

her arms to the outside of the circle. Following this, she might repeat the directions verbally ("Move your arms in") without doing the action, and she would repeat this procedure with "Move your arms out." Next, she would sing the first two lines of the song without doing the actions, watching to see whether the children could follow the directions in the song without the visual demonstration. She would continue with this pattern while presenting the rest of the song. Keeping actions and verbal descriptions separate in this way helps children attend to the directions.

• *Simplify.* You can make movement tasks more manageable for children by breaking them down into steps or **simplifying** them. To use the simplify technique with the "Hokey Pokey," for example, put your arms "in" and then pause for the children to copy you before putting your arms "out." This simplifies the sequence of two movements by making them two single movements with a pause in between. Take out the pause step later when the children are comfortable performing the sequence. The use of two arms instead of one in this sequence is another element that simplifies it for children, since movements that use both arms or hands at once are simpler for children than movements involving a single arm or hand. Another example of simplifying is to present the *movements* for an action song before adding the *words* and/or the *melody.* Children then can participate even if they can't say all the words or sing the entire melody.

• *Facilitate.* The **facilitate** component of the Teaching Model is designed to help children become active participants in the learning process by encouraging them to describe the movements they have experienced. Adults can encourage children to reflect on their movements by asking appropriate questions. The questions that provoke the most thought are divergent or open-ended ones that don't call for a single correct answer or a yes/no response. For example, in the Hokey-Pokey demonstration discussed above, after the children have practiced the in-and-out movement, the teacher might ask the question "Where did we put our arms?" The responses to this would probably vary; for example, children might say, "In and out," "In front of me," or "I made them really straight." Accept all of children's responses. You can indicate your interest in children's ideas by making comments that repeat some of the children's words ("Jacob made his arms really straight").

Teaching Strategies

Keep the following general teaching suggestions in mind when selecting and presenting movement and music activities for preschoolers and kindergartners.

• **For preschoolers who are having their first experiences with group movement activities, select activities that have only a few simple movements** or leave out some of the less important movements until children are familiar with the song or game. A good rule of thumb for those working with 3- and 4-year-olds is that movement sequences should contain no more than four movements. Using this strategy, a teacher presenting the "Eensy, Weensy Spider" song would sing all the words, but might demonstrate only four simple movements: the spider going up, the rain coming down, the sun coming out, and the spider going back up. She would not try to demonstrate the rain washing the spider out or the sun drying up the rain.

For preschoolers, keep movement sequences simple; select activities with just a few movements.

• **At first, select rhymes and action songs in which children remain in their personal spaces** or only one child (or part of the group) is moving about the space, rather than using activities that have all the children moving about the space. Space awareness takes time to develop in beginners of all ages. Providing a carpet square for each child to stand on and move on is one way to define personal spaces for the children. For example, this strategy can be used with the activity "Sally Go Round the Sun" from the High/Scope Press book, *Movement Plus Rhymes, Songs, & Singing Games.* In one variation of this activity, children step to the beat on their carpet squares as a child leader moves around the inside of the circle. (Substitute the child's name for "Sally" in the song.) On the word "BOOM" the leader freezes in a statue shape that the others copy. Another variation of this activity that is appropriate for beginners is to have all the children choose their own shapes to freeze in, rather than asking them to imitate the shape assumed by the child who is leading.

Encourage a child leader to set the tempo for the movement or to offer ideas for the group to follow.

• **Encourage movement experiences in which children explore the movement ideas in their own ways and at their own pace.** Give children opportunities to share their movement ideas with the class or to lead the activity. "Let's move like wiggly worms to the music," the teacher might say, not specifying how wiggly worms should move. Next, she might give the children the chance to suggest other creatures to imitate.

• **Remember that in beginning movement experiences children should not be required to understand the directions "right" and "left" or to mirror the movements of the leader.** These skills are more appropriate for older students (grade 2 and above) who have already tried doing the movements in their own ways.

• **Do the movements for a rhyme or song *before* adding the words and/or melody for that rhyme or song.** You can either go all the way through the song or activity sequence before adding words and/or melody or you can do a line or phrase or two at a time, as illustrated in the "Hokey Pokey" example.

• **Use the concept of "Learner SAY & DO" to help children organize steady beat movements and movement sequences.** With this strategy, children say words that define actions or body parts touched (SAY) and match the movement to the words (DO). The synchronization that occurs develops the cognitive-motor link to learning. For example, the teacher could have children tap a steady beat on their knees with short sticks in both hands while saying "Knees, knees, knees, knees" to the beat.

• **Encourage a child leader to set the tempo for the movement** and then add the rhyme or song to the movement in that child's tempo. If the child leader begins in a tempo that is too slow or too fast for the other children, encourage that child to make the movements faster or slower: "Trevor, could you pat your knees a little slower, so we can all do it together with you."

- **Pause in the rhyme or song at the ends of phrases or sentences** to enable all the children to execute the movement or the sequence of movements. For example, after singing "The eensy, weensy spider went up the water spout," pause and wait until most of the children have tried the climbing movement, then sing the next line.

- **As you plan an activity, think about ways in which you might encourage children to be aware of their movements.** Ask questions such as "What are some ways we can. . . ?" "What do we mean when we say we are. . . ?" "How were you. . . ?" "How did you know you were keeping steady beat?" You will notice that these types of questions do not have one correct answer. It is important to pause after asking a question to give children a chance to think and respond. Then you can facilitate and encourage several different answers.

ॐ

Use these tips as the basis for effective experiences with rhymes, action songs, and singing games. For ideas for such experiences see *Movement Plus Rhymes, Songs, & Singing Games:* 2nd ed., by Phyllis S. Weikart, High/Scope Press, 1997.

Chapter Five

Meeting the Needs
of *All* Children

• •

*H*igh/Scope teachers approach a child with special needs by emphasizing the broad cognitive, social, and physical abilities that are important for all children, rather than by focusing on the child's differences. The articles in this chapter illustrate how High/Scope teachers meet children with special needs where they are and provide a rich range of experiences appropriate to that level.

In the first article, "Supporting Children's Home Language in the Classroom," Eileen M. Storer (with Marilyn Barnwell, Chantal LaFortune, José Velilla, Lucinda Godinez, Sahra Yusef, Ursula Ansbach, and Ofelia Maskell-Ruiz) explains how to communicate with children of diverse cultural and lin-

guistic backgrounds by creating an atmosphere of acceptance where children can try new languages and where teachers and children can be resources for each other. Each approach is consistent with High/Scope's commitment to the principle of shared control. In the second article, "Many Ways to Plan," Storer provides several ideas that will help you encourage children with varied language backgrounds to participate actively at planning and recall times.

In the next selection, "High/Scope's Approach for Children With Special Needs," Katie Gerecke and Pam Weatherby remind us to focus on who children are—individuals with core needs and interests—rather than focusing on their specific problems or the specific aids they may need. Gerecke and Weatherby provide several concrete examples of how to help children with specific special needs engage in the High/Scope identified key experiences that all preschoolers should have an opportunity to enjoy.

In the fourth article, "Classroom Adaptations for Children With Special Needs," Katie Gerecke expands on this theme by providing specific curriculum strategies (adaptations) developed within the framework of the High/Scope approach that take into account the special needs of an individual child. Gerecke also offers suggestions on how adults with different philosophies on working with children with special needs can overcome the conflicts that occur when they must work with the same children in the same classroom. In "General Teaching Strategies for Children With Special Needs," Gerecke provides general strategies to use when working with children who have a wide variety of special needs. In "High/Scope Strategies for Specific Disabilities," Katie Gerecke and Pam Weatherby provide strategies designed for children with specific kinds of disabilities, including hearing and visual impairments, orthopedic handicaps, and autism.

In the next article, "Books Come Alive for Children," Pam Weatherby describes how she uses a well-loved children's book as a springboard for a number of activities for both children with special needs and typically developing children. In the final article, "Using Dolls to Build Disability Awareness," Weatherby explains the benefits of using "adapted" dolls that closely match the characteristics of individual children with special needs in her classroom. Using these dolls in presentations to children and their families, Weatherby emphasizes the strengths represented by the children with special needs in her classroom and all the ways they are like their peers rather than different.

Supporting Children's Home Language in the Classroom

By Eileen Storer

This article was written in collaboration with Marilyn Barnwell, Chantal LaFortune, and José Velilla, educators at Bloomingdale Family Program in New York City; Lucinda Godinez, principal at Little Singer School, Bird Springs, Arizona; Sahra Yusef, a family service worker at Washtenaw County (Michigan) Head Start; Ursula Ansbach, a High/Scope Field Consultant; and Ofelia Maskell-Ruiz, a High/Scope staff member.

• •

*P*reschoolers Tommy, Nathalie, and Christy are sitting in the block area with *their teacher, José. Nathalie has been crying. Tommy tells José that he wants the keys Nathalie has been playing with: "Yo quiero ese [I want these]," Tommy says as he reaches out and gently touches the cradle of José's hands. José responds, "Tú quieres ese. You really want those." Then he turns to Nathalie and says, "Tommy dice que él lo quiere. He really wants these keys." "He could use mine," Christy offers, holding up another set of keys. José responds, "He can use yours? Tommy could use your keys?" "Yes," Christy says.*

§

The above conversation (part of a scene that appears in the High/Scope video, *Supporting Children in Resolving Conflicts*) occurred at Bloomingdale Family Program, a New York City Head Start center that uses the High/Scope approach. Like many of today's preschool programs, this program serves young children with rich and diverse cultural and linguistic backgrounds.

The teacher in the example, José Velilla, supports children's problem solving by restating what children say in both English and Spanish. This is one way of supporting children who have varied language backgrounds; teachers in High/Scope settings are discovering many others. While the strategies used may vary, depending upon the needs of the children and the teacher's own language background, a common element that unites all of these approaches is a commitment to the principle of shared control.

In the High/Scope early childhood approach, teachers open themselves to children's initiatives and ideas by sharing control of classroom events. In doing so, they provide children with opportunities to describe or portray themselves realistically, make decisions, and solve problems. When adults share control with children, they enter into give-and-take

interactions that are authentic and focused on strengths (for a full discussion of this strategy, see Hohmann & Weikart, 1995, pp. 52–56). Sharing control with children of varied language backgrounds (including nonverbal learners, children who speak only English or another native language, and children who speak more than one language) means viewing their differences as strengths to be valued and respected rather than problems that interfere with learning.

Language develops through cooperative play. As this child gets a pretend haircut, he may hear a language spoken that is different from the first language of his family.

In the opening vignette, José shares control with the children by providing them with the opportunity to express themselves in the language of their choice. He affirms their language choices by reflecting their words back to them in their own first languages. When Tommy chooses to speak in Spanish, José responds accordingly, in Spanish. Similarly, José supports Christy, who expresses herself in English, by responding in English. In addition, he makes the conversation accessible to all the children by restating each child's words again in the other language. For example, when Tommy tells José, "Yo quiero ese [I want these]", José responds, "Tú quieres ese. You really want those." This is important both for Tommy, who has been speaking only Spanish, and for Christy, who has been using only English, so that they can feel supported in working together to find a solution.

Affirming Children's Ways of Expressing Themselves

In this example, José not only supports the language choices of children who are speaking but also affirms Nathalie's choice to participate *nonverbally.* Nathalie has been crying, and José offers Nathalie comfort and contact by rubbing her back gently while she listens to Tommy and Christy. When necessary, José checks in with Nathalie and communicates her wishes to the other children. An example of this occurs later in the conversation when Tommy tells José that Nathalie is finished with the keys. José says to Nathalie, "Nathalie, ¿tú todavía quieres esto, verdad [Nathalie, do you still want these]?" Nathalie nods yes. José turns back to Christy and Tommy and says, "Nathalie says she still wants these keys."

Though José's ability to translate for the children is clearly helpful here, this is not the only way to create a climate of shared control for language expression. Below is another vignette from the same High/Scope video, this time illustrating a different teacher and a different classroom from the same center. In this example, Chantal LaFortune, a teacher who is not fluent in Spanish, provides support to both English and Spanish-speaking children by using just a word of Spanish along with English:

§

Chantal is kneeling in the art area between Darel and Sury, holding a green ball of modeling compound. Both children want to play with the green modeling compound in Chantal's hand. Responding to a suggestion one of the children has made, Chantal turns to Darel and says, "Would it be okay if you and Aseret and Sury worked together with this?" Darel nods. Chantal then turns to Sury, saying "How are you going to work with this? ¿Comó [how]?" Sury pauses for a moment and then responds, "Aseret will play with me." Chantal answers, "Aseret will play with you? But, what about Darel? He wants to play with it too."

§

By her use of just one word from Sury's home language, Chantal communicates her empathy and support. This helps to calm Sury, who then expresses how she wants to solve the problem.

In these two examples, José and Chantal use different strategies to create a classroom climate where children from diverse backgrounds can communicate, develop language skills, and feel comfortable initiating and carrying out plans.

Guidelines for Adults

Again, teachers do not have to be fluent in a second language to provide support to children who speak a different home language. What is required instead is a process for identifying the resources of the teaching team and deciding how best to work with families to support the strengths of individual children. Some guidelines for this planning process are presented next.

 • **Meet with parents to identify their children's strengths as well as the areas where they may need additional support.** Marilyn Barnwell is one of the education directors of the Head Start program where José and Chantal teach. Of the children in the program, 85 percent speak Spanish as their first language; the program also includes some children who speak Chinese, French, and Creole. Many of these children come to the classroom already speaking English as their first or second language, while others come to preschool speaking only Spanish or another language.

Marilyn says that while program staff strive to have one native-speaking teacher in each classroom, this isn't always possible for children who speak languages other than Spanish. In addition, the program serves some children whose first language is American Sign Language. To enhance communication with all these children, Marilyn stresses the importance of working closely with the parents, who in Marilyn's words are the "windows into the child." For example, at the program's open house in the beginning of the year, Chantal and her co-teacher talk informally with parents to determine what languages they are comfortable speaking and identify areas where their child might need support. In addition, they observe the language and interaction styles parents and children use with each other. The teachers often ask parents for a few "words of comfort," or "helping words" in the

Familiar Words

While teaching at a full-day child care center serving families from 65 countries, High/Scope consultant Beth Marshall and her co-teacher developed this communication strategy:

The teachers asked each child's parents for familiar words in the child's native language, such as "comfort words" (terms of endearment, the child's names for special stuffed animals or toys) and the words used in the home for everyday routines such as eating, sleeping, or using the bathroom.

The teachers listed the names of the children in their classroom. Next to each child's name, they wrote a few words familiar to that child. Copies of this list were posted in several places around the room, clearly visible to teachers as they went about their daily routine.

Beth says the teachers found that using these personal words with children helped to improve communication and eased children's transition from home to school.

child's language, such as the words in Spanish for a child's special blanket or the names of family members ("Nana" for Grandma, "Papa" for Dad). They might also ask for often-used phrases like "How?" or "Look!" in the child's language. During times of the day when the child might be unhappy, such as when separating from the parent in the morning or at other transition times during the day, teachers, regardless of their language background, can use these familiar words to provide comfort and reassurance (for more on use of familiar words, see far left).

• **Use information from parents to plan as a team around children's strengths.** Once Chantal's teaching team has had a chance to speak to the parents, the team incorporates parents' input as they plan ways to support the children in the classroom at different times of the day. For example, when deciding which children will be grouped together for planning, recall, and small-group times, Chantal and her teaching partner discuss the children individually and look for children who can be resources for one another. For example, there might be a child who speaks mostly Chinese who has a friend who is comfortable speaking in both English and Chinese. The team might put those children in the same planning group so they can provide language support and reassurance to each other. Chantal also said that she and her teaching partner look for times of the day when they can

The presence of familiar items from home can ease the home-school transition when there is more than one language spoken in the classroom. Toddlers at a child care center on the Choctaw Reservation in Conehatta, Mississippi, use materials donated by parents.

include the child's native language. For example, at large-group time they plan songs they can sing in both English and Spanish.

• **Look for teachers' special strengths for supporting children of different language backgrounds.** Though Chantal does not speak Spanish fluently, she works with a co-teacher who is comfortable in both Spanish and English. During team planning at the beginning of the school year, Chantal and her teaching partner decided to put those children who needed additional support in Spanish in the partner's planning group. However, Chantal points out that grouping children in this way does not mean that planning or recalling in either group is always done in Spanish or English. Instead, each child decides, on a moment-to-moment basis, which language to use for planning. Often, Spanish-speaking children decide they want to practice their English, so they give their plans or answer questions in English. When possible, the teacher supports each child's language decision by responding in the language the child has just used, reflecting back some of the child's words.

When teachers recognize the strengths they each bring to the team, it enriches the experience for the children. Chantal emphasizes that although the Spanish-speaking children naturally appreciate her teaching partner's ease with Spanish, her own use of Spanish "comfort words" communicates to children that she also is there to support them. The children learn that they have two teachers to whom they can express their plans, ideas, and problems. In addition, the teachers can be resources to each other in supporting children's language. For example, at work time Chantal will sometimes call her partner over to help if a child is communicating an important feeling or idea in Spanish. Likewise, Chantal's co-teacher often calls upon her to provide other resources.

• **Look for meaningful ways to involve parents in providing a supportive and inclusive atmosphere.** Lucinda Godinez is the principal of Little Singer Community School, an elementary school in Bird Springs, Arizona, that uses the High/Scope approach. A high percentage of the children at Little Singer speak Diné (the name for the Navajo language used by native speakers) as their primary language. Lucinda views this language situation as an opportunity to bring parents who speak the native language into the setting and actively involve them in their children's education. Many features of active learning settings, she says, enable parents to feel welcome and comfortable about coming into the classroom to work directly with the children. In Little Singer classrooms, as in all High/Scope early childhood settings, there are a variety of manipulative materials that children can choose to use in many different ways. For example, a kindergartner might make a plan to pour colored water into different-sized containers at the water table. Lucinda says that regardless of language background, children and parents can see what is happening in such activities and these common experiences give them a concrete, nonverbal reference point for stimulating verbal communication. At small-group workshop time, Lucinda says teachers use English and Diné as children work with manipulatives related to the workshop topic. Thus, children get a "double shot" of language, she says, plus the opportunity to relate language to concrete experience. One of the kindergarten classrooms, for example, focused on counting

Bilingual Signs and Labels in the Preschool Setting

I am a Head Start teacher. Almost half of the children in my classroom speak Spanish as their first language. Recently, some of the children have been asking for the words that go with some of our labels. Should I add English and/or Spanish words to the classroom labels for areas and materials?

—A preschool teacher

In High/Scope settings, labels are placed on containers, shelves, or racks to identify where materials are stored. At the preschool level, labels are primarily nonverbal (consisting of pictures, drawings, outlines, or actual objects) but you may add words to *some* labels (in either or both languages), provided you don't remove the pictures, symbols, or objects. Interpreting the symbols (or words) on classroom signs and labels provides a beginning literacy experience.

At Bloomingdale Family Program in New York City (a program in which the majority of children speak Spanish as their first language), teachers use the following labeling strategies. According to teacher Chantal LaFortune, Bloomingdale teachers initially use pictorial labels to identify the materials, storage spaces, and areas in their room. Chantal says the pictures or symbols serve as a universal language that all the children understand (regardless of the language they speak) and enable children to negotiate their environment successfully and carry out their plans. As children become more comfortable using the labels in the classroom, Chantal reports they often request that words be added to the labels. At this point, she says, the teachers respond to the ideas children have initiated by adding Spanish and English words to some of the signs or labels. For example, the words *Art Area* appear in both English and Spanish on that area's sign, along with the art area symbol. When labeling the classroom some years, teachers write all the English words with one marker color and all the Spanish words in another. In other years, they write the Spanish word above the symbol or picture and the English word below it. Either way, children who want to copy or read a word learn to identify whether a word is English or Spanish by its color or position.

A final word of caution: Avoid going overboard with word labels for preschoolers—it's not necessary to add words to every label in the classroom. Keep in mind that most children at this level will be "reading" the pictures or symbols on the labels, not the words.

during a math workshop. The teacher and an aide worked with small groups of children inside the classroom, exploring counting with beans or dice, while a parent took one small group outside to count pebbles or leaves, facilitating language in both Diné and English. Experiences like these give the children opportunities to process information nonverbally and in their home language while hearing the new language.

According to Marilyn Barnwell, the rationale for sharing control with children from different language backgrounds "is not so much about language as it is about providing comfort, acceptance, inclusion, and opportunities for learning." As we have seen in this article, we support children who are acquiring English as a second language when we create an atmosphere of acceptance where children can try new languages and where teachers and children can be resources for each other. In such a supportive atmosphere, we provide children with opportunities to hear their own language spoken in the classroom, even if this is only a few words. We provide children with comfort when we offer physical contact and closeness and invite parents and familiar faces from the community into the classroom. In addition, when we share control with children, we allow them to communicate in ways that are comfortable for them, whether in their first language, their second language, or nonverbally.

REFERENCES

Hohmann, M., & Weikart, D. P. (1995). *Educating young children: Active learning practices for preschool and child care programs.* Ypsilanti, MI: High/Scope Press.

High/Scope Educational Research Foundation. *Supporting children in resolving conflicts.* Video. (1998). Ypsilanti, MI: High/Scope Press.

Many Ways to Plan

By Eileen Storer

• •

The ideas listed in this article will help you encourage children with varied language backgrounds to participate actively at planning and recall times. As you read them keep in mind that children who are not fully comfortable using a second language such as English feel most successful when allowed to start planning with concrete activities that accommodate both verbal and non-verbal plans (such as pointing to an area or going to get a toy).

Most of these suggestions can be adapted for either planning or recall times:

• **Children plan and recall in pairs.** Children take turns telling their plans to their planning partners. Children who are most comfortable in their native languages might be paired up with children who are comfortable in both languages. (However, even if a partner who speaks the child's first language is not available, the presence of a partner will still help the child feel more comfortable with planning.) Children may choose to share their plans in the language of their choice, a second language, or by using actions and no words at all. For example: *Kristie takes her partner, Jackie, by the hand to the house area, pointing to the dolls she wants to use there. Hannah picks up a picture of the block*

Planning partners exchange plans.

area, puts her finger on a block in the picture, and says to Spencer, her planning partner, in Somali, "Dhisaya guri [build a house]."

• **Children act out (pantomime) their planning and recall ideas for the group.** This strategy can be used with children working together in pairs or in small groups. For example, while pantomiming, Jessie may also decide to supplement her gestures with words (using the language of her choice). Some children may enjoy having the rest of the group guess what they plan to do (or what they did). With this strategy, Jessie, the child who is about to act out a plan or experience, may choose to give a verbal clue first, using a few words in her native language or English, then using gestures or motions to convey her plans or experiences. Likewise, the children in the "audience" may give their guesses either in their native languages or in English. For example: *At planning time, Jessie walks over to the house area and points to the dolls in the doll bed. Calvin exclaims, "Va a jugar con las muñecas [She is going to play with dolls]." At the same time, Brian says, "Jessie's gonna play with dolls."*

• **Children plan and recall with symbols.** Classroom symbols, such as children's personal symbols and the symbols on the interest area signs,

provide a representation of children's choices and actions that can serve as a springboard for conversation between children and teachers. (Children's personal symbols are simple shapes or outlines used as a written code to identify a child's cubbie, artwork, and other

	Juice	Napkins	Cups	Snack Basket
Monday				
Tuesday				
Wednesday				
Thursday				
Friday				

Symbols and pictures provide a rich visual language that all children can understand, regardless of language background. Some of the pictures and symbols children use in High/Scope classrooms include outline labels for storage spaces in a music area (shown above); children's personal symbols on a daily snack chart, (above); and pictorial daily announcements on a message board (at right).

personal belongings; the interest area symbols typically depict a material found in that area, such as a house shape for the house area or a pair of scissors for the art area.)

These symbols can be used in a variety of ways. Children may use the symbols without much language, for example, by simply pointing to the symbol for the desired play area; or they may choose to talk about their plans as well. Children may hang or tape their symbols on a material they want to work with or draw a line on a classroom map from their personal symbol to the symbol for their chosen play area. Teachers can support children by interpreting children's actions and putting them into words. This is a time when teachers may use "helping words" from the child's native language when describing what they see children doing. For example: *"Sarah, mira [I see] you put your symbol on a block in the block area. It looks like you are making a plan to work with the blocks today."* Sarah replies: *"Yes, I'm making a zoo."*

• **Children plan and recall with puppets.** Some children who are learning a second language are more comfortable when they can tell their plans or experiences by talking through a puppet, stuffed animal, or doll. Props like these shift the focus from the child to the puppet, creating a "safety net" in which children have the freedom to communicate plans and ideas in their native language or to practice speaking in a second language. For example: *At recall time Jake holds up a dragon puppet to peer through a Styrofoam "TV" and says, "I played computers and then I played with Jesse at the water table."* Remember that some children may choose not to express themselves through a puppet, preferring instead to simply talk or make gestures.

High/Scope's Approach for Children With Special Needs

By Katie Gerecke and Pam Weatherby

• •

All children have individual *intentions and interests* that result from their personal experiences, play preferences, and the specific social, physical, and cognitive abilities that are emerging at any given point in their development. In High/Scope classrooms, the core of the curriculum is the same for all children, including those with special needs, because High/Scope teachers recognize that these *individual intentions and interests* lie at the heart of childrens' identities, *not* their *special needs.*

Children with special needs may require additional support—extra time to accomplish their intentions, physical aids to support their mobility, a supportive adult who is aware of alternatives to standard verbal communication. But as we provide for these special needs, we must remember to provide for their core needs and interests as well, as we do with all children. As supporters of development, we need to focus first and foremost on who children are, rather than on the specific aids they may need or the special problems they may have. (See p. 232 for a comparison of the High/Scope approach to traditional methods.)

Identifying Individual Needs

A key principle of the High/Scope approach is that as adults work with children throughout the day, they take time to **identify each child's status on a developmental continuum** and **provide experiences** suited to the child's developmental level. These experiences help the child exercise emerging abilities and eventually challenge the child to try

Regardless of a child's special needs, the core of the curriculum is the same for all children.

Contrasting the High/Scope Approach With Traditional Methods

Traditional Approach	High/Scope Approach
Assessment by testing:	**Assessment by observation:**
Identification of deficits (what the child currently cannot do) is the basis for specific instructional objectives.	Identification of strengths (what the child currently is able to do) is the basis for monitoring development.
Goals and objectives:	**Goals and objectives:**
Specific skills, behaviors	Active engagement with people and materials
Above child's present level of functioning	Matched to child's present level of functioning
Tied to chronological age	Tied to developmental age
Curriculum:	**Curriculum:**
Direct instruction	Children's initiatives and key experiences in child development
Predetermined teaching and learning activities	Adult-planned, child-planned, and spontaneous experiences within consistent routines
Adult-initiated	Child- and adult-initiated
Adult-controlled	Shared control by children and adults
Performance-oriented	Process-oriented
Extrinsic reinforcement	Intrinsic motivation

out the "next steps" in development. Adults encourage children to use and practice abilities that can be generalized to many other experiences and situations. The **High/Scope key experiences** provide a framework for identifying both **where children are** in their development and **what kinds of experiences** will enable children to practice the important abilities that are emerging. Adults follow this same basic approach of **careful observation, interaction, and assessment** for *all* children in High/Scope classrooms and centers, including those who have special needs. The following examples illustrate this point.

In one classroom, the teacher observes that Daniel, a child with cerebral palsy, is banging a felt pen on a tin carton of art materials. To support Daniel, the teacher decides to tap another piece of metal in the same manner. By

matching Daniel's action and pace, the teacher communicates with him and encourages further explorations with sound and movement. At large-group time, the teacher offers additional opportunities for Daniel to continue these explorations with different materials in a group setting (by providing drums and drum sticks for everyone to try and by picking up and maintaining children's steady beat).

§

During such experiences, key experiences naturally emerge; in these particular activities, for example, Daniel is *feeling and expressing steady beat, building relationships with children and adults,* and *playing simple musical instruments.*

The High/Scope approach assumes that children can take an active role in defining the appropriate match between their skills and the learning activities in which they engage. Thus, the child is encouraged to make a conscious plan each day, and the adult assists the child in formulating and carrying out this plan. Perhaps Kevin, a child with a language delay, walks to the art area and then stops. The teacher might join Kevin, commenting that he is in the art area and then asking him to get out the things he would like to work with. Brenda, a child with a visual impairment, provides another example of how the adult supports learning within the context of the child's plans.

§

At planning time, Brenda states, "I'm going to the blocks." The teacher goes with Brenda to the block area and encourages her to handle the various blocks until she finds the ones she wants. The teacher also keeps Brenda's needs and interests in mind in planning subsequent group experiences. For example, in observing Brenda's block play, she records this observation: "Three times, Brenda stacked four cube blocks and then accidentally knocked them over with her hands. Then, with a sigh, Brenda stopped stacking blocks." Noting Brenda's apparent frustration at not being able to make a taller tower, the teacher plans a small-group time with Bristle Blocks®, which stay firmly fastened together. Though these blocks have been available in the block area, Brenda may not have been aware that they could provide a solution to her difficulties. During the subsequent small-group activity, Brenda makes a stack of five Bristle Blocks® and the teacher notes: "Brenda counted her five-block stack and said, 'They're up there.'" At the close of small-group time the teacher encourages Brenda and another child to go to the block area to put away the Bristle Blocks®. This will make it easier for Brenda to find the blocks the next time she wants to build.

§

Through these experiences with the Bristle Blocks®, the teacher might note that Brenda has engaged in specific key experiences—for example, *counting objects* and *experiencing and describing positions, directions, and distances in the play space, building, and neighborhood.*

Working With Children Who Have Developmental Delays

In the High/Scope approach, children's special needs are seen in the context of their overall developmental needs. In this perspective, **when the child's disability involves developmental delays,** the best way to promote growth in the child is to **provide a rich variety of experiences keyed to the child's developmental level rather than his or her chronological age.** These experiences would include opportunities to work directly with materials as well as the chance to hear and use related language. For example, for 4-year-old Chelsea, whose developmental level is equal to that of a 2-year-old, appropriate experiences would be the same as for a typically developing 2-year-old. At cleanup time, the teacher might use body language and words to indicate that she wants Chelsea to bring a ball to her. Then the child and teacher could take it to the ball box together (key experiences: *recognizing objects by sight, sound, touch, taste, and smell; sorting and matching.)*

Working With Children Who Have Sensory or Motor Impairments

On the other hand, **when the child's disability is the result of sensory or motor impairments that cannot be corrected or improved,** the best way to promote growth is to **mobilize the child's existing resources toward achieving developmentally important intellectual and social abilities.** For example, when working with a child with a hearing impairment, communication may include signing as well as oral language, but the *base* is the availability of interesting things to talk about, empathic peers and adults, and invitations to communicate in all kinds of ways. When the child with impaired hearing points to a kitten in a book, the teacher might say the word "kitten" slowly and clearly, facing the child and signing at the same time. This experience is enriched if the teacher states or asks what the kitten is doing (possible key experiences: *recognizing objects by sight, sound, touch, taste, and smell; relating models, pictures, and photographs to real places and things.)* Similarly, a child in a full body brace who plans to work at the sand table can be positioned safely at the sand table to work alongside other children. From a developmental point of view, this experience has the same potential for promoting growth for the child in the body brace as it does for the child who is able to stand unaided at the sand table. For both children, a wide range of High/Scope key experiences could result from this activity.

To conclude, let's examine another classroom incident that offers many insights. It had been suggested that 4-year-old Leslie should be placed in a special program because of delays in her development and a family history of mental retardation. Instead, Leslie was placed in a Head Start classroom that served a wide range of children, where the following incident occurred.

§

*Leslie had been watching a turtle cross the floor to the art area. She handed the teacher a piece of chalk and said, "Teacher, write **turtle**." The teacher wrote "Turtle" on the blackboard. "No, **big turtle**," said Leslie. The teacher wrote "Big turtle." "No, **BIG TURTLE!**" shouted Leslie, waving her outstretched arms. The teacher wrote "Big turtle" in very large letters. "There!" Leslie said with a satisfied smile.*

§

Many lessons can be learned from this story. Although Leslie's family history and statistical forecasts may have suggested the possibility of mental retardation, as a supportive adult, her teacher did not make assumptions about Leslie's "special needs." Instead, as we should with all children, she observed Leslie closely and responded to what she saw her doing in order to help her learn.

Leslie's behavior in this incident reveals many strengths. She could distinguish and talk about the size of the turtle, and she also realized that her idea could be represented in written words. Leslie also seemed to envision that a big turtle called for big letters. Her thinking was on target, but her ability to communicate her thoughts was less developed. This is not unusual in preschool children—their thoughts, feelings, and ideas appear faster than the words they need to communicate them. Because the teacher was

Both for children with special needs and typically developing children, adults promote language development by offering lots of interesting experiences for children to talk about and by supporting them as they converse about their experiences.

Adapting Group Times for Children With Special Needs

When a small- or large-group activity includes children with special needs, it is important to consider whether modifications are needed to give all the children access to the experience. Below, we consider ways to help children with specific disabilities participate in some typical group activities. All the activities listed here are adapted from activities described in *Educating Young Children: Active Learning Practices for Preschool and Child Care Programs* (Hohmann, M. & Weikart, D. P., 1995). The page references given for each activity refer to that resource.

For a child with impaired vision:

• **Making rubbings *(creative representation)*.** Provide all of the children with thin paper, chalk or crayons, and a very textured object to place under their paper, for example, a veiny leaf, an embossed greeting card, a piece of bark, or a stencil. For children with visual impairments, make sure the objects used have very prominent textures (p. 317).

• **Moving to live music *(music)*.** Many large-group activities involve children in moving to music. In some activities, children spontaneously move in their own ways to a musical selection. In this type of activity, you might pair a visually impaired child with a child who has bells attached to his shoes or wrist and encourage the two children to hold hands as they move. In this way, the child with the visual impairment can gain an impression of how the other child is moving to the music. If the experience is planned so that all children are imitating the same movement, as when children take turns suggesting different movements, be sure that the movement is explained verbally: "Let's twist our shoulders" or "Let's make punching motions with our arms"(p. 435).

For the child with impaired hearing:

• **Imitating story characters *(language and literacy)*.** This type of group activity involves imitation of or singing about the characters encountered in stories or songs. During this activity, position yourself so the child with impaired hearing can see your actions and see the signed communications that describe the action. If the child initiates an action, you can respond by imitating it. Another way to help the child with a hearing impairment understand the actions you are imitating is to show a video of the story or song, possibly even one made of the children re-enacting the story (p. 319).

For a child with a body board, body cast, wheel chair, leg braces, or a prosthesis:

• **Doing cooperative projects *(language and literacy)*.** Cooperative small-group activities (for example, washing toys and trikes or filling wagons with sand) are often planned to encourage interaction and conversation among children who might not otherwise interact. In such activities, place the child with limited mobility near the equipment needed, then work alongside that child until the children have become involved with one another (p. 350).

• **Learning to use tools** *(initiative and social relations).* The opportunity to use real tools like those adults use is appealing to all children. "Real" tools can be the basis for many small-group times. Try planning an outdoor small-group time in which children work the soil in a garden with short-handled spades, rakes, diggers, and spoons. This may be done in preparation for a later small-group time in which children plant bulbs, seeds, or bedding plants in the garden. Consider a raised outdoor garden (in a box) for children who cannot sit or kneel on the ground. Children with various mobility problems can manage this activity; for the child with a hand or arm prosthesis, be sure to include some tools that can be picked up or used with the prosthesis (p. 284).

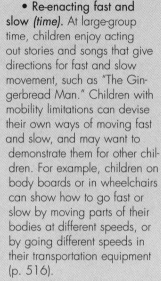

• **Distributing materials** *(number).* When tools such as glue or felt pens need to be distributed or collected before or after small-group activities, give all children a chance at this task, even those with mobility limitations. For example, this activity can be modified for a child with a body cast by having that child distribute or collect the tools from a stationary position so the other children come to the child in a body cast for materials to use or to hand in their materials (p. 481).

• **Taking walks** *(space).* Short walks to locations near the school may be planned for small or large groups. Take wagons to provide a break for children who have leg braces; let all the children take turns riding part of the time. Listen to children's conversations during the walk and later observe how they use the experience in their play (p. 503).

• **Re-enacting fast and slow** *(time).* At large-group time, children enjoy acting out stories and songs that give directions for fast and slow movement, such as "The Gingerbread Man." Children with mobility limitations can devise their own ways of moving fast and slow, and may want to demonstrate them for other children. For example, children on body boards or in wheelchairs can show how to go fast or slow by moving parts of their bodies at different speeds, or by going different speeds in their transportation equipment (p. 516).

For a child who is non-verbal or language-delayed:

• **Playing position games** *(movement).* In "Statues," a common body position game, children move to music in a variety of ways, freeze when the music stops, and then describe how they are positioned. Adults can expand on the descriptions offered by children with limited language development or provide them with a description that incorporates sign language with verbal language. For a child in a wheelchair, plan part of the game to focus on arm and head positions (p. 413).

• **Guessing sounds** *(music).* Play sound-guessing games in which one child chooses an instrument to play (or chooses from sound-making materials) and stands hidden from the rest of the group. The other children then guess

Continued on p. 238

Continued from p. 237

which instrument or material the child used to make sounds. Provide pictures of the instruments/materials so that verbal and non-verbal children can use both oral and sign language in making their guesses (p. 437).

• **Using shapes** *(classification).* Provide art or scrap materials in regular shapes (for example, buttons, paper strips, sticky-backed cardboard disks) and then encourage children to make collages with them. As children work, note whether they describe and name the shapes they are using. When conversing with language-delayed children who are using the collage materials, be sure to use the words and signs for the shapes they are using or the collage they are making (p. 451).

• **Creating series and patterns** *(seri-ation).* Give children beads and strings and observe as they make "necklaces." Some children will use the beads randomly, while others will make patterns. Encourage children to describe or show you their patterns, encouraging both verbal and nonverbal demonstrations. For example, some children may describe their pattern (two red, one blue), some may point to sections of their necklace, others may point to the first bead of each series in a repeated pattern (pp. 469–70).

For a child with an attention deficit:

• **Unpacking and storing new materials** *(time/classification).* When new materials are to be added to the classroom, children can help unpack the materials, decide where they should go, and even make labels for them. This process can help a child with an attention deficit develop the ability to organize materials and remember where materials are kept. For a child with this special need, keep the activity short and simple, unpacking just a few items and labeling them one at a time. Stop before the child becomes frustrated. When you repeat this activity, you can gradually increase its complexity, if the child shows readiness. At first, for example, you might take instant photographs of the new material and encourage the child to think about how to attach the photograph label to the shelf or container. Another time, you might encourage children to create their own picture labels, as long as you are willing to accept each child's unique interpretation of what a label looks like (p. 521).

REFERENCES
Hohmann, M., Weikart, D. P. (1995). *Educating young children: Active learning practices for preschool and child care programs.* Ypsilanti, MI: High/Scope Press.

attuned to Leslie's thinking, she was able to support her in persisting with her idea. The teacher focused on Leslie's strengths, interpreting her shouting as the desire to communicate, rather than as misbehavior. And, because the teacher recognized the importance of literacy to all children, she made every attempt to act on Leslie's request for written words.

Whether or not Leslie had special needs really doesn't matter in this incident. Leslie's pressing need here was not to have someone focus on her problem areas; rather, she needed an adult who would support her in a helpful, observant manner. By providing interesting materials (a turtle and chalk) within a social setting, the adults in this classroom set the stage for Leslie's learning and development. In addition, in this particular incident, the teacher took specific actions to support Leslie's expressed interests, and did not let preconceived notions about Leslie's mental abilities (or preconceived notions about polite behavior, or the correct ways to teach reading and writing) prevent her from offering Leslie the assistance she requested.

This is the essence of the High/Scope approach, both for children who have special needs and for typically developing children. The bottom line is that **regardless of special needs** *all* **children need access to the core of the High/Scope Curriculum:** opportunities for active learning; stimulating experiences with "real" materials, peers, and adults; times for planning, working, and recalling; supportive adult-child interaction; and careful observation and assessment of children to determine what each child **can** do.

Classroom Adaptations for Children With Special Needs

By Katie Gerecke

• •

Children with special needs are more like other children than they are different. They have personal experiences and specific social, physical, and cognitive abilities that educators seek to match with interesting activities and curriculum experiences, just as they do for other children.

These special children also have needs that require extra attention and support from adults in the classroom. In focusing on the child's special needs, however, there is a danger of overlooking the more important intentions and interests of the "whole child." This article will discuss how to consider childrens' special needs in the classroom in relation to their overall abilities. Although much of the article assumes an inclusive approach, in which special needs children participate in the classroom alongside normally developing children, most of the strategies presented are also appropriate for classrooms serving **only** children with special needs.

Key Principles for Using the High/Scope Framework

As High/Scope educators we must provide the balance preschool children need to develop to their fullest potential. Key principles in using the High/Scope framework to work with children with special needs include the following:

• **Involve children with special needs in active learning** by adapting materials and activities to suit them, within the framework provided by the plan-do-review process and other elements of the High/Scope daily routine.

• **Remember that choices are just as important for children with special needs as they are for other children,** even if at times you may need to provide a limited number of choices.

• **Use the High/Scope key experiences and your observations of children** to identify their personal interests and where they are in development.

• **Seek learning activities that enhance and extend the child's emerging abilities and personal interests,** just as you would do for other children.

• **Carefully observe, interact with, and assess all children,** including those with special needs.

Criteria for Making Curriculum Adaptations

Classroom "adaptations"—specific curriculum strategies developed within the framework of the High/Scope approach—take into account the special needs of an individual child. Such adaptations enable the child to gain access to a particular learning experience or material that is part of the overall curriculum for all children. For example, if a child with impaired vision is in the classroom, the book area might be adapted to include story tapes and multi-sensory books (texture and smell books). These would be placed in the book area alongside other books so that all the children could have access to them.

In making adaptations of any curriculum to accommodate the child who has special needs, teachers consider the following criteria, derived from the literature of special education.

The goal of curriculum adaptation is to give the child with special needs access to universally important experiences like listening to stories that provide the foundation for life-long learning.

1. *The adaptation is respectful of the chronological age of the child and retains and enhances the child's self-esteem.*

2. *All of the children in the classroom have the opportunity to use or to understand the reason for the adaptation.*

3. *The activity or experience brings the child as close as possible to what other children are doing.*

4. *The activity or experience relates to the child's interests and developmental age.*

5. *The timing and sequencing of the experience are attuned to the child's readiness, motivation, and capabilities, including his or her capacity for self-control.*

6. *Successes are built into the experience. Graduated levels of difficulty are built into the experience as the child can handle them.*

7. *Experiences are meaningful to the child rather then contrived, and develop relevant, generalizable skills rather than "splinter" skills.*

8. *The adults have a clear focus on the purpose for the materials and activities used, taking into consideration the child's intentions.*

These criteria are readily achieved within High/Scope programs because of their "close fit" with the principles of the High/Scope approach. A major strength of High/Scope's programs is their ability to deliver a high-quality, individualized education to children with a wide variety of needs, including those with special needs. The High/Scope approach allows teachers whose classrooms include children with special needs to "flex" activities and schedules with strategies that meet individual needs yet do not detract from the program for all children.

This is possible because High/Scope teachers emphasize child-initiated activities, plan the setting to offer a great many choices of materials and activities, and carefully observe each child to determine which materials and experiences might best meet the child's strengths and needs. Assessment is accomplished using the broad developmental goals of the High/Scope approach and the High/Scope key experiences to develop the individualized educational plan (IEP) objectives and criteria for meeting them. To provide the data for this type of assessment, teachers on a daily basis record anecdotes describing each child's natural performance in classroom activities. This approach to assessment for special needs children is described in more detail in other High/Scope resources (Gerecke, 1997b;

Slack, 1996; Tompkins, 1991). Note that school authorities may require additional activities to supplement the findings from this observational assessment process.

In the field of special education, the trend is toward flexible and child-focused approaches like High/Scope's because they work well in inclusive classrooms. For example, Suzanne Winter (1997) recommends that to plan for inclusion of children with special needs in regular classrooms, educators should do the following: select a flexible curriculum, match the teaching to the child's strengths, adapt activities as necessary, use the child's interests to target relevant skills, and use systematic observations to connect learning to assessment. This is essentially the same as the High/Scope approach to inclusion described here.

Adults Working Together

In making curriculum adaptations, another important set of issues to consider arises from the need to collaborate with specialists who work with the child. Part of the strength of inclusion programs for young children is their integration of expertise from both early childhood education and special education. When this integration is successful, it greatly enriches the program for all children. Special education personnel contribute their knowledge of disabling conditions and specific services, while preschool educators contribute their understanding of the "whole child" and their curriculum training in working with young children. It takes thoughtful considera-tion and hard work by all of the adults in the program to make this rich collaboration work in the most positive way.

Authentic assessment in which IEP goals are stated in terms of the child's natural performance in classroom activities ensures that skills assessed are relevant to "real life."

The "clinker" comes when viewpoints about how to work with children clash. Professionals trained in special education and those trained in the High/Scope approach often have difficulty coordinating their efforts because their basic philosophies are different. These difficulties can be worsened by the administrative expectations and legal demands of the educational system as it relates to children with special needs.

How do adults dealing with each other in the classroom everyday overcome the conflicts that result from these differences and outside pressures? Here are some suggestions:

• **Recognize that each person cares for children.** This is the "common denominator," the reason why you are "in this together" (Terdan, 1997). For example, suppose that a High/Scope-trained teacher is working with a teacher who has had many years of experience in special education. The first teacher insists that Joan, who has autism, participate in circle time, while the co-teacher feels that Joan needs more time before she becomes involved. The first teacher could encourage more discussion by making a comment that points to their shared concerns about the children. (Teacher A to Teacher B: "I know we both want to help Joan become involved in the regular program. Let's sort out our goals for Joan as well as our general goals for all the children at circle time.")

• **Respect each other's point of view.** This is an essential step in resolving disagreements. Acknowledge the background and strengths of each person. (Teacher A to Teacher B: "I notice that most of the children are very involved when you lead circle time.")

• **Listen carefully to the other person's point of view.** Be open to new ideas. Start by stating where each of you are in your thinking (Teacher A: "I understand that it's hard to lead circle time when Joan is wandering and making noises." Teacher B: "Yes, I feel I might lose the whole group.")

• **Articulate your beliefs clearly.** Use "I" messages instead of "You should" messages. Be clear about your commitment to active learning, the key experiences, and other aspects of the curriculum. (Teacher A: "I feel that Joan is ready to come to circle time for a brief period. She needs this opportunity to take an active part in a group activity." Teacher B: "Well, I'd like to see *her* make the decision to come to circle. Could you help her by offering circle time as one of two choices?"

• **Look for areas of agreement.** Recognize your common ground as you plan together. (Teacher A: "We both want to help Joan participate. If she does choose to come to circle time, why don't I stay near her while you lead the group?" Teacher B: "That may work; let's try it for a few days, then we can evaluate.")

• **Search for solutions together.** Explore options that can meet your common goals. (Teacher B: "What if Joan starts to get over-excited?" Teacher A: "If Joan cannot stay in circle time, how will it be if I move with her to the toy area?" Teacher B: "I think that's too close. Can you give her the choice of the art area, working with crayons and paper? Or perhaps you can sing with us from there.")

• **After you have tried out the idea, jointly evaluate the results.** Continue to communicate about what is working and what is not. If problems arise, discuss them—don't shut down your communication. (Teacher B: "I notice Joan has been coming to circle, but not participating. What can we try next that will help Joan to join in?" Teacher A: "Yes, let's just watch, look for something that sparks her interest, and then use that idea as often as we can. Also, let's keep circle time short, as you are doing now.")

As suggested by Mary Hohmann and Jackie Post (1998), the conflict resolution steps you use with children (see list at left) are also useful for resolving disputes with adults. By reviewing these strategies and adapting them to yourself and your fellow adults, you can be an agent for change.

Steps in Conflict Resolution

1. Approach calmly.
2. Acknowledge feelings.
3. Gather information.
4. Restate the problem.
5. Ask for ideas for solutions, and choose one together.
6. Give follow-up support as needed.

Personal Characteristics

The personal qualities of the teacher are a final "ingredient" necessary for making successful curriculum adaptations. Adults who work in classrooms that include children with special needs must of necessity have affective characteristics that help them to be especially aware of individual children and their behaviors and needs (see Heward, 1996). Most important of these characteristics are differential acceptance; a capacity for empathic relationships; the ability to communicate directly and honestly; and the ability to serve as a role model for the children.

Differential acceptance means being able to receive and witness many extreme behaviors without responding in kind, but rather by accepting those behaviors and working with the child to change them. Accepting does not mean approving the behaviors, but understanding them without condemning. This requires a capacity for *empathy,* the ability to see things from

Using the High/Scope Approach in an Inclusive Classroom

I am a special education teacher. I work alongside a Head Start teacher in an inclusive classroom (that includes typically developing children as well as children with diagnosed special needs who meet Head Start criteria). How can I work with the children with special needs on specific skills or behavior problems when the class is using the High/Scope approach?

—*A preschool teacher*

This is a complicated question that has several facets. First, you need to understand the agreement made between the school district and the Head Start agency and know the legal parameters within which each group must work. Then you, the Head Start teacher, and the whole team need to communicate very carefully and thoroughly about the High/Scope approach and the learning needs and interests of each child in the room. To meet the needs of all the children in the classroom, all the adults on the team will need to plan together daily.

For children with special needs, the advantages of being in this classroom are many. When children with diverse skills and behaviors are placed together in small-group time, and when teachers encourage children to work together, chil-dren with special needs will tend to imitate the behaviors of other children. This allows specific skills and behaviors to develop in a natural manner and setting, rather than through teacher demonstration and direction. The skills learned in this way are more easily generalized to other situations.

For example, at work time teachers can arrange for the special education teacher to be in the area where a child with special needs chooses to work. This teacher can follow and imitate what that child initiates, in order to encourage practice in a skill. She will also encourage other children to participate in these activities. If a behavior conflict occurs, the teacher can use the High/Scope steps in problem solving at a level appropriate for the child, thus stopping problem behaviors as necessary, by using language the child can understand and encouraging as much discussion as is possible for the child. Again, the other children involved should be included in this process. The teacher should also look for the positive behaviors that occur and comment encouragingly and specifically on these behaviors. The changes that occur can be observed and documented to meet IEP requirements.

another's point of view. When a teacher has an *empathic relationship* with a child, that teacher is able to recognize and understand many nonverbal cues that the child presents and to use those cues to reach the child. In addition, *direct and honest communication* is required to gain the child's confidence that he or she is in safe hands and will be treated fairly. And finally, the teacher who demonstrates maturity and self-control is a good *role model* for children who are often frustrated and who, as a result, experience frequent non-acceptance. By observing the teacher's self-control, children gain confidence that the efforts they make can produce personal change.

Agreeing on Discipline Policies in the Classroom

We are teachers in a Head Start classroom using the High/Scope approach, working in partnership with a special education agency to include children with special needs in our class. These two agencies have different policies regarding discipline for children with special needs.(For example: One agency says that a teacher cannot physically restrain children and that time-out should be used. The other agency feels that teachers must at times restrain children and that time-outs should not be used.) How do we find a discipline approach that is consistent for the children and compatible with High/Scope principles?
—*Preschool teachers*

These collaborations take work—there is no "easy fix" in resolving issues like these! Sometimes after a program has begun, problems result from misunderstandings of each agency's policies. If this happens, it is better to meet and look objectively at the situation than to let the problems grow.

The best process for resolving this type of issue is for the classroom staffs and administrators of both agencies to review all relevant policies together before the classroom opens. Joint policies can emerge from this approach. Throughout this process it is very important that the High/Scope approach be stated clearly to all concerned.

Don't give up if these discussions don't resolve all the issues. The next step would be to ask some *specific* questions, leading to a new way of working with the children when problems occur. Discuss these questions:

• **Are preventive measures in place in the classroom?** In your discussion, consider the *problem prevention practices* common to High/Scope classrooms (for example, consistent routines; caring, supportive adults; choices for children; acceptance of a wide range of developmental levels in children's behaviors; balance of child-initiated and adult-initiated activities; carefully planned transitions; agreed-upon rules, limits, and expectations). Point out that, like all children in High/Scope classrooms, children who are having problems should be observed carefully. What does the child actually do, when does he or she do it, and to whom? Are there any patterns in the child's behavior? What triggers unacceptable behavior?

• **How can we stop harmful physical behavior in a way that is acceptable?** It must be clear to everyone in the agencies that aggressive, destructive behavior, (hitting, biting, kicking, throwing, hurting in any way, bullying) must be stopped immediately by the use of words and actions. Certainly all agencies accept this. But it may be harder to reach agreement on appropriate ways to remove and/or restrain a child in such situations. Some agencies specifically state that adults can restrain children only from behind, with a "hug" approach. This encloses the child in a firm, but gentle way. Other agencies recommend use of "four-point restraint": (arms, legs, hold secure, keep talking). Discuss such policies in terms of overall child development goals.

• **If time-out is to be used, what principles should govern its use?** Discuss whether time-out can be used in developmentally appropriate ways. High/Scope uses a problem-solving approach to conflict that avoids time-out altogether, but some agencies may insist on using time-out as a very last resort. If so, attempt to define some limits for this practice. For example, if time-out is to be used, the adult should give the child a choice of where time-out is to occur ("You may go to the rocking chair or sit on the stool by the window"), the adult should be near the child (aware of the child but not giving attention), and the time-out should last no more than one minute for each year of the child's age. After time-out, the child and teacher may plan together what the child is going to do upon returning to the group.

After clarifying short-term policies like these, explore using High/Scope's con-flict-resolution process as a way to bring about long-term change.

In addition to clarifying such policies to be used at crisis times, practices for modifying children's behavior over the long run can be discussed. Explore High/Scope's conflict resolution process as such a long-term solution, pointing out that children with special needs may need to be introduced to this process using just a few steps at a time.

In this article, we've presented some of the "ingredients" that allow teachers to successfully adapt the High/Scope approach to working with children with special needs. These ingredients include an understanding of High/Scope principles and the criteria for successful adaptation, the ability to resolve differences with other professionals who work with the child, and the personal qualities of the teacher.

The next article in this chapter, "General Teaching Strategies for Children With Special Needs," offers some general adaptation strategies High/Scope teachers have found useful when serving children with special needs in inclusive classrooms.

REFERENCES

Garrett, J. (1997, Spring). Activity-based intervention: A strategy for inclusive practices. *Association for Childhood Education International Newsletter, 9*(3), 1–3).

Gerecke, K. (1997, January-February). High/Scope's approach for children with special needs. *High/Scope Extensions, 11*(4), 1–3.

Gerecke, K. (1997, January-February). Writing child-focused IEPs. *High/Scope Extensions 11*(4), 6.

Heward, W. L., & Orlansky, M. D. (1996). *Exceptional children: An introductory survey of special education.* New York: MacMillan Publishing Co.

Hohmann, M., & Post, J. (1998). When we disagree: Creating problem-solving dialogue with staff and parents. In *1998 International High/Scope Registry Conference proceedings* (pp. 81–82). Ypsilanti, MI: High/Scope Press.

Slack, S. (1996). Rethinking the IEP process. In N. A. Brickman (Ed.), *Supporting young learners 2* (pp. 293–302). Ypsilanti, MI: High/Scope Press.

Terdan, S. (1997, May). Passion is the frosting on the cake. Presented at California High/Scope Educators Breakfast.

Tompkins, M. (1991). "Special" children: Building on their strengths. In N. A. Brickman (Ed.), *Supporting young learners* (pp. 53–62). Ypsilanti, MI: High/Scope Press.

Winter, S. (1997, summer). "SMART" planning for inclusion. *Childhood Education, 73*(4), 212–217.

General Teaching Strategies for Children With Special Needs

By Katie Gerecke

• •

This article provides general strategies to use when working with children who have a wide variety of special needs; the next article in this chapter provides additional lists of strategies designed for children with specific kinds of disabilities. Though these strategies are designed with inclusive classrooms in mind, they are also helpful for classrooms serving only children with special needs. Many of these suggestions will be familiar to High/Scope practitioners, since they are variations on basic guidelines from the High/Scope Curriculum.

Planning and Preparation

• Just as you would do with other children, get acquainted with the parents of children with special needs before school begins (make home visits, if possible). As you visit with the families, use the High/Scope Family Information Sheet (see p. 316) to record information about their children's interests and family life.

• Use the lists of strategies and materials in *Educating Young Children: Active Learning Practices for Preschool and Child Care Programs* (Hohmann & Weikart, 1995), checking the ideas that might be useful for children in your class who have special needs. (Note: many of the strategies in this article are adapted from ideas in *Educating Young Children*.)

• Analyze tasks or skills (break them into a sequence of steps) to clarify where children will be successful and where you will need to offer support. For example, to paint at the easel, children need to grasp the brush, aim for the paint, lift the brush, place pressure on the brush, and move it. Therefore, you may want to provide wide-top jars of paint, big sheets of paper, and sturdy, wide brushes for children who have difficulty coordinating hand movements. As they paint, you can gently support their hands, but only as needed. A good place to have them start painting might be on a very big piece of butcher paper taped to a fence outside.

• Provide a variety of materials and activities that will allow children to work at a given skill in equivalent situations (e.g., using measuring cups or sauce pans in graduated sizes in the house area might be seen as equivalent to stacking nesting blocks in the block area.)

• Invite adults with special needs to share in your classroom whenever possible.

• Plan ways to work in partnership with any specialists or therapists who work with your children who have special needs. For example, if you have learned from Abigail's parents that she really likes to go camping with the family, place a back pack, camping cook set, and a magnet fishing game in the house area to encourage her to become involved there. Perhaps a specialist who comes to the classroom to work with Abigail on hand coordination would be willing to use the fishing game or cook set as she works with the child (and classmates who may want to join in). Likewise, ask the specialist for additional ideas that you can incorporate into your classroom and daily routine.

Room Arrangement

• Use large, clear labels in all areas and for all tools and materials. Make sure the room is uncluttered and the room layout is simple and easily understood.

• Use easy-to-replicate shapes for children's symbols.

• Use a multi-sensory approach (e.g., providing modeling compound with scent as well as color).

• As a small-group activity, work with a group in one interest area for about a week at the beginning of the year (or when a new child arrives) to acquaint children with the choices that are available for work time.

Daily Routine

• Have a consistent daily routine for all children. This is especially helpful for children with special needs.

• Post the daily routine in pictures as well as in words. Show the sequence of events in a simple chart, for example, consisting of photos or clear line drawings representing each part of the routine. Arrange the pictures horizontally from left to right. Keep in mind that photos are the most concrete representation and easiest for developmentally young children to understand. Place the chart in the area where you have your greeting circle, and point to it as you talk about what will happen in the various segments of the day.

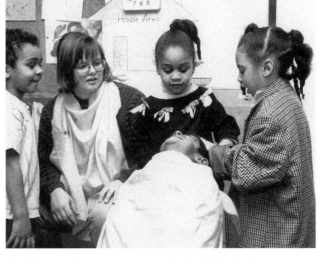

A rich and well-organized array of materials in the house area invites all children to communicate, pretend, and develop friendships.

• During planning time, offer photos of the different areas (or props) so that children can point to them to indicate what they want to do.

• To help children with special needs learn about possible play activities, take them with you as you join in play at work time and encourage them to take part in the activity with you. Be sensitive to their preferences and to their acceptance by the other children. Do not force the issue. (For example, "I'm going to see what Doctor Marie is doing in the House Area. Mike, shall we ask her if we can be nurses?" If Mike says, "No," that's all right. Try again another time.)

Interaction

• Interact and converse with children who have special needs as you would with others—matching their level and interests whenever possible and extending on their chosen activities. Allow extra time for children with special needs to respond, either verbally or non-verbally.

• Make good use of small-group time to enhance communication. For example, as you are moving around the group to reflect with each child on what he or she has done, use a similar approach with a child who does not have speech. Describe what the child without speech has done, using the same tone and perhaps encouraging the child to nod, "yes" or "no." Do not skip the child.

Inclusion

• Prepare children for the inclusion of a new child. (For example, you may read a story describing a child with disabilities. This may help the children feel comfortable asking questions about the ways in which the new child may seem different.)

• Help other children to be aware of a child's special needs and to respond helpfully. (This is a sensitive issue—it's important for the child with special needs to feel empowered to obtain help as necessary without being "smothered.") Help the children to relate to each other in a playful, child-to-child way. (For example, a classmate could push a child in a wheelchair, saying "I'm the engine. You're the driver. Rrrr.")

• Whenever possible, include other children in any special activities designed for children with special needs, including those done with therapists.

• Include children with special needs in regular classroom activities throughout the day. When possible, allow children without disabilities to test (with care) any special equipment, such as a wheelchair.

• Encourage another child to join the child with special needs in his or her chosen activity, especially when that child is new to the classroom, if that is acceptable to both children. (For example, "John, is it okay for Amy [the new child] to build with you?" If this is not okay with John, then encourage Amy to build with you nearby.)

• If necessary, maintain different limits for children with special needs, according to their level of development. Help other children understand this need. (For example, "Max needs to leave our group to rest—he'll be back at snack time" or "John will be at the sand table or with the trucks while you are running your race—you can join him later.")

REFERENCES

Hohmann, M., & Weikart, D. P., (1995). *Educating young children: Active learning practices for preschool and child care programs.* Ypsilanti, MI: High/Scope Press.

Marshall, B. (1996). Family information sheet. In N. A. Brickman (Ed.), *Supporting young learners 2* (p. 140). Ypsilanti, MI: High/Scope Press.

High/Scope Strategies for Specific Disabilities

By Katie Gerecke and Pam Weatherby

• •

The following strategies are helpful for High/Scope teachers working with children who have specific disabilities. They incorporate strategies and suggestions from High/Scope's preschool manual, *Educating Young Children: Active Learning Practices for Preschool and Child Care Programs* (Hohmann & Weikart, 1995), with practices developed by special education professionals. These beginning strategies are just a small sample of the many possible teaching strategies and adaptations. As you develop teaching ideas for your own program, you are limited only by the needs of your particular group of children and your imagination.

Learning Disabilities

Children with learning disabilities need extra help in organizing information and performing tasks. The following suggestions for adult support help to prevent frustration, anger, and the tendency to give up when upset.

- Eliminate or reduce background noise and clutter as much as possible.

- Post picture sequences of schedules and routines (washing hands, flushing the toilet, setting the table, using the drinking fountain) in prominent places.

- Observe and imitate children's actions in play.

- At points of frustration, provide enough assistance to enable children with learning disabilities to continue their activities or to follow through on their intentions. (If a child is having trouble squeezing a glue bottle, offer an open container and a cotton swab.)

- Make suggestions that give children clues or choices for the next step in the activity. ("Will you need a paintbrush or a felt pen to make your picture?")

- Use lots of water play. (It's very calming.)

- Use action songs and stories.

- Use the conflict resolution process, introducing a few steps at first, then adding more steps gradually.

- Build choices into all activities, even when children's choices have to be limited.

- Use especially calming activities to end large-group time and other physically active times of the day.

- Time large-group activities so that they stop while children are still involved.

- Have quiet places in the room.

- Sequence activities from simple to complex whenever possible. (For example: Offer puzzles with frames and handles on the pieces before offering frameless puzzles with conventional pieces.)

- Keep directions simple and specific. Describe no more than one or two actions at a time. For example, "First, get your hands wet, then rub the soap on them." (Pause.) "Now you can run them under the faucet."

- Show children how to use the tools and materials in the classroom.

- Use clear cues for transitions and keep transitions to a minimum.

- Repeat back and expand on the child's language.

Cognitive Impairments and Developmental Delays

Children with cognitive impairments and developmental delays learn at a slower pace. Concrete modeling and demonstration are key strategies.

- Follow and imitate children's actions and sounds in play, using the same pace.

- In conversation, play, or organized experiences, allow lots of time for children with cognitive impairments to respond with actions or speech.

- Use simple room arrangements with clear traffic patterns and storage spaces that are clearly labeled, organized, and defined.

- Use lots of repetition and demonstration throughout the day.

- Have clearly defined spaces for personal and group activities.

• In prominent places, post picture sequences for routines and schedules (washing hands, flushing the toilet, setting the table, using the drinking fountain).

• Use action songs and stories.

• Give frequent feedback: ("I see that you put the truck back on the shelf.")

• Provide visual cues with verbal directions (pointing to the red ball as you say, "Please bring me the red ball"). Gradually separate visual and verbal cues as a child's ability to interpret verbal cues increases. Check often to see which type of cue the child is using.

Eye contact enhances communication, as does imitating the child's actions and words.

• Use open-ended questions and collaborative activities to encourage children to think through problems. ("How can you and Harry carry that big board together?" "What other way can you think of to get your trike out of the corner?")

• Sing directions for a task ("This is the way we wash our hands").

Speech and Language Impairments

Communication in any form is the most important goal for children with speech and language impairment. To encourage communication, plan for experiences that will motivate them to give and receive messages.

• Offer quiet, secure places where children with speech and language impairments can retreat in times of frustration (Bunnett & Davis, 1997).

• During planning and recall, allow children to lead you to the chosen play area. Verbalize what they are telling you with their actions.

• Use lots of water play. (It promotes language among children.)

• Make sure all learning experiences offer children with speech and language impairments opportunities to directly observe, explore, and experiment with materials.

• Give only one verbal direction at a time.

• Reduce background noise as much as possible. (Avoid background music.)

• Provide language experiences with repetitive sounds, phrases, and sentences. (Use lots of simple poetry, repetitive stories, action stories, and songs.)

• Imitate the sounds children make.

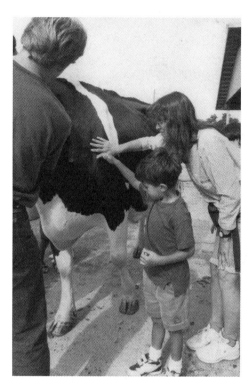

Provide multisensory experiences.

• Have conversations with children about things that interest them, pausing and waiting for their responses. (At snack or meal times, for example, food is often a good topic.)

• Listen with interest and look at children who are speaking, even when their language is unintelligible to you.

• To encourage them to talk about recent experiences, show pictures of what they have just been doing.

• Be aware of whether children are receiving speech therapy, and work closely with their therapists.

• Provide dress-up clothes to match a story—this helps with concepts and words (Bunnett & Davis, 1997).

• Use lots of actions and gestures to accompany your own and children's words, particularly during planning and recall.

• Encourage children to show objects as a way of communicating, particularly in planning and recall, and accept a child's non-verbal communication as a form of recall.

• Use all forms of communication—both verbal and non-verbal, including gestures and communication aided by devices and materials (computers, music, tapes with spoken words or music, flip tablets, charts, microphones, and so forth).

• Use communication boards with pictures of important objects, times, and events, including individual planning boards for the plan-work-review sequence. Communication boards should have pictures of both school and home materials and people.

Hearing Impairments

Children with hearing impairments need visual attention-getters to help orient them to what is happening.

• Use a simple room arrangement; defined areas; clear traffic patterns; large clear labels for areas, tools and materials; and organized storage.

• Avoid background noise.

• Use manual gestures or motions when singing (Bunnett & Davis, 1997).

• Face children with hearing impairments whenever possible, using a clear voice and facial expressions.

• Use lots of actions and gestures to accompany your own or their language, particularly during planning and recall.

• Show objects to demonstrate what you are talking about. Accept children's non-verbal communications.

• During music and movement activities, increase children's opportunity to hear, feel, or see the beat by patting it on a hard surface, playing a drum, or using cassette tapes with a loud beat.

• Sing along with song tapes to encourage children to lip-read.

• Use individual communication boards (containing pictures of the areas and materials, both in home and school) for plan-do-review and other activities of the day.

• Use "total communication." Use and encourage speaking, signing, and use of residual hearing whenever possible.

• Be aware of whether children are receiving speech therapy, and work closely with their therapists.

• Use sign language for the areas of the room, introducing new signs for specific objects and actions as appropriate. (If a sign for an action or material is not listed in your reference book, make up an appropriate sign and share it with both the class and parents.) This will encourage child-to-child communication.

• Learn a few basic signs (for *yes, thank you, please, stop,* and so forth) to use to communicate with children and model appropriate social behavior.

Visual Impairments

Children who have visual impairments need opportunities to use hearing and touch to explore their environment, before they can make use of the tools and materials in it.

• To help children with visual impairments move with confidence, be sure the pathways into the areas of the room are wide enough and remain consistently located.

• Use Braille for the child's name or initial as appropriate.

• Use large, clear, tactile labels to identify areas, tools, and materials. (Actual objects with distinctive textures are one useful kind of label.)

• Make children's personal symbols out of simple shapes that do not bend. Use a raised or textured shape to identify the child's cubby.

• Use lots of play dough and other molding materials, sensory materials, construction materials, and glue.

• Provide many put together/take apart building sets (Bristle Blocks®, connecting blocks); place in the art area as well as in the block area and toy area.

• Provide many tactile-auditory experiences, using language in conjunction with the experiences whenever possible. ("I'm giving you the rough sandpaper; can you feel the fine sandpaper on the table?")

• Encourage children with visual impairment to use touch to explore all parts of an object. (This is important for understanding the relationship of parts to the whole.)

• Converse with the child as you would with any other child. Use *specific* words for objects and actions, avoiding words like "this" or "here."

• Help children with visual impairment to feel motions that other children can see. (For example, if the group is swaying to music, put your hands on the child's shoulders so he or she can sway with the group. Ask the child's permission first.)

• Describe what you are doing as you do it. Label actions as well as things. Also describe to the visually impaired children what others around them are doing at small-group or work time.

• Use activities that involve spatial concepts (*on/off, up/down, in/out,* and so on), sometimes using toys to demonstrate.

• Help visually impaired children to use auditory processing whenever possible: provide sequenced verbal instructions, games that require memory, sequenced stories. Include other children when using this strategy.

• Use an individual planning board with specific objects glued on it to represent the areas. (Introduce this when children have become very familiar with the area so that they can generalize from the object to the whole area.)

• Encourage other children to be observers for visually impaired children by explaining what they are doing and how. (This is mutually beneficial.)

• Encourage other children to identify themselves as they approach.

• Make a recording of each child's voice and have children guess who it is; this helps the visually impaired child match names with voices and is fun for the other children, too.

Health Impairments

Chronic illnesses and health conditions are often less visible, but can significantly affect a child's performance and social acceptance. Due to periods of low energy and absences, there may be many day-to-day variations in how well the child functions. Work to keep children with health impairments a part of the group, allowing for rest as needed.

• Assume everyone can participate in all activities: make plans to modify an activity only as necessary. If some children can't participate, perhaps they can lead or monitor the activity. Always check the weather to accommodate sensitivity to heat.

• When a child is absent for long periods, save representative objects and pictures to help the child share in classroom experiences or be aware of changes.

• Keep in touch with children during absences, for example, by sending them letters or pictures (from both children and adults).

• Provide health-care-related props for doctor, nurse, or hospital play.

• Pay special attention to the cleanliness of room, toys, and so forth.

Orthopedic Impairments

There are many types of orthopedic handicaps, each associated with specific problems in moving or responding. Keep in mind that physical disabilities are not necessarily linked with cognitive losses.

• Be sure pathways into the areas are wide enough for wheelchairs or body boards (Bunnett & Davis, 1997). Make sure the classroom is uncluttered, with easy-to-reach shelves, cubbies, sink, and so forth.

• Use positioning equipment to provide ways for children with orthopedic handicaps to reach into equipment from a wheelchair or body board or when using braces (at the sand table, water table, "goop" pans, and so forth) (Bunnett & Davis, 1997). Check with therapists for safe ways to work this out.

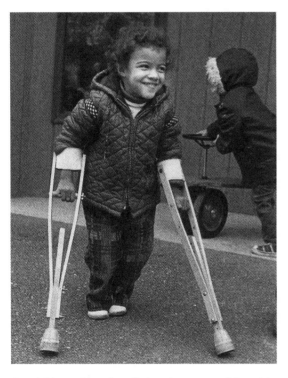

For children with orthopedic impairments, modify activities only as necessary.

• Use lots of non-locomotor movement activities (involving anchored movements, such as moving the arms with the feet in place).

• Provide enough space at large-group time so children can move their wheelchair or body board in imitation of the other children's movements.

• Provide dress-up clothes that open up and down (some in back), so all children can use them.

• Modify classroom tools and materials by adding handles or grips so items are easier to grasp (for example, adding triangular grips to brushes and felt pens, rubber bicycle handles over handles and knobs).

• Find specialized equipment that children might need in order to participate in activities as others do. (For example, provide body boards for mobility, or attach a tray to a wheelchair so a child can use toys, making sure that the tray is large enough for two children to play on.)

• Provide opportunities for other children to support the child with an orthopedic handicap as needed and desired by the child. (For example, if a child with a hand prosthesis cannot pick up a crayon, encourage another child to put a crayon in the prosthesis.) Encourage children who want to help to ask directly whether help is needed. (If Jamal asks you, "Can I help Zack move over to the block area?" encourage him to ask Zack whether he needs some help.)

• If a child with an orthopedic handicap can be on the floor, plan floor activities that include all the children.

• Use adapted battery or electrical toys (such as remote-controlled cars) to allow children with orthopedic handicaps to control actions—allow other children to share in their use. (These are especially useful for pretend play.)

• Be aware of whether children are receiving occupational or physical therapy and work closely with the therapist.

• Involve all children in active play as much as possible. If a child can't participate, perhaps he or she can lead or monitor the activity.

Severe Behavior Problems and Emotional Disturbance

Children who have frequent episodes of difficult behaviors over a long period of time, an inability to develop satisfactory interpersonal relations, and a pervasive mood of unhappiness (Heward, 1996) require a consistent, logical, and predictable routine.

• Offer extra support as needed to help children with behavior problems participate in routines. For example, shadow them inconspicuously. Use encouraging smiles and phrases. Develop mutually understood signals to indicate the need to stop a behavior.

• Note a child's "trigger points," and avoid them when possible. When outbursts occur, treat them with an objective response.

• Use extra warmth, understanding, and tolerance.

• Provide for calming activities: Offer sensory materials, water play materials, soothing music.

• Allow a withdrawn child to watch activities from a "safe" distance.

• Include children in activities at the level that they can tolerate.

• Reassure anxious children about their safety and their abilities.

• Talk to all children as appropriate. Do not ignore a child because the child does not respond, but rather be aware of his or her comfort level.

• Use encouragement freely.

• Prevent aggressive children from hurting others.

• Observe how children with behavior or emotional problems learn best, using that modality frequently for the whole group. For example, if a child does well outside, plan extra outdoor activities.

• Provide options during group times. (For example, if large-group time becomes stressful, give the child with an emotional disturbance the option of looking at books.)

• Provide adult support at transition times. Give clues and choices about how to transition. Use songs or movement activities during transitions. Keep transitions to a minimum.

• Provide soft lighting and cozy spaces. (Bunnett & Davis, 1997)

• Label the feelings behind a child's actions.

• Read "angry" books and discuss them with the group.

• Be a "buffer of stress" (Dimidjian, 1986, as quoted in Hohmann & Weikart, 1995, p. 388), providing a safe haven and modeling coping strategies when a child feels overwhelmed.

• Build choices into activities whenever possible, even when setting limits on a child. ("Will you go inside by yourself or would you like me to help?")

• Be flexible about the ending times for activities, giving some children extra time to finish an activity as needed, while allowing other children to move to the next activity in the routine.

• Provide cues to alert the child to the need to control an action (an agreed-upon signal, a statement to the child about the behavior). Encourage the child to think of ways to control his or her own behavior ("What will help you to not push?").

• When you notice the child behaving appropriately, acknowledge this with a smile or a few words ("That worked"; "You did it"; "You played with Jim today"). Comment even on small improvements.

• Help children deal with the logical and natural consequences of inappropriate behavior. (For example, stay nearby as Robbie picks up the blocks he has thrown.) For all children, avoid using time-out.

• Shorten activities as needed.

• Introduce the conflict resolution process to all children. Include the child with severe behaviorial or emotional problems as much as possible, introducing the process one step at a time with this child.

• Some children with severe problems don't handle a lot of language well when they are having trouble, so keep language to a bare minimum. If behavior escalates, you may need to remove the child briefly and problem-solve later.

• Be aware of the child who is withdrawn. Give this child as much appropriate attention as you give to the aggressive child.

• Imitate and take your cues from the appropriate play actions of the child.

Autism

Children with autism need many sensory experiences within a calm and predictable environment. Their behaviors are often very different from those of other children. Rigid, repetitive responses like head banging or rocking are frequent.

• Use a wide variety of sensory materials (certain musical instruments, flexible building materials such as pipe cleaners, paper to crumple, and if the child will accept them, modeling compound, water, and "goop"), and encourage children to explore them in a free-form way.

• Children with autism are often sensitive to noise, so limit background noises as much as possible.

• Avoid materials that encourage repetitive behavior, such as castanets.

• Encourage a buddy to work with the child with autism.

• Children with autism may latch on to a particular "feely" object (such as a Koosh ball). This can help them settle down at group times.

• Keep the environment simple, quiet, and uncluttered.

• Stick to a very consistent routine; children with autism are upset by even the slightest change.

• Keep routines and group activities as short as possible, but avoid unnecessary transitions. When transition is necessary, keep changes to a minimum (nearby location, similar activity).

• Use simple words and directions and simple signing (one thing at a time). As aids to communication, use photos and pictures of areas and objects in the room and especially of other children in the room.

• Use music, especially familiar songs, both to interest children with autism and as a way of giving directions.

• Keep choices simple, but do offer choices.

• Imitate actions that are not repetitive or self-destructive. Repeat self-stimulating actions at first, then change one part of the action to see if the child follows.

• Encourage turn-taking, both in conversation and actions.

• Use simple photos or line drawings to make a daily routine chart. Prepare the child with autism for any changes in the routine, such as field trips or special visitors. Practice the changes using the chart as an aid.

• Gradually increase oral sensory experiences.

• Provide a cozy, comfortable space as a retreat. Children with autism often like small, enclosed spaces.

• Introduce real, self-care materials and activities (such as dressing oneself) and practice using them with other children.

• Remove nonedible, small materials.

• Work with a communications specialist/speech therapist on alternative communication methods (sign language, picture book, using communication board with speech).

REFERENCES

Bunnett, R., & Davis, N. (1997, March). Getting to the heart of the matter. In *Beginnings workshop: Environments for special needs* (pp. 42–44) [pamphlet]. Redmond, Washington: Child Care Information Exchange.

Dimidjian, V. (1986). Helping children in times of trouble and crisis. In Nancy E. Curry (Ed.), *The feeling child: Affective development reconsidered.* New York: The Haworth Press.

Heward, W. L., & Orlansky, M. D. (1996). *Exceptional children: An introductory survey of special education.* New York: MacMillan Publishing Co.

Hohmann, M., & Weikart, D. P. (1995). *Educating young children: Active learning practices for preschool and child care programs.* Ypsilanti, MI: High/Scope Press.

Books Come Alive for Children

By Pam Weatherby

· ·

In my 25 years as a special education teacher I've become convinced that language is perhaps the most important curriculum area for children with special needs. Experiences with children's literature play an important role in the development of language and literacy skills, both for these "special" children and for typically developing children.

In approaching experiences with books, the challenge for all preschool teachers is to instill in children a love of literature. As children listen and respond to stories, they are also developing the ability to express their own thoughts and feelings in words. Here are some techniques I use in my own classroom to help good books come alive for children; the strategies are well suited to settings like my own that include both children with special needs and typically developing children. To illustrate these strategies, I'll use my experiences with one of my favorite books, *Frosty the Snowman* (as retold by Annie North Bedford).

• **Start by choosing books carefully.** First, consider the literary qualities of the story, the quality of the themes, illustrations, and structure. Choose books in which the illustrations clearly and sequentially follow the narrative. It's also important to look for "child appeal." Choose stories that will interest children because they are related to things children have personally experienced or interests that have recently arisen in the classroom. Also look for the educational potential of the book; consider, for example, which key experiences may arise as children listen to the story, re-enact it in play, or engage in related group activities.

• **When you have selected a book, prepare a "prop box" containing objects related to the story that children can use to experience the story more actively or to re-enact it in role play.** This is especially helpful for children with limited language skills who may need help in understanding the vocabulary of the story.

• **Read the story to children with inflection and drama, holding the book so that children can see the pictures as you read.** (This advice may seem obvious yet I have visited many classrooms in which teachers seem to be reading the book to themselves without drawing the children into the story or showing them the pictures.)

• **Select books in which most of the vocabulary is meaningful to children, and help them understand words they do not know.** As you read, use the props you've collected as concrete illustrations of the words in the story; if necessary, simplify or explain the language of the story as you go along. Explain that the props will be available later for children to play with. For example, the word *coasting* that appears in *Frosty* is unfamiliar to many young children and to children who have always lived in warm climates. When I read the story I explain that "coasting is like riding," and I may also bring in a real sled for children to sit on and lay on. I might also take children "coasting" by making a sled out of cardboard and/or blocks.

• **Plan follow-up small- and large-group times related to the story.** During these times, give children opportunities to explore and play with the props you've collected, to create their own story illustrations and models of story characters, and to move and communicate like story characters. During these group activities, consider whether there are opportunities for the key experiences, and watch and listen for children having fun with language, describing experiences orally, comparing, counting, classifying, seriating, drawing, painting, making models, and moving to music.

In following these strategies, I've planned and encouraged many active experiences related to the *Frosty* story, which I read to children every year. I've collected a wide range of props to use with *Frosty:* lots of winter hats and shoes, boots, ice skates, a sled, changes of clothes to dress Frosty for various occupations, pretend food for the store that Frosty visits when he goes to town, many sizes of blocks for building "snow houses," small cars and trucks to represent the traffic in the story, butcher paper for making roads. I introduce some of these materials the first time I read the story to children; other materials are introduced later during group experiences.

Over the years, we've tried many different small- and large-group experiences to follow up with after reading *Frosty.* A favorite group activity we do every year is to build our own full-sized classroom Frosty out of papier-mâché, since we do not have real snow in our part of southern California unless we drive to the mountains. The creation of Frosty is always a joy to share with children. Papier-mâché constructions are time-consuming

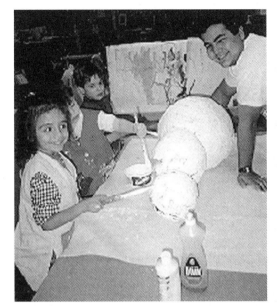

Painting the dry papier-mâché is one of the final steps in the creation of a large Frosty model, a time-consuming process that fosters cooperation.

to create and take days to dry, but the final product is worth the wait. When time and classroom space haven't been available, we've made our Frosty out of stuffed white trash bags.

The processes for making the papier-mâché snowman and the trash-bag snowman are similar: children work in small groups, and there are individual sets of materials for each child. For example, for the papier-mâché snowman, each child has the opportunity to mix flour, salt, and water to make the paste solution and each child has a bowl for dipping newspaper strips in the solution. To decorate and dress our snowman, we use charcoal for the eyes and nose, a scarf around the neck, sticks for arms, boots for shoes, a real corncob pipe, and a broom. We like to use red yarn or red pipe cleaners for the mouth because the children can have fun changing the expression on Frosty's face to match the changes in Frosty's emotions in the story. (This also presents a valuable opportunity to discuss feelings.)

Along with their part in constructing one large snowman, children sometimes choose to draw and paint pictures of snowmen or make individual Frosty models out of papier-mâché, modeling compound, stuffed paper bags, and other materials. One group of children enjoyed wrapping big blocks in white paper during small-group time. Then, at work time, they decided to build "houses for Frosty" out of the white blocks.

Large-group language, music, and movement experiences are another way to build on stories you have read. For example, we sometimes introduce a "magic hat" to children at large-group time to represent the magical hat in the story. Often, we'll reread this part of the story, and this leads to a discussion of the meaning of magic as it relates to Frosty putting on the hat, coming alive, and dancing around. Following this, children often enjoy singing the song "Frosty the Snowman." All the children are given the opportunity to learn to sing the first verse of the song and some children choose to learn all the words. Children especially enjoy singing the "Thumpity, thump, thump; thumpity, thump, thump" part of the song, sometimes patting the beat with rhythm sticks or other instruments as they listen to, sing, or dance to this part.

These are just a few examples of the many ways that story-reading can be a springboard for all kinds of activities in classrooms that include children with special needs. By encouraging active experiences that center on children's literature, teachers provide important opportunities for children to develop abilities in language and literacy as well as other curriculum areas.

Using Dolls to Build Disability Awareness

By Pam Weatherby

• •

It is important for children identified with special needs to understand as much as they can about the nature and causes of their physical and/or cognitive strengths and weaknesses. This is especially important for preschoolers; young children who have some understanding of their disabilities are better equipped to communicate with curious peers who will ask many honest questions about the unusual characteristics they notice in their classmates.

For the past ten years, we have been using adapted dolls to help children learn more about disabilities. Moreno School is an integrated setting serving both children with disabilities and typically developing children in preschool through sixth grade. Many of our children with special needs are included in regular classrooms, and the dolls have been helpful in facilitating the inclusion process. We not only use the dolls in communicating with children but also in inservice presentations and presentations to parents and siblings.

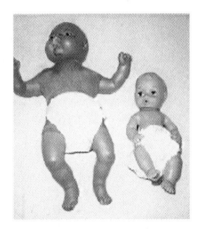

Dolls are modified to match the characteristics of specific children with disabilities. These dolls represent children with cerebral palsy.

I've found that the best communication tools are dolls that closely match the characteristics of individual children with disabilities, including the individual child's appearance, ethnic background, and specific disability. Many of the dolls that have been most effective for me have been purchased in local variety stores and then adapted. While dolls representing children with special needs may be purchased through educational catalogs, these are expensive and may not match the actual children in your program.

The dolls I've created to represent children with spina bifida are a good example of our approach to disability awareness. Spina bifida is a birth defect in which there is a cleft in the spinal column. In the most severe form of this disorder, the spinal cord becomes tangled in a fluid sac on the baby's back. The sac is usually surgically removed within the first few weeks of life, but the child is paralyzed from the point of the lesion down. Many children with spina bifida need to wear diapers because the nerves to the bowel and bladder are affected. To represent children with this impairment, I purchased four cloth dolls at a local variety store. Two dolls were the size of infants, one was the size of a toddler, and one was about the size of a 3-year-old. All the dolls were female and were used to represent the same child growing up. To adapt the dolls, I dressed the infant dolls in diapers only. I sewed a "bump" on one infant doll's back and a "scar" on the back of the other infant doll to represent the child before and after surgery. I sewed "scars" on the backs of the bigger dolls and dressed them in clothes, but kept them in diapers to represent the fact that even older children with spina bifida might need to wear diapers. Using these dolls helped children and adults visualize spina bifida and usually generated some thoughtful and insightful questions.

I took a similar approach in adapting dolls to represent cerebral palsy. Since prematurity is the leading cause of this disability, I bought one very small baby doll and one baby doll about the size of an eight-pound baby. In introducing the dolls, I tell children that not all newborn babies are the same size and that some babies born too early are called "premature" or "preemies." I emphasize that most premature babies are just fine, but that some of them have damage to the part of the brain that helps them walk, move, and talk like other children. I explain that some of these children may need to wear braces, or use walkers, wheelchairs, and other equipment to help them get around. When possible, I use real examples of these kinds of equipment in our presentations.

I've also used dolls to help children and adults understand more about blindness and deafness and the wide range of individuals who have visual and hearing impairments. During these presentations, I ask children to put their hands over their eyes or ears to simulate these disabilities. To help children understand the absence of sound, I ring a loud school bell and then sneak the clapper out and "ring" it again. I also show children real hearing aids, books in Braille, and other such specialized equipment. As much as possible we include books about the disabled in our book area, and crutches, wheelchairs, and dolls with disabilities in the house area to make awareness of disability a normal part of the classroom.

In all of our special needs presentations, I emphasize the **strengths of the people represented by the dolls** and all the ways in which they are like their peers rather than different. One favorite doll represents a beautiful Hispanic girl with thick curly hair and a beautiful smile. This doll resembles a child we had in our classroom who looked very normal but had a severe disorder

in language. She often exhibited fearful, erratic behavior accompanied by lots of screaming. At the same time she was an accomplished artist who often communicated through pictures. She could dance to any kind of music. She made choices during planning time by pointing to pictures. As I illustrate these disabilities and strengths with the use of the doll, I explain that this child was a very special friend to all of us.

For preschool children, explanations about specific disabilities are best received and most concrete when given in response to children who ask questions about their own peers or the children they see regularly in their school or agency. Having dolls like these available when children ask questions makes the answers we give much more meaningful to children.

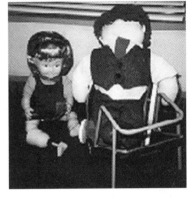

At top are dolls we modified to represent a child with spina bifida. Two other infant-sized dolls were also used to represent the same child. The dolls and equipment in the bottom photo were purchased from catalogs.

Chapter Six

Active Learning in the Elementary Grades

· ·

*T*he active learning approach described earlier and used successfully in High/Scope preschool settings is also an important part of High/Scope elementary settings. Elementary school children "learn by doing," often working with hands-on materials and carrying out projects of their own choosing. High/Scope's approach encompasses all aspects of elementary children's development and involves both teacher and parents in supporting and extending children's emerging intellectual, physical, social, and emotional skills and abilities. This chapter focuses on active learning in the elementary classroom.

The first article, "Making the Transition to Hands-on Materials," by Charles Hohmann and Diana Jo Johnston, outlines steps teachers can take when making the gradual transition from a traditional textbook-and-workbook elementary classroom into a classroom organized according to High/Scope guidelines. In the next article, "Tune In to Children's Interests," Diana Jo Johnston shows us how to find out what children's interests are, and how to use this information when planning reading and writing experiences for each day's program. "Active Small-Group Workshops," by Charles Hohmann and Diana Jo Johnston, provides an outline for planning small-group activities (workshops) for elementary classrooms. Three sample workshop plans are also provided.

In the next selection, "The Play's the Thing: Facilitating Child-Created Dramas," Ursula Ansbach presents an approach to child-created drama that was used successfully in a multi-arts program targeted to improve achievement test scores in an urban public school. In "Getting Excited About Art," Nancy Brickman offers techniques for introducing well-known works of art to children during small-group workshops.

The article "Encouraging Young Problem Solvers," by Cathy Albro and Diana Jo Johnston, provides strategies adults can use to encourage independent problem solving during small-group workshops in the elementary classroom. In "Active Learning—An Experience Base for Acquiring Language," Charles Hohmann explains how the High/Scope "ingredients of active learning" (materials, manipulation, choice, language from children, and support from adults) support children whose first language is not English. In "Reading Research: New Findings," Hohmann discusses phoneme awareness, an awareness of the smallest sound units that make up spoken words, and their importance in helping children learn to read.

Finally, in the article "Effective Conferences for K–5," Diana Jo Johnston provides tips to help teachers prepare for and conduct efficient and informative parent/teacher conferences for elementary programs.

Making the Transition to Hands-on Materials

By Charles Hohmann and Diana Jo Johnston

• •

Teachers who are shifting to the High/Scope elementary approach usually make dramatic and visible changes in their classroom learning environments. Changes in the kinds of learning materials selected and the organization of the classroom reflect the program's goals of involving students in hands-on, active learning experiences and helping teachers develop alternatives to traditional paper-and-pencil instruction.

High/Scope elementary classrooms, like preschool classrooms, are organized in clearly defined **interest areas** (for example, art, building/construction, reading/writing, math, science, and social studies areas). Each area is stocked with appealing materials that allow children to learn through direct, hands-on experiences and encourage children to use academic skills in real-life contexts. For example, a math area would contain lots of manipulatives, such as sorting trays, shells, pebbles, dice, base-ten blocks, and many practical tools such as number lines, rulers, scales, measuring cups, compasses, and calculators.

Transforming a traditional textbook-and-workbook classroom into a classroom organized according to High/Scope guidelines is a big job, and one that continues throughout the school year. To be successful in this task, teachers will need to be well organized and willing to continuously reevaluate their settings.

At a gathering of High/Scope elementary teachers who had recently implemented the approach in their classrooms, the following suggestions were offered for handling the transition to a High/Scope classroom:

• **Start slowly,** setting clear goals for each phase of the process and building on what seems to work and is comfortable for you. Be prepared to experiment.

• **Establish the interest areas first.** The plan-do-review process depends on having the basic interest areas in place. Be sure that each area has enough materials and is clearly defined. This will enable children to have a variety of choices and to see what is available to them.

• **Learn about the children.** Find out as much as you can about the children who will be in your classroom, so you can individualize your classroom arrangement. For example, if you have lots of animal lovers, live pets are a natural for the science area. Consider each child's special needs, abilities, or talents, making sure your materials offer a challenge for every child.

• **Involve children in decisions about materials.** This will increase their feelings of ownership in the classroom (e.g., "Does anyone have an idea where we can keep this new box of inch cubes?").

• **Consider what you teach.** As you select materials, take a systematic look at your curriculum. Consider how it relates to your group of children as you begin to know them better. Use the materials in each area to support each curriculum goal.

• **Identify lines of administrative support.** If your school district's purchasing department is most familiar with filling orders for workbooks and other traditional materials, they may not know how to handle your requests for High/Scope-style materials. This can cause delays. Locating administrators who can help you deal with the bureaucracy is a necessity. Don't hesitate to ask for help from a supportive administrator.

• **Inform the parents.** Don't keep your activities and plans to yourself. Parental concern is legitimate and should be respected. The success of any change can be jeopardized by negative reactions from parents, so take time to cultivate their support. At the earliest opportunity, offer parents accurate information about what is being planned and how it can affect their child's learning. For example, send a classroom newsletter to parents containing a brief description of your plans. Then invite parents to come to a room meeting if they wish to find out more about the changes in the classroom. Parents may be asked to help by finding materials (e.g., a collection of bottle caps) or even by making needed equipment or furniture.

• **Maintain classroom organization.** As you add more things to your room, the potential for clutter increases. Remember, because of the public nature of the classroom, first impressions to outsiders are very important. It is possible to have both an orderly environment and a wide variety of interesting materials, if the materials are added systematically.

Establishing clearly defined interest areas is the first priority of teachers new to the High/Scope elementary approach. Each area should have enough materials for several children to choose and use, especially during the daily plan-do-review process. These dramatic and visible changes in the classroom learning environment signify High/Scope's active approach to educating children.

• **Use plan-do-review to improve.** Once the plan-do-review process is established, use it to continually evaluate and revise the areas and materials. Listen to and observe children to see what worked and what didn't.

• **Don't forget the school custodian.** Consider how the custodian will perceive the changes in the room, and accept input on such issues as how to make the classroom easier to sweep at the end of each day.

• **Involve specialty teachers.** Art and music teachers, for example, may have good suggestions for improving your art and music areas. They may welcome the opportunity to give input since it enables them to have an impact beyond the one or two hours per week when they have direct contact with your students.

• **Capitalize on local resources.** The unique resources of your community—businesses, libraries, parks, museums, community groups, and local government agencies—can be used to enhance the classroom learning environment. Keep your eyes open at rummage sales. Keep in mind that it takes time to acquire plentiful and interesting materials. Don't forget that many businesses donate freely to schools.

As the year progresses, consider your accumulated knowledge of children's interests, strengths, or weaknesses as you continue to make additions to and changes in the classroom.

Tune In to Children's Interests

By Diana Jo Johnston

• •

In High/Scope programs, the opportunity for children to pursue their personal interests is not seen as a frill or reward that is given after "the real learning" is out of the way. Instead, teachers make a concerted effort to find out about their students' specific interests, and they use this knowledge as they plan instructional activities. Whether children are interested in animals, sports heroes, particular kinds of music, or artwork, knowing about these interests is essential for planning learning experiences that engage children.

Let's illustrate how this observation and planning process might work in planning for **reading and writing experiences** for elementary children. The first step in this process is to **find out what children's interests are.** The key is to watch each child and ask everybody who has contact with that child for their observations. Here are some ideas:

➻ **During the silent reading times in your classroom, observe each child for clues about personal interests.** What do children pick up to read? Do they go straight to the travel or animal magazines? The small biographies of sports heroes? Do they like books with elaborate illustrations? Books that focus on rhymes, word play, or jokes? Do they like to read with a friend or two or do they prefer to read alone?

➻ **During plan-do-review time, observe what each child tends to do and what interest areas they prefer.** Do art supplies go quickly in your classroom? Are there children who love to play games? Do some children always go to the animal pets and science materials?

➻ **At parent conferences, pass out a form for the parent to fill out while waiting to talk with you.** On this form, or as you meet with parents, ask them what books they have been reading recently with their child. Does the child have favorite books or authors? What magazines and newspapers are available in the home? Do the parents like to take their child to the library? What kinds of books do they take out? What hobbies, play activities, sports, and games does the child enjoy? What kinds of activities does the family enjoy doing together?

↦ **Ask the "special" teachers (music, art, PE, library) and support staff (playground helpers, after-school program staff) what they know about each child's interests.** Ask the school librarian to print out a list of the books borrowed by each child in your class. (Most library computers will do this.)

↦ **Find out from the students themselves about their interests and preferences.** For example, plan a small-group workshop in which children discuss, then list, their vacation activities, hobbies, and so forth. Help them compile the information in a chart or booklet form, which you can save and refer to as you plan.

Here are some additional ways to use information on children's interests as you plan reading and writing experiences for each day's program:

• **Add reading materials related to students' interests to all areas of the classroom** (including, but not limited to the book and writing area). For example, add animal or sports magazines (with sensitive material removed) to the science or math area, or add catalogs related to students' interests. Put travel brochures and maps from children's family trips in the geography or social studies area. In choosing such high-interest materials, don't worry too much about matching students' reading levels, since students will work especially hard to read something that really interests them.

• **Tailor language arts workshops to students' interests.** For example, if an activity centers on students searching through printed text to find prefixes, suffixes, or homonyms, don't ask them to do their searches on workbook pages. Instead, provide a selection of magazines or copies of book pages related to students' interests. Have the children choose reading matter that interests them, and then have them highlight the relevant words in the chosen text. This helps students see that reading and writing skills are connected to "real life."

• **Choose formats for workshop activities based on the interests you've observed.** For example, if you are planning to do a story retelling workshop and you have observed students playing with the puppets in the classroom, have them use puppets to retell the story. If students are interested in drama, have them make the story into a play. If students are interested in building or making artwork, have them make models or paintings based on the story.

• **While it's a good idea to choose materials related to students' interests, avoid restricting the range of interests represented** in your classroom. Don't organize all the learning activities, resources, or reading matter in your classroom around specific themes or units—for example, don't assume that all children will be interested in circuses, insects, or zoo animals. Students' interests are still developing and many students do not know yet what they are interested in. To give children an opportunity to develop strong and wide-ranging interests, expose them to a broad range of children's literature and nonfiction books, as well as to a variety of magazines and other print resources (written for both adults and children).

Once you get "hooked" on the process of discovering students' interests and planning around them, you will think of many more ideas. As a result, all of your learning activities will be more engaging for your students.

Add magazines and catalogs reflecting students' interests to the reading rack, as well as to the interest areas.

Active Small-Group Workshops

By Charles Hohmann and Diana Jo Johnston

• •

In elementary classrooms using the High/Scope approach, many of the instructional activities take place in small-group activities called "workshops." Each workshop group involves four to eight children who work independently much of the time. Two examples of first-grade workshops are provided in this article. In addition, a science workshop for first and second graders is provided (p. 287).

Small-group workshops promote active learning in several ways. **Active learning materials** (such as tools, manipulatives, art materials, and computers) are more practical to use in small groups, and **choices** are more easily offered. In a small group, children can use the materials at the same time without having to wait for a turn. Since small-group activities don't require silence, they can talk to one another about what they are doing. Such **conversation** supports and extends children's thinking and creates a more relaxed working environment that (brain research and everyday experience tell us) allows the mind to be more engaged and active.

Small-group workshops require considerable **organization and preparation** to operate successfully. Each workshop activity generally involves a quarter or sixth of the class working on a task designed and assigned by the teacher. During a workshop period, each small group of children works at one of the activities for

Math Workshop

Before beginning this first-grade math workshop, the teacher works with the whole group doing two or three graphs together (examples: graphing children's favorite ice cream flavors, television shows, or kinds of pizza). At workshop time, the small groups rotate among the following activities:

Group 1. Children work with teachers on problems from the math text.

Groups 2–6. A different set of supplies (see list), plus crayons and 1-inch graph paper, are placed at each activity station for students to use in making their graphs. Students may work either individually or in groups of two or more to do their graphs.

Supplies
Unifix blocks
Colored paper clips
Sea shells
Nails, bolts, screws, nuts
Play money
Pattern blocks

Reading and Writing Workshop

A typical first-grade reading and writing workshop involves four small groups of students in the following four activities. In this example the book report activity was new, so the teacher took 5 minutes before the workshop to demonstrate to children how to draw a set of sequence pictures with captions. At workshop time, the small groups rotate among the following activities:

Group 1—Children engage in guided reading with the teacher; children then pair up, choose books, and read with their buddies.

Group 2—Children write in their journals about the recent class visit to a farmer's market.

Group 3—Children represent a book they've read by drawing a sequence of pictures.

Group 4—At the computer area, children practice letter-sound combinations with Davidson's *Kid Phonics* software.

a pre-set length of time (typically 15 to 30 minutes). A few minutes after the warning signal, the group rotates to the next activity and begins working. The workshop period may allow for a complete rotation so that each small group completes each of the 4–6 activities during the workshop period. However, since some workshop activities are time-consuming, it may take two or more workshop periods over two or more days for all the small groups to complete the rotation.

Workshops generally require some introduction and explanation, especially when new materials, concepts, or skills are involved. This introduction takes place with the group as a whole; it can be an extended lesson related to the skills to be practiced in the workshop, a briefer mini-lesson or review, or a demonstration of some of the tasks to be performed. After the introduction, children can break into the small groups to explore and apply the concept or skills introduced in the large-group setting. As children work in small groups, the teacher may conduct one of the activities or may circulate among the activity groups.

For children who have never experienced small-group workshops and rotations before, it is best for the adult to focus first on getting children familiar with the workshop **process.** During this initial phase, keep the actual workshop activities simple: painting, working with clay, listening to story tapes, or playing games like dominoes, bingo, or Boggle. It will take children 5 to 10 days to learn the workshop process: how the rotation works, where to go and when, what the start and stop signals mean, how to clean up. Once children are comfortable with the process, teachers can begin to plan instructional activities with more substance. Another way to simplify planning for workshops during this initial phase is to have only two activities going at once, for example, having 3 of the 6 groups working on each activity.

Science Workshop:
A Litter Survey

This activity, in which children analyze the build-up of unwanted materials in the natural environment, is designed to help elementary-level children understand the environmental impact of littering. It is excerpted from *High/Scope K–3 Curriculum Series: Science*, by Frank Blackwell and Charles Hohmann (Ypsilanti, MI: High/Scope Press, 1991), p. 104–105.

Materials:
Litter collection bags for each pair of children; plastic gloves for each child; materials for making a graph

Activity:
Working in pairs and wearing plastic gloves for safety, children visit an outdoor area (playground, park) and gather litter. (Children are warned not to collect any broken glass or other sharp objects.) Then they decide what different categories of litter they have, and after sorting the litter into these categories, they create graphs comparing the incidence of various types of litter.

This activity illustrates how the beauty of the human environment can be upset by the build-up of unwanted materials.

Questions to Ask:
Why do we consider some things to be litter in our environment? What different kinds of groups did you sort your litter into? What type of litter did you find the most of? The least of? Can you think of any reasons for this? What happens to litter if no one picks it up? Who leaves litter behind? What can you tell about the lives of those who have left this litter?

Extension:
1. Children investigate alternatives to littering. They learn about recyclables and biodegradeables, about landfills and recycling centers.

2. Children collect and analyze litter from other environments, such as the school hallways or the school cafeteria. They also choose to help beautify an area of the school building or grounds by analyzing and then disposing of all the litter and then mounting a campaign to reduce the most predominate type of litter.

Key Experiences:
- Analyzing: separating and measuring the parts of a mixture to describe its composition

- Classifying materials into small groups based on common attributes

- Using bar graphs

REFERENCES
Pringle, L. (1986). *Throwing things away.* New York: Thomas Y. Crowell.
Shuttlesworth, D. & Cervasio, T. (1973). *Litter: The ugly enemy, an ecology story.* New York: Doubleday.
Weiss, M. (1984). *Toxic waste* ("The Good Old Days," pp. 9–14). New York: Franklin Watts, Inc.

The experiences High/Scope elementary teachers have had in planning workshops has led to several more **tips for effective workshops:**

• **Mixed ability groupings work best.** Teachers should also consider the personalities and styles of individual children in making up the groups.

Graphing the Results

This is a sample data sheet students might make after collecting and sorting the litter. Students then make a picture or bar graph from the data. Another approach might be to weigh or measure the volume of each type of litter and to create a new data sheet or graph showing the volume or weight of each type of litter.

Sample Litter Data Sheet

Place where the litter was collected:

_____

Number of pieces of each type of litter:

Candy & snack wrappers_____

School papers_____

Newspapers_____

Bottles_____

Cans_____

Other metal items_____

Plastic items_____

Cigarette butts_____

Other_____

• It's a good idea to provide recognizable but low-key signals (rattles, bells, and so forth) to remind children when to rotate. A 5-minute warning signal before the group comes to an end is especially important to ease the transition.

• With kindergartners and first-graders, playing a music tape as children move from activity to activity makes the transition much smoother.

• In many classrooms serving children in grade two or older, teachers appoint a child as the weekly leader for each small group. The child's responsibilities are to remind the other children about the time signals, to make sure materials are available, to be a liaison with the teacher when problems arise, and to make sure cleanup is complete.

The Play's the Thing: Facilitating Child-Created Dramas

By Ursula Ansbach

· ·

Creative play-making is a valuable learning experience for elementary-level children. In this article, we describe an approach to child-created drama that was used in a multi-arts program targeted to improve achievement test scores in an urban public school. The arts program also included music, visual arts, and teacher-developed games. Children's reading scores improved dramatically after their participation in this program.

Creative drama experiences for elementary-level children may be conducted either as whole-group or small-group experiences. In creating a play, children may use all the basic elements of theater: a setting, interesting characters, a plot, props, and costumes. The teacher usually works directly with the group during the development of the story and characters, but parts of the process may be carried out by children working independently in small groups.

To get children started in creating their own drama, begin by introducing the elements of a dramatic story—beginning, middle, and ending. Talk to children about how most plots have a beginning, in which the characters experience a problem situation; a middle, in which the problem reaches a crisis; and an ending, in which the problem is resolved.

Then invite children to make up their own story. They can start with any element that attracts them, building the rest of the play from there. They might start with a setting (a circus, for example); a prop (a magic walking stick); or a situation (a problem arising between two brothers).

Here's how the play-making process worked with one group of second-grade children. They decided to make up a play about a boy who was upset because he wanted to play basketball with his older brother and the brother's friends. The older brother didn't want to include the younger boy and didn't like it when the younger boy tried to tag along.

The class decided that the first scene of the play would show the small boy and his mother as they watched the older brother go out to play with his friends. The mother and son would talk about the younger boy's wish to go along with them. Once the group had agreed on this basic situation, the teacher asked open-ended questions to help the children develop the story line: For example, she asked, "What would the boy say?...What would the mom say then?...What happened next?"

Each time the children thought of a new development for their drama, the teacher asked for volunteers to act it out. They continued using this process to develop a second scene, in which the class imagined what the group of older boys was saying and doing outdoors on the playground, and a third scene, which showed what happened when the small boy sneaked out, found the older boys, and tried to tag along.

The whole process of creating and refining the characters and story line for this play took place over the course of 5 or 6 days, with the group spending about 20–30 minutes a day on the effort. (The time needed to develop a play will vary, depending upon the age of the children and the complexity of their inventions.) From time to time, the group broke into smaller groups to carry out specific activities, such as locating or making props and costumes or developing particular characters or scenes further. Eventually, the children knew the plot, story, and characters well (having settled disagreements about which plot lines should be included), had all the necessary props and costumes, and were able to act out their play consistently.

In the play-making approach described here, children use language that comes naturally each time they act out their plot. Though teachers or children may write down a story line at some point in the process, a memorized script is not recommended because children learn more by generating their own language. Children's invented dialogue tends to be rich, vivid, and appropriate to the context. And because the basic plot line and characters are developed through a shared process, each "performance" is surprisingly consistent in language.

This kind of play development experience can be extended in many ways. Children can make illustrated storybooks based on their play, or you can bring in related books for the group to read together. Children may want to do "research" to help them develop more realistic settings, costumes, or situations. Another possibility is to invite parents or another audience in to see the performance.

At this stage, however, performing for others should not be the primary goal; children are primarily developing the play for themselves and for the skills and abilities they can develop through such experiences.

Getting Excited About Art

By Nancy Brickman

· ·

Young children can and do get excited about the works of great artists, according to Cathy McFerrin, a High/Scope certified trainer based at the Child Study Center in Forth Worth, Texas.

McFerrin, who works with K–8 and preschool teachers, has developed techniques for introducing well-known works of art to children.

Her approach integrates High/Scope's active learning strategies with the art education ideas of Mary Ann F. Kohl and Kim Solga (*Discovering Great Artists,* Bright Ideas for Learning, 1997).

McFerrin advises teachers to introduce great art to children in the context of hands-on art experiences. This helps children understand and recognize what an artist does and the value of thinking and talking about art. These "making and appreciating art" experiences can be offered during K–6 small-group workshops or preschool small-group times.

McFerrin recommends opening the small-group experience with a discussion of certain artworks. For example, in elementary classrooms the teacher could read a children's book about a particular artist to the whole group, and one of the small groups could then explore and discuss the book's reproductions with the teacher. Or the group could explore and discuss a book or collection of artwork on a particular theme (such as paintings of people with their pets or mothers with their children). In discussing such art with children, teachers should be attuned to children's interests and levels of development. For example, teachers may want to use a storytelling approach to convey information about an artist. McFerrin notes that older children may become very interested in discussing the details of the artist's life; showing children a picture of the artist can often stimulate this curiosity, she says.

After this introduction to a particular artist or type of art, the teacher might hand out a set of related art-making materials. For example, after showing children a book about the works of Dutch artist Piet Mondrian (an artist whose works depict brightly colored rectangles with black borders on white backgrounds), the teacher might pass out the following materials: white paper, black paper strips, glue sticks, scissors, and colored markers. Or, the group might explore reproductions of Henri Matisse's paper cutouts, with the teacher explaining that as the artist got older, he was disabled and could no longer paint on canvas so he made pictures by cutting and arranging pieces of brightly colored paper. Then the teacher would distribute colored construction paper, glue sticks, and scissors for children to make their own paper-cutout pictures.

With lots of hands-on experiences, children begin to recognize and understand what an artist does and the value of thinking and talking about art.

As the teacher passes out the hands-on materials, he or she may casually suggest (using child-level language) that children may want to create works that are similar to the artist's in style, technique, or content ("You might want to try making some swirls, like Van Gogh did" or "Perhaps you'd like to make your own pet picture"). Children should not be pushed to use the materials in any particular way, of course.

As children work, and after they have finished their creations, the teacher might encourage them to discuss, share, and reflect on what they did. To encourage thoughtful discussion, the teacher could make descriptive comments ("You used the side of the chalk"; "The swirls seem to be moving"; "These squares remind me of the ones in the painting") and ask open-ended questions ("What did you use?" "What were you interested in doing here?" "Where did you start?" "How did you make that?").

McFerrin says that this combination of doing and discussing art encourages children to deepen their interest in the artwork of others and also to see that they are "great artists," too.

Encouraging
Young Problem Solvers

By Cathy Albro and Diana Jo Johnston

• •

In High/Scope elementary classrooms, much of the academic instruction in language arts, math, science, and other academic areas takes place in **workshops.** At workshop times children work in small groups of four to eight, carrying out tasks planned by the teacher. Usually, several different workshop activities are going on at once, so children are working without direct teacher supervision for much of the workshop period.

When children work independently, it is natural that they will encounter problems. "Where can I get some more masking tape?" "I don't understand how to do this math problem." "Taping the pebbles on the poster didn't work—What can I use instead?" These examples are typical of the problems and stumbling blocks children often encounter during workshops. More examples are listed at the right.

How do teachers help children with such problems? At the elementary level, teachers are not able to provide one-to-one help to every child who has a problem. Instead, the emphasis is on setting up a management system that enables children to solve problems independently or with the help of peers. This shift in approach is necessary for practical reasons (one teacher can't attend to all the problems faced by 25 or 30 children). In addition, this approach reflects the curriculum's goal of preparing children for independent problem solving by giving them problem-solving opportunities, as they are ready for them.

Typical Problems Children Face During Workshops

- What do I do about the paint I spilled on the table?

- I forgot the directions for the second science activity.

- How do I get the paper out of the printer?

- What activity do we rotate to next?

- What kind of a graph does the teacher want to see at the end of the workshop?

- I just finished this great-looking book cover, and I really want the teacher to notice it.

Here are strategies teachers use to encourage independent problem solving during small-group workshops:

- **Use a consistent room arrangement,** familiarize children with it, and involve children in deciding where materials should go. Let children know it is their job to get out additional materials they may need for the workshop activity (more tape, a pair of scissors), and to put them away.

- **Limit the demands on the teacher** by setting the expectation that children who have problems should turn to peers first, then to the teacher. For example, some teachers have an "Ask three children before me" rule. You might also have a sign-up sheet for students who haven't been able to solve a problem by working with a classmate. The teacher then attends to these students at the first available moment, working down the list.

- **Focus first on the workshop rotation process.** At workshop times, each small group rotates through several different activities. This can be confusing for children at first. To help children learn how the rotation works, start with simple activities, like story tapes or games. Once children understand the workshop process, add more academically challenging tasks.

- **Plan for a range of developmental abilities in each small group.** This way, children who are capable in particular areas can help other children out. This builds a sense of community in the classroom.

- **Appoint child leaders for each small group.** The leader is responsible for knowing about the materials and directions for particular workshop activities. Have children take turns being the leader.

- **Whenever possible, post written instructions** for workshop activities (or tape record the instructions), so children who are confused about the directions can check them independently.

- **Use large-group time to discuss repeated problems** and to plan with children how to solve them.

In classrooms that use these strategies consistently, children gradually become self-sufficient problem solvers, and teachers can spend more of the workshop period focusing on children's important learning needs.

Active Learning—An Experience Base for Acquiring Language

By Charles Hohmann

• •

Many teachers in High/Scope elementary settings work with children whose first language or home language is not English. Fortunately, teachers who are implementing the High/Scope approach already have in place many of the practices they need to work with these children, because the approach emphasizes thinking and language acquisition.

The High/Scope "ingredients of active learning" are basic features of High/Scope settings and a "natural fit" for children who are in the process of acquiring English (or, for that matter, any second language). The ingredients (materials, manipulation, choice, language from children, support from adults) support these children in the following ways:

• **Materials.** Active learning environments provide a rich array of materials and equipment for children to experience and work with in a hands-on, "minds-on" way. This emphasis on direct experiences is especially important for children who are acquiring English, since such experiences promote the use of **"referential language"**—language related to active experiences with physical objects and communication with others. Activities that focus on language itself (such as phonics, spelling, punctuation, rhyming, or poetry activities) and activities that rely completely on language (such as history readings or lectures) are more abstract for everyone, but especially for those with a limited knowledge of the English language. Learning about the English language *system* through such activities is important, but these experiences are secondary to experiences with referential language for acquiring English language *facility*.

• **Manipulation.** Children in active learning settings have materials to work with, create from, and think about—to "experience directly." Thinking can proceed in any language (and without language) but requires an experience base. Manipulating materials in the context of "real" events gives children who have a limited knowledge of English an experience base for thinking, developing concepts, and communicating with peers and adults. For example, many topics in mathematics (such as grouping and sorting, arithmetic operations, measuring, and working with shapes and patterns) lend themselves to the use of manipulatives. By emphasizing hands-on experiences with such concepts, High/Scope programs open such topics to investigation by children with a limited knowledge of the English language. Science, too, is conveyed through concrete experiences with materials, systems, and equipment. Children with a limited ability to converse in English may communicate their science findings nonverbally, through pictures, drawings, and graphs, as well as verbally, through writing, speech, or dictations in their first language or in English.

I spent the last 30 min. in the art center. I made a birthday card for my mother. Tomorrow is her birthday. I will give her the card I made when I get home.

Tádlin dah'alzhin ji' na'ach'ąąh bit hazlǫ́ǫ́ji' nąashnish ni'ęę'. Shimá yiskáǫǫ binahaah biniiyé naaltsǫǫs bá íishtaa. Hooghan di nánísdzáago baa deesh hééł nisingo íishtaa.

At a school in Bird Springs, Arizona, a kindergartner recalled what she did in Diné (native speaker's term for Navajo language). The teacher wrote down her words in Diné and English.

• **Choice.** Choices provide a "wrap-around" for intentions and initiative, the motivational aspects of learning. By making choices, children transform experiences into opportunities for thought, problem solving, and reflection. In addition, children are more likely to enjoy activities that they have chosen, and new research on brain function shows that this positive emotional dimension adds to the richness of mental connections—concrete evidence that the experience of making choices enhances learning. In a High/Scope classroom, all the learning benefits that stem from making choices are available to children with a limited knowledge of English, because High/Scope elementary programs incorporate choices into all learning activities. Children with a limited ability to converse in English can communicate with adults and peers about their choices using pictures, drawings, or words (in the child's first language or English when possible).

• **Language from students.** Another basic principle of the High/Scope approach is to support all children in expressing themselves as fully as they can. This applies to children who come to the classroom with all degrees of English language ability—ranging from none to fluency with English. Teachers in High/Scope settings encourage children to use speech and writing (in either language) to communicate about their choices, feelings, needs, creations, and discoveries. If the adult (or peers) can respond in the child's first language, *this provides a bridge from the first language to English.* If others in the classroom cannot speak the child's first language, the shared environment of materials and experiences provides the best possible conditions under which children and adults can learn one another's languages.

• **Support from adults.** The last ingredient of active learning refers to the adult's role in supporting all of children's learning experiences, including those that involve the acquisition of language. For the child whose knowledge of English is limited, this means again providing the rich referential language environment that we've alluded to above. Within this environment, the wide range of materials and opportunities to use them provide many occasions for communicating with classmates and adults in pictures and words (English and otherwise). Adults support children who are acquiring English by "meeting them where they are." This means allowing children to express ideas in their first language when this best meets the needs of the moment. It also means encouraging these children to use the limited amount of English they have learned (along with drawings, work samples, gestures, and pantomime) to communicate with others.

Reading Research: New Findings

By Charles Hohmann

· ·

The effectiveness of fluoride in preventing tooth decay was discovered when dental researchers observed that children in some towns had significantly fewer cavities than children in other towns. The researchers eventually realized that the differences between the towns in tooth decay rates were associated with the amount of fluoride in their water supply. They also found that adding fluoride to town water supplies that lacked this element could prevent cavities.

Preventing Reading Difficulties in Young Children, a report released by the National Academy of Sciences (NAS) in 1998, relates a similar kind of story about a "missing element" that explains why some children have difficulty learning to read. Research has found a component of language learning that is always present in children who read well and is often weak or missing in children who are slow learning to read. In a similar vein, the research also shows that adults can improve success in reading for children having difficulties (as well as for children at risk for reading problems in the future) by adding the "missing element" to their learning experiences.

This mystery component of language learning is called **phoneme awareness.** It is an awareness of the smallest sound units that make up spoken words. The sounds /s/, /a/, and /t/ are the phonemes of the word *SAT.* (The slash symbols are used to distinguish a sound from its print representation in a letter or letters.)

When infants hear and begin to speak their native language, the phonemes of their language are recorded or "mapped" in their brains. This happens for most children before they come to school. This mapping allows children to hear and comprehend words and then to begin to produce them as speech. Even though most children are able to understand speech and have begun to produce it by the age of 2 years, they are not consciously aware of the phonemes themselves. Their knowledge of phonemes is subconscious and the processing of speech that involves these sound elements is done automatically by the brain.

To learn to read effectively, children apparently must acquire a conscious awareness of the phonemes of individual words. Even though children may be learning letters, recognizing some words in print, or even writing words, they may still be unaware of the individual phonemes. In light of this information, teachers from preschool on should make a conscious effort to help children develop an awareness of phonemes in spoken language.

Phoneme awareness is not quite the same as phonics awareness, although these two areas of learning are related. Phonics involves the alphabetic relationship between printed letters and speech sounds and, according to the Academy's report, is an important part of effective reading instruction. Phoneme awareness, however, starts largely with spoken language and is most easily approached through activities involving oral language. Since print is not necessarily involved, learning about phonemes can and should begin quite early—preferably in preschool—and then should continue in kindergarten and the early elementary grades.

As preschool and early elementary teachers, how can we start young children moving toward phoneme awareness? For some teachers, this may require some additions to the activities they are providing for young children. Fortunately, these activities are quite brief and many can be provided in familiar contexts.

Activities that help children develop an appreciation of rhyme—a familiar type of activity for most High/Scope teachers—are among the early activities that can be important for phoneme awareness. For example, teachers can emphasize the rhyming words in songs and chants such as "Eensy Weensy Spider" and "Hickory Dickory Dock." As children enjoy and respond to rhymes, they can begin to predict rhyming words as adults read them stories like *Noisy Nora* (by Rosemary Wells) and *Over in the Meadow* (by John Langstaff and Fedor Rojankosky). They can also make their own rhymes—again, orally—by combining rhyming words ("fat cat" or "cool pool") or by completing or making up silly sentences ("Did you ever see a snake in a lake?"). Children can also begin to detect the sounds that make up words. At first, teachers should focus on the initial sounds. For example, they could select a child by saying "The next person to plan is someone whose name begins with /b/" (pointing to Bernice) or "/t/" (pointing to Tonya)". As they do this, teachers should be sure to say the /b/ sound rather than the letter name. Once children catch on to the idea, they can take turns leading such activities.

As children's phoneme awareness grows, they develop the ability to break words into sound subunits—first showing they recognize syllables, and later the phonemes themselves. At this stage, for example, you can encourage children to enunciate the syllables in each other's names (Ton-ya, A-bra-ham, Chris-to-pher), clapping once on each syllable. Counting the syllables can also help build awareness. You can also break words into syllables in movement and music activities.

Important though phoneme awareness is, both the NAS report and much of the other literature on these discoveries emphasize the importance of teachers providing a balanced combination of all literacy elements—reading books, writing, oral language activities, as well as phonics and phonemic awareness. Phoneme awareness activities only work when they occur in a print-rich environment and are accompanied by a range of experiences such as reading to children, writing daily messages, and talking with children about what is important and interesting to them.

REFERENCES

Adams, M. J. (1996). *Beginning to read: Thinking and learning about print.* Cambridge, Massachusetts: MIT Press.

Adams, M. J., Foorman, B. R., Lindberg, I., & Beeler, T. (1998). *Phonemic awareness in young children.* Baltimore: Brookes Publishing.

Snow, Catherine E., Burns, M., & Griffin, P. (Eds.). (1998). *Preventing reading difficulties in young children.* Washington, DC: National Academy of Sciences. (Available at www.nas.edu)

Effective Conferences for K–5

By Diana Jo Johnston

• •

In High/Scope elementary programs, parent/teacher conferences focus on children's strengths and developmental accomplishments, just as they do at the preschool level. However, elementary-level children are now old enough to participate in parent conferences, so these meetings take a somewhat different form than they do in the preschool.

Before the Conference

As with parent conferences at the preschool level, **preparation is the key to a successful meeting.** You should prepare for conferences in several ways. **Start by informing parents.** Send home a flyer describing how you expect the conference to unfold. Explain that children will participate and ask parents to come 5-10 minutes early to "tour" the classroom with their child. Explain that the conference will focus mainly on the child's schoolwork, and that you are also interested in hearing from the parent about the child's accomplishments and interests at home. You might include a questionnaire about the child's pastimes, hobbies, favorite TV shows or games, and/or ask parents to come prepared to talk about two or three of the child's home accomplishments. Explain that a separate meeting can be arranged if parents have special concerns that might be better discussed without the child present.

Prepare materials to use in your discussions with parents. Go through the child's portfolio of work samples and select a small number that show the child's progress. Assuming you are using some system for recording observations of important child behaviors, you should also have a stockpile of child anecdotes to draw from as you search for materials that document children's progress. Prepare a parent report for each child that pulls together a few child anecdotes for each curriculum area. Be sure you have two copies of the report—one for you and one for the parents. Depending upon your school's requirements, you may also need to have the child's report card on hand at the conference.

Anticipate questions parents may ask. "What can I do to help my child learn?" is a concern of many parents. Be ready to respond with concrete suggestions: prepare schedules of upcoming exhibits, plays, or other events that the parent and child can attend together; put together reading lists of books the parent and child can read together at home (make sure you have lists appropriate for children at different levels in reading); and prepare handouts with suggestions for "real-world" math problems. **Be ready for tough questions that challenge your curriculum approach.** Expect that many parents will ask questions such as, "How does my child compare with the other children in the classroom?" "Is he below grade level in math or reading?" Be prepared to respond to such questions by explaining that our approach focuses on developmental change and the child's individual progress rather than on comparisons like these.

The Conference Unfolds

Once you've laid the groundwork by following the above suggestions, here's how a typical conference might go:

The conference opens as the child "tours" the classroom with his parents. At this time the child shows the parent his desk, the classroom displays, the computers and other interest areas, samples of his work, and so forth. To allow you to concentrate on finishing up the previous conference, be sure you have a separate, quiet place to meet with parents.

Once you are seated with parents and child, open the discussion by showing parents something that documents a special accomplishment or interest of the child, such as a piece of a child's writing or an anecdote about the child. Starting on a positive note makes both parents and child feel comfortable and sets the stage for a frank discussion.

Using your parent report, work samples, and report card as springboards for conversation, move systematically through a discussion of each curriculum area, starting with the area in which the child is strongest. Stay focused, remembering that you have a lot of ground to cover. Converse with, rather than "talk at" the parents. Encourage the child to share two or three work samples per curriculum area—have the rest organized for parents and child to discuss at home (you may get bogged down if you try to show parents too many work samples). At some point in the conversation, invite the parents to share information on the child's interests, pastimes, and accomplishments at home.

As your discussion draws to a close, take some action that points to the future. This may be the time that you give parents a book list or a schedule of upcoming community events to share with their child. You can also offer to bring in a special resource for the parent at some future time—however, if you make such a promise, write it down so you can be sure to follow up later.

As a closing note, ask the child to share something he or she has especially enjoyed about school this year—for example, a recent field trip, a science activity, or something made at plan-do-review time. This final event is a fitting way to end a conference that focuses on the child's strengths, interests, and achievements.

Close the conference by inviting the child to show a photo or work sample that highlights a special accomplishment: "I worked on this airplane for three days at plan-do-review time."

Chapter Seven

Collaborating
With Parents

· ·

In the High/Scope approach, teachers and parents form a collaborative part-nership to support and extend the education of young children. The articles in this chapter focus on this type of parent involvement and how this partner-ship benefits all—children, parents, and teachers.

In the first article, "Building Bridges With Parents," Pam Lafferty explains how, through trial and error, she and her team developed support strategies that encourage parents to come into the early childhood setting to work with children. Lafferty outlines the benefits of parent participation and provides guidelines and other tips.

Carol Markley's "Staying in Touch With Parents You Don't See Regular-ly" provides some valuable tips on how to stay in touch with parents through personal notes, journals, e-mails, photographs, and videotapes, as well as reg-ular telephone conversations. In the next selection, "Preparing for Successful Parent Conferences," Markley reminds us that parent/teacher conferences can be productive for teachers and parents without a great expenditure of prepara-

tion time. Throughout the article, Markley provides tips for organizing the process, from building relationships with parents to choreographing the conference itself.

In the next article, "Involving Parents in Curriculum Planning: A Head Start Story," Nita Banks describes how the parents and staff of a 23-classroom Head Start program worked together to incorporate the High/Scope curriculum approach into their setting. Banks gives specific examples of steps her team took to help parents overcome their reservations and become active participants in the planning and observation process.

Finally, in "Answering Parents' Computer-Related Questions," Charles Hohmann helps teachers field parent questions about home computers and software.

Building Bridges With Parents

By Pam Lafferty

• •

"The school should grow gradually out of the home life; it should take up and continue the activities with which the child is already familiar in the home . . . . It is the business of the school to deepen and extend the child's sense of values bound up in his home life."

—John Dewey, 1897

More than 100 years ago, educator John Dewey wrote of the importance of building bridges between homes and schools. Today, most early childhood educators would agree that the need for continuity between home and school is just as strong. Over the years, teachers and parents working together have built many bridges, yet there is still a need to strengthen and extend these links.

Effective parent-teacher partnerships are based on a mutual understanding that each party has something unique to contribute. While parents know much more about their children than teachers ever can, teachers come to the partnership with professional training in child development and education. When both parents and teachers understand the importance of each role, a sharing process can begin. This exchange of information about individual children leads to the richest possible environment for children's development.

A preschooler enjoys a quiet moment reading with Mom in the book area.

This article explores strategies for promoting this sharing process between program staff and parents. While the parent involvement strategies suggested here are based on experiences in the United Kingdom (U.K.), they are relevant in many contexts and cultures. Many of the suggestions grow from my work with teachers and parents as a trainer/consultant for High/Scope UK. These experiences have included providing training programs for teachers and home child care providers who work in areas of social deprivation in the U.K. and overseas countries, and helping to develop the *Caring Start* materials for parent workshops (*Caring Start* materials can be purchased from High/Scope Press.) The strategies also draw on my own teaching experiences working in a part-day preschool program in a small village outside London, England. This program serves a diverse group, which includes children of families who have lived in the village for generations, children who qualify for services because of low income or special needs and are transported to the program from other communities, and children of international families who are transient workers in the area.

Parents as Classroom Volunteers

Throughout my career, I have sought to encourage parents to come into the early childhood setting to work with children. When parents contribute directly to the educational program by serving as everyday classroom volunteers or by sharing a special skill or talent, the program is enhanced for all concerned. This article focuses on how to encourage and support this kind of direct participation.

The benefits that come from parents participating in the classroom are many, including the following:

- **The adult/child ratio immediately becomes more favorable.**
- **The curriculum is shared with parents in an authentic way.**
- **Parents see firsthand what their children are doing in school.**
- **Parents have opportunities to offer additional ideas to the staff.**
- **Parents experience the routine and interaction strategies for themselves.**
- **Siblings may also be introduced to the preschool approach.**
- **The staff learn a great deal about the families.**
- **There is an opportunity for a strong and trusting relationship to develop between parents and staff.**

Despite these many benefits, however, regular participation by parents in the classroom represents a level of parent involvement that many programs never achieve. Because of outside commitments, many parents are unable to take a direct role in the classroom; however, even parents who have the time may feel uncomfortable participating in this way. Teachers, too, sometimes feel uneasy about parents taking part in the classroom program. They may feel threatened by the prospect of being "watched," or they may feel that if a parent is present, they will be expected to know everything about that parent's child.

My own experiences with having parents as volunteers in the classroom have convinced me that the doubts and fears parents and teachers have about this practice can be overcome. I'm convinced that the benefits of this kind of parental participation justify the extra efforts teachers must make initially to insure parents' comfort and effectiveness in this role. We have found that parents' experiences in the classroom will be successful if teaching staff prepare carefully for their visits, using the approach presented in this article.

This approach has evolved over a number of years, and has been affected by changing views about parent involvement. When I was a young teacher in the early 1960's, there was often a feeling among school personnel that "home is home and school is school." It was common at that time to find a notice on the door of a school saying "NO PARENTS BEYOND THIS POINT." As time went on, attitudes changed. Gradually, both professionals and parents began to realize that the care and education of a child could not be separated into pockets—both parties were important to children's development and children would benefit if parents and teachers worked together. This point of view was new to many teachers, some of whom felt it meant a downgrading of their status as professionals. It was also new to some parents, who wondered what they could tell a professional to enhance the development of their child. The barriers between parents and "teacher-experts" thus took some breaking down, but eventually the consensus moved toward a "parents as partners" philosophy.

The best way to implement this new philosophy was often not clear, however. One thing we tried in our preschool was to post carefully thought-out notices near the entrance. These were renewed regularly. A typical notice might read: *We would love for you to come in and work with us. Please let one of the staff know which day you would like to come.* These notices got some responses from parents, but never as many as we'd hoped. Another thing we tried was to put up a list of dates and invite parents to sign up for a date that was convenient for them. Again we got some responses, but we had the feeling that there were additional parents who might have come in, if the right kind of support had been offered.

Often, too, those parents who did agree to participate arrived in the classroom wanting to be useful but unsure of what to do. The teachers believed the parents' presence was a good thing, but were unclear as to how to connect with them. The teachers often resolved this by inviting parents to do "helping jobs," such as cutting up paper, washing up dishes, and clearing out cupboards. Gradually, however, teachers realized it might be better to encourage parents to work directly with the children. But this change in policy was accompanied by an unrealistic expectation that because children attended the setting, their parents would somehow know what to do once there themselves.

Gradually, it dawned on us that parents needed more specific information about what they could do. We needed to offer them a wide range of choices and support from the staff team so that they could plan a way of contributing. At this point a new notice appeared on the outside door: *This Nursery is for you and your children. You are welcome at any time, and if you would like to come in and work with us, there is a list of suggestions on the wall inside. Please make your choices and then talk to your child's teacher about when you would like to come in.*

Inside the reception area we posted a comprehensive list of choices. These included both housekeeping tasks (washing up dishes in the kitchen, filling up the baskets in the writing and drawing area) and suggestions for getting involved with children (sitting in the book area and sharing books with children).

Initially, some of the parents felt most comfortable coming in and washing dishes. Gradually, as they became more confident, they would extend their plan to include working with the children. To help in this process, the teachers produced short pocket-sized lists of guidelines (see p. 314) so that parents could use the adult-child interaction strategies the staff were using. This produced the added benefit of parents using the same interaction strategies at home.

Eventually, as we implemented our new policy of providing both choices and specific support to parents, many parents participated for many different reasons and with many different plans. At last, we were building bridges together. For a description of how a parent newsletter can convey to parents what's happening in your classroom, see the sidebar on p. 315.

Parents Contributing Talents

A particularly rewarding way in which parents can participate directly in the education program is to share a special skill, talent, or interest with children. To encourage this kind of sharing, make a conscious effort to identify parents' special interests. Sometimes you can gain this information by asking parents directly during informal conversations, during home visits, or through your parent newsletter; sometimes parents spontaneously offer to share some aspect of their lives and talents. The High/Scope Family Information Sheet on page 316 can be a helpful tool in this process of inviting parents to share special talents.

Often these very personal contributions by parents become the bridge to fostering positive home-school relationships for both child and parent. Three-year-old James, for example, had been in our setting for some weeks but was not yet speaking to any of the staff team or other children. The family lived on a farm with no other houses nearby, and although James had one younger brother, meeting other children was a new experience for him. It had been hard for his mom to even consider sending him to a nurs-ery school, and she stayed with him at school on a regular basis, wondering if she was doing the right thing. One day, the teachers invited the family to bring one of their animals into the program, and a few days later, James and his mom arrived with a white chicken. The chicken became the focus of large-group time as it sat calmly

On a home visit, the teacher asks about the parents' special talents.

in the middle of the floor surrounded by children. James and his mother were quickly engaged in conversation by the children as they asked ques-tions like "What is the chicken's name?" "Does it lay eggs?" "Where does it live?" The family's talent for working with animals was shared regularly after that. Eventually, the whole group paid a visit to the farm.

Similarly, at a preschool in an urban inner-city setting, another parent's contribution grew from his son's interest in wheeled toys. Four-year-old Wayne's plans would often include going outside to have a turn on one of

Sample Guidelines for Parent Volunteers

Volunteering in the classroom is often easier for parents if they have explicit guidelines. They need to know what their choices are and how to interact with children once they've made a choice. To help parent volunteers, post guidelines on small signs or cards, and place  *them in the areas of the classroom where parents may choose to work. For example, below are two sample cards, one describing what volunteers can do in the book area and a second giving general interaction strategies that parents can use in all the areas.*

Working and Talking With Children in All Areas

- Approach calmly and quietly.

- Put yourself on the same level as the children. This may be standing, kneeling, sitting, or sometimes even lying on the floor.

- Listen to what children are saying.

- Watch what they are doing.

- Show pleasure, enjoyment, or disappointment in your face to match their mood or feelings.

- Describe what they are doing, for example, "You're using the red paint on your picture."

- Occasionally ask questions or wonder aloud about what they are doing. Avoid "quiz questions" like "What color is this?" Instead, ask real questions that express genuine curiosity or a need for information. For example (in the computer area), "Can you show me how to make the printer work?"

Working in the Book Area

- Follow children's cues. If children invite you to read to them or to look at a book together, do so.

- You can also invite children to choose a book to read with you.

- Feel free to read to one child or several at a time.

- Sit at the children's level to read the book.

- Make sure children can see the pictures as you read.

- Pause occasionally for conversation as you read. Encourage children's comments. You may want to ask open-ended questions about the book, for example, "What do you think is going to happen when we turn the page?" "What do you think about that?" "How do you think (name of character) felt?"

- Answer any questions children may have, as they ask them (you don't have to wait until the end of the story).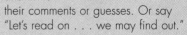

- If you don't know the answer to a child's question, say so, and invite their comments or guesses. Or say "Let's read on . . . we may find out."

- As you share books with children, some children may want to "read" the book to you. They may do this by talking about the pictures as they turn the pages, reciting parts of the book they know, or pointing to letters or words they recognize. Encourage all these forms of "reading."

Parent Newsletters

One of the simplest strategies for encouraging parent involvement is to send home a regular parent newsletter. The newsletter can convey information about what is happening in the setting as well as engage the parent in a two-way dialogue. Teachers can build parents' sense of "ownership" in the newsletter by inviting and publishing their contributions: for example, favorite recipes, tips on things to do at home with children, or items they may have available for sale or exchange. The newsletter can also be used to solicit ideas for upcoming school events; you might want to include a form requesting suggestions for future field trips or parent meeting topics.

If appropriate for your group of families, publish the newsletter in more than one language and encourage parents to read the newsletter together with their children. Build this newsletter-reading time into your day; when parents come to pick up their children, hand the newsletters to the children, and encourage parents and their children to sit down and share it before they leave. If some parents in your group are not fluent in English, or have limited literacy skills, they may view this informal reading time as an opportunity to observe how other parents share the newsletter with their children. This can be a non-threatening way for some parents to learn about the program.

Make your newsletter clear and fun to read by including lively graphics, pictures, photos of classroom events and children's work, graphs, children's drawings, and so forth. A sample opening could be as follows—

Dear Parents,
As the leaves pile up in our garden I know it must be autumn. Our first piece of news is that we must say goodbye to Anne Seymour on Friday and hello to Linda Simmie, who is returning after maternity leave. May I take this opportunity to thank Anne Seymour. We hope she will continue to come in and see us— her skills as a pizza maker have been much enjoyed!...

Over time, parents will become familiar with the newsletter and may come to rely on it for communicating with teachers and with the rest of the parent group. At this point, you might ask for a parent volunteer to take over the production of the newsletter.

Note: High/Scope Press offers a series of newsletters titled *You and Your Child* and a series of fact sheets titled *All About High/Scope* designed expressly for parents. See page 397 for further information or call 1-800-40-PRESS.

the wheeled vehicles. When, as inevitably happened, wheels came off or other faults developed, Wayne would examine the vehicle carefully and try to mend it. The tools we possessed for repairs were limited, and Wayne began to say things like "You need a wrench to fit that nut" or "You need a better screwdriver than that—my dad's got one at home." Dad was unemployed at the time, and I asked Wayne if he thought his father might lend

Family Information Sheet

Adult's name: _____ Adult's name: _____

Relationship to child: _____ Relationship to child: _____

Place of birth: _____ Place of birth: _____

Occupation:_____ Occupation: _____

Hobbies/special interests: _____ Hobbies/special interests: _____

_____

_____

Child's name: _____ Place of birth:_____

Special interests (What does the child like to do? What kinds of outings does he/she

enjoy? What toys or play materials does he/she enjoy?):_____

_____

_____

Other family members living in the household (please list names, ages, and relationship

to the child): _____

_____

Family lives at_____

Family has lived there for (length of time)_____

Other places they have lived: _____

_____

Ways the family celebrates special events (please list the event and the way it is cele-

brated): _____

_____

_____

Things in family's home that are special to the family and that they would be willing to

share with the class (for example, Grandma's potato pancake recipe, Mom's rock col-

lection, Dad's conga drum): _____

_____

_____

Possible additions to classroom: _____

_____

_____

some of his tools to help us repair the vehicles. Soon Dad arrived with a tool bag in hand and offered to do the repairs. Over a period of time whenever he was available, Wayne's dad would come in and work together with the children to fix the vehicles. He demonstrated a great deal of patience with them, showing them what to do and inviting their suggestions. Children made lists of things to do with Wayne's dad and eventually began to build the activity into their plans—a true partnership!

Sharing talents not only enhances the self-esteem and confidence of parents and their children but also enriches the curriculum. Like the other avenues of parent involvement we discuss in this chapter, it is a way to "build bridges."

To conclude, I'd like to share a recent teacher-training workshop experience in which participants were invited to suggest 50 ways of connecting with parents. The teachers identified many actions that in themselves seemed small—making eye contact with a parent, a smile, a wave, noticing a new hairstyle, eating together, listening sensitively, knowing the child's name before the start of the session, and so forth. However, gestures such as these small, spontaneous contacts give the message that staff are interested in the children and family as individuals. Such contacts often form the initial relationships with parents and create an ethos and firm foundation upon which to build other contacts. Their impact in building bridges with parents cannot be overestimated. This brings us to a parting thought. As you use any of the strategies suggested in this issue, keep in mind: HOW we approach parents will have much more impact than WHAT we do!

§

Rhyanna Powell is a parent whose two children attended Teams Family Centre, a nursery school program in Gateshead, England, managed by Pam Graham, a High/Scope UK Endorsed Trainer. As part of the program, Graham conducted parent workshops, which Powell attended. This "Reflection" illustrates the changes in parent attitudes that often result from parent workshops and involvement with a High/Scope-oriented early childhood program.

When Alex (my 3-year-old) was small and we lived in Mansfield, I used to take her to the local parent and toddler group. At the time, I thought it was wonderful. When the other mothers and I arrived, we'd find everything set out on tables. Each table had a different set of materials, and each group of children would spend 20 minutes at each table before moving on to the next one. This way, every child got a turn to try everything.

I've already said that I thought it was wonderful, but let me put you in the child's place. . . .

You are 2 years old. Your mum has told you you're going to a terrific place that is specially set up for kids. It's full of toys and games, and she says you're going to have a great time.

When you get there, you have a tremendous feeling of anticipation as you walk through the door. As you take off your coat, you can look into the playroom. You are so excited by what you see! There are tables, chairs, children—and so many toys! The tables are covered with all kinds of great-looking things. There are paint and play dough, balls and building bricks, dolls and toy animals, puzzles, a sand and water table, and even a climbing structure with a slide.

The first thing you want to do is race over to the sand table. So you do. But before you get your hands on that sand, someone, some strange woman, takes you by the arm and leads you away from it. So, being a normal 2-year-old, you throw a tantrum and try to get back to the sand, but the grownups raise their voices and tell you not to be silly. After all, they say, you'll get a chance at everything before you leave. Then they lead you to the table with the building bricks on it—it's boring, but after a while you get quite interested. And when you are right in the middle of building the tallest tower in the history of the world, the adults do it again—they tell you it's time to move on to the next table! You're upset, but today you've learned something—you can fight against the grownups, but you can never win. Even when you're having fun, it has to be on their terms. By the time you go home, you've had a turn on everything but all that wonderful enthusiasm you had when you arrived is gone.

Organizing everything for children is convenient for adults. But children who never have the opportunity to plan activities for themselves will grow up lacking the confidence to try new things. These children may never develop the ability to make decisions without instructions. As a parent, I would see such people as robots.

Following our experiences with the parent and toddler group, Alex and I joined the program at the Teams Family Centre at Gateshead, which was implementing the High/Scope approach. The first thing I noticed when I got there was that it's not just mums that go there with their children. Fathers go too.

Toys aren't set out beforehand. Instead, they are always within easy reach of the children. Children are encouraged to plan for themselves what they want to do, and parents and staff are there in a supporting role. These children are dictated to in so many aspects of their lives—so to see them doing just what they like, for as long as they like, is great!

They learn how to play together as well as alone, they learn how to share as well as to assert themselves, and they learn how to behave in polite society. But probably most important is the fact that they learn to do things for themselves whenever possible. This makes them feel like important people in their own right.

Staying in Touch With Parents You Don't See Regularly

By Carol Markley

• •

In describing strategies for building relationships with parents, the opening article emphasizes the need for early childhood staff to use the times when parents drop off and pick up their children as opportunities to get to know parents and to exchange information about their child. But some parents—because children are bussed to school or dropped off by another caregiver—do not appear at the school on a daily basis. What can early childhood teachers do to stay in contact with these parents?

Written Communication

One way to keep in contact with parents is to send them written messages about what their children are doing in the classroom. These could be **brief notes** that you write and send home with the children (possibly safety-pinned to their clothing to ensure that they do get home) or notes that are written in a **small notebook or journal** that children bring back and forth from home to school in their back pack. One advantage to the notebook or journal idea is that parents can be encouraged to make entries in response to the teacher's notes. For example, the teacher might write, "Today Renee spent most of work time in the house area playing with a doll that she called Katie. She changed Katie's diaper,

Christopher's parents don't come to the classroom daily, so the teacher sent them this photo of Christopher and his friends watching the "TV" they had built out of hollow blocks.

fed her, rocked her, and put her to bed. Does Renee know a baby named Katie?" In return, the parents might write to explain that Renee's afternoon child care provider has a baby named Katie, and that lately Renee has been very interested in the care of Katie while she is there in the afternoons. Parents might also share information about other experiences the child is having at home: "Lately, Corey has been listening to his *Dumbo* story tape over and over. He is fascinated with everything related to Dumbo." As you write in a child's journal, keep in mind the guidelines given on page 329 for writing anecdotes. Like the anecdotes you record for classroom evaluation and planning, the notes you send to parents about their child's activities should be specific and objective and should highlight the child's strengths, abilities, and interests. Another alternative to individual child journals is to have one journal/photo album for the whole class that circulates in turn to all the program families (see left).

With more and more people using computers at the work place as well as at home, **computer-aided communication** with parents is another possibility. For example, it may be possible to communicate with *some* parents through **e-mail,** which they may be able to receive at their home or work place. In addition, if you have the COR-PC or COR-Mac, computerized versions of the High/Scope Child Observation Record for Ages 2½–6, you already have your classroom **anecdotal notes** entered into computer files. These can easily be e-mailed to parents or printed out to be carried home by children.

Circulating Photo Album

At a Michigan child care center attached to a large hospital, staff provide a circulating photo album as one way to keep in touch with program families. The album is part of the parent lending library at the center, and is available to be checked out for a day or two at a time. Included are pictures of children taken during different parts of the daily routine: during small- and large-group times, meal times, work time, outside time, and during special events such as field trips. In addition to the photos, blank pieces of paper are scattered randomly throughout the album, and parents are invited to record their comments on the blank pages. Parent comments include things their children have told them about the photos as they look through the album together, general comments about the album ("This has made the time my child spends away from me come alive"), and questions about things shown in the pictures ("What exactly is slime and can you print the recipe in the next parent newsletter?"). Parents and children alike are enthusiastic about the album.

Other Items to Send Home

In addition to written communication with parents, many visual items can be sent home. For example, send home children's **artwork,** with a sticky note attached containing an anecdote about the process the child used in creating the artwork or a description the child gave of his or her creation. Another option is to send home **photographs** of children's block structures or dramatic play activities, preferably with anecdotes attached. (Instant photos are best because the photo goes home when the play incident is fresh in the child's mind and is easily recalled to share with parents.) **Videotapes** of the children in action in the classroom are another possibility.

Other Ways to Communicate

Though it is helpful to communicate with parents by sending home written messages and other items, there's no substitute for an actual conversation with parents. You can arrange to make brief **telephone calls** to a parent's work place or home on a regular basis to stay in touch with parents you don't see regularly. You can also arrange for occasional face-to-face meetings with parents at times that don't conflict with the parents' work obligations. For example, scheduling periodic **home visits** in which the teacher interacts with both the child and the parents helps to establish a relationship with the parents that is further strengthened at the occasional **parent conference.** Occasionally holding weekend or evening **family events** (potlucks, sing-alongs, pizza parties) and inviting parents to accompany the class on **field trips** are additional ideas. Of course, all of these kinds of events must be scheduled well in advance and in consultation with the parents.

Using all of these communication strategies with every family, every day would be impossible or impractical, but choosing one or two and using them at regularly scheduled intervals does much to establish relationships with the parents you don't see regularly.

Preparing for Successful Parent Conferences

By Carol Markley

• •

"Parent/teacher conference time is coming up again and I'm really nervous."

"I never feel like I'm prepared to talk to parents."

"I feel like conferences are a waste of time for me and the parents, especially when all I do is show them their child's checklist. A list with a few skills checked off doesn't give us much to discuss."

§

If you've ever found yourself making comments like any of these, don't be discouraged. You *can* have parent/teacher conferences that are productive both for you and for parents, without spending loads of time preparing for them. *How* you prepare is more important than the *amount* of time you spend. This article describes a variety of strategies that help you prepare for successful conferences.

Building Ties With Parents

While most teachers recognize the need to establish positive and authentic relationships with children, they may not recognize that, for an effective program, good relationships with parents are just as important. Communication with parents shouldn't begin at the parent con-

Taking the time to communicate in meaningful ways at the beginning and end of the day fosters positive parent-teacher relationships.

ference; instead, the conference should be just one event in an ongoing relationship. To set the stage for effective conferences with parents, begin your preparations on the first day of school as you **establish a relationship with the parents of the children in your classroom.** Here are several ways to strengthen relationships with parents.

✓ **Show a genuine interest in the parents.** Learn parents' first names and use them as you greet them at drop-off and pick-up times or when you talk to them on the phone. Show your interest in parents by **asking honest questions.**

Preschooler Alissa's mom, Abigail, makes a 25-minute drive over country roads to bring Alissa to preschool. On a snowy morning, after greeting Alissa, the teacher said to Abigail, "Good morning, Abigail, was the drive in difficult?"

✓ **Organize your daily routine to give you unhurried opportunities to speak with parents.**

In the High/Scope Demonstration Preschool, outside time is the last event in the daily routine. Near the end of outside time, one of the two teachers works with children near the gate of the playground so she can greet and talk to parents as they come in to pick up their children. This arrangement usually works well in encouraging parent/teacher conversation, except on snowy winter days. When children are using the sleds, the teachers have found they both need to work directly with children to insure their safety while sledding. As a result, on days when the sleds are out, the teachers have decided to give children a 2-minute warning and then have the children put the sleds away a few minutes before parents begin arriving. They have found that this makes it easier for teachers to talk with parents.

✓ **Respond to the parents' interests and concerns.** Parents, like their children, want to be seen and heard for who they are. If you are aware of a parent's personal interests, pastimes, or occupation, occasionally make a related comment or ask a personal question, and if appropriate, share a bit of yourself as well.

One morning at work time 3-year-old Jordan said to his teacher, Nancy, "Me and my dad are goin' to the Eastern [Eastern Michigan University] football game tomorrow." Later, Nancy asked Jordan's father, Marty, if he had ever gone to Eastern. Marty explained that even though he had never been a student there, he and Jordan enjoyed going to the Eastern football games together, especially to watch the band at halftime. Nancy responded by telling him that she was going to the University of Michigan game the next day. They talked for a few moments about strategies for dressing for football games during really cold weather.

Along with responding to parents' interests, part of a teacher's job is listening attentively to parents, especially for the unspoken concern that may be behind a parent's question or comment. Once you have "drawn out" parents and encouraged them to express the feeling behind the question, it's important to respond in a way that shows you hear and acknowledge their concern, even if you have no solution to offer. If their real worries have been acknowledged, parents will be more ready to "hear" the teacher's answer to the original question.

Sarah's mother, Joanne, said to the teacher one morning, "Sarah sometimes says she is writing her name when she is working with paper and markers, but she isn't really writing the letters of her name. How is she going to learn to write 'real' letters?"

The teacher paused for a few minutes to encourage Joanne to say more. Then Joanne said, "I'm worried about Sarah's writing, because her older sister Chelsea—she's in second grade—seems to be behind schedule in learning to write." "I can understand how concerned you must be about Sarah's writing," Sarah's teacher answered. "Our experience tells us Sarah is on her way to writing 'real' letters. Just the fact that she says she is writing her name when she makes these print-like marks shows that she has an understanding of what writing is. Also, since she writes her marks in a line instead of randomly on her paper, she is showing that she knows that letters are written in a line from left to right. Making these kinds of letterlike marks is an important stage in learning to write that we see many preschoolers go through. With our support and encouragement, her print-like marks will become more and more like 'real' printing."

✓ **Give the parents specific information about what their children have been doing.**

One morning Matthew's teacher shared this story with Matthew's mother: "Matthew and Whitney spent most of work time together pretending to be detectives. They walked around the classroom with notepads and pencils asking children and teachers if they knew anything about a missing purse. After questioning each person, Matthew pretended to write the person's phone number on a piece of paper—actually writing the numbers '1010.'" This kind of factual description of a play incident is much more meaningful to the parent than a general statement like *"Matthew had a good day today."*

✓ **Listen carefully and respectfully to parents.** Parents have valuable insights into their children's behaviors. If you give parents plenty of time and space to share their experiences and observations, you will receive lots of helpful information about the child.

Sue, a teacher, had noticed that Cassie had recently become withdrawn and quiet in her play. Cassie had suddenly begun spending a lot of time in the book area, exploring books and doing puzzles by herself. In a conversation with Cassie's father, Sue happened to find out that Cassie's parents had been keeping her up later in an effort to spend more 'quality time' with her. Sue then realized that the change in Cassie's behavior did not indicate a problem—she was just a tired child. When she shared this observation with Cassie's parents, they decided to look for another way to make special time for Cassie.

✓ **Provide opportunities for parent participation.** Another important way to strengthen relationships with parents is **to let parents know they are welcome in the classroom at any time.** Encourage parents to visit for all or part of the day to play with their children and their children's friends.

At the High/Scope Demonstration Preschool, children listen to stories and explore books at the opening of the morning session. Parents often stay for a few minutes to read with children.

Parent Meeting Survey

Parent meetings are another way for program staff to stay in touch with program parents. Meetings can focus on general child development topics or on helping parents understand the center's program. To find out which topics are of most interest to parents, circulate to parents a survey containing a list of suggested topics, and ask parents to choose the topics that seem most interesting. Invite them to suggest other topics not included on the list. Here are some parent meeting topics that you might suggest in your survey:

• What is active learning?

• Overview of the center's daily routine

• How your child learns though play

• The High/Scope key experiences

• Supporting your child in learning to read and write

• Problem-solving approach to conflict (including both child-child and child-adult conflicts)

• Small-group time: What is it? Why do we do it?

• No fuss, no muss bedtime tips

• Pros and cons of video viewing— How much is too much?

• What happened to family meals?— Sure-bet dinner options

• Reading with, instead of at, your children

• Helping children deal with the illness or death of a loved one

• Remaining calm during public temper tantrums

For more information on planning parent workshops see *The Essential Parent Workshop Resource: The Teacher's Idea Book 4,* Michelle Graves, High/Scope Press, 2000.

In addition, **schedule parent meetings** prior to conference time. The meetings can focus on describing your program to parents, as well as discussing general child development topics. When parents have had these opportunities to become familiar with the program, teachers will spend less time during conferences explaining the curriculum and the program in general and more time talking specifically about what each child is doing in the program. To see how a parent meeting survey can help you determine what topics are of most interest to your parents, see p. 328.

✓ **Take anecdotal notes on children's behaviors.** In High/Scope classrooms, teachers gather information for daily planning and child assessment using an anecdotal note-taking system. As they observe and interact with children during normal classroom activities, teachers take brief notes describing play incidents that highlight the abilities individual children are developing. Later, the child anecdotes gathered through this process become the basis for assessment using the High/Scope Child Observation Record for Ages 2½–6 (COR) assessment instrument. (For more information on anecdotal note-keeping see right. For further information on writing child anecdotes and the COR assessment process see *Supporting Young Learners 2,* Nancy Altman Brickman, ed., High/Scope Press, 1996, pp. 277–292.) The accurate and specific information gathered through anecdotal note-keeping provides a wealth of concrete examples of children's strengths and abilities that can be used in reporting to parents during parent conferences. One time-saver that is used in High/Scope's demonstration classroom is the computerized version of the COR (COR-PC or COR-Mac). When teach-

Basic Guidelines for Anecdote Writing

9/13 At work time in the sand table, Reid and Alex worked together to build an "electricity."

Anecdote Format

1. **Date**

2. **Beginning**: When, where, who

3. **Middle**: What the child did and said, with child's language in quotes

4. **Ending**: When applicable, a statement of the outcome

Writing Objective Anecdotes

1. Focus on what the child **did** and **said**.

2. Be factual.

3. Be specific.

4. Be brief.

Examples

2/17 At work time in the art area, William used a marker to draw a picture of a person that included a head, a torso, two legs, two arms, eyes, eyelashes, a nose, a mouth, ears, and hair. He said to Carol, "Look, I made a picture of you."

2/19 At small-group time, Demetrius sang the alphabet song as he used a marker to make a line of marks on his paper. He held up the paper and said, "Carol, I made the ABC's."

ers prepare for conferences, the computerized COR quickly generates a parent report summarizing the child's progress and providing a few anecdotes about the child's behavior in each of six basic developmental areas (initiative, social relations, creative representation, music and movement, language and literacy, logic and mathematics). Whether you are using the COR or some other system of documenting and evaluating children's progress, it is helpful prior to the conference to **prepare a similar brief report on each child that contains child anecdotes organized by general child development categories.** The High/Scope **key experience categories** may also be used as a way of organizing your child observations.

✓ **Save children's work.** In addition to taking anecdotal notes, you may want to save and date samples of children's drawings, paintings, and writing as another source of information which can be used at conference time. Photographs can also be taken of children's structures and dramatic play.

✓ **Give parents ample advance notice of conferences.** Notify parents of the dates and times of conferences well in advance, so they can make plans around these dates. Be flexible in accommodating parents' schedules by offering several different choices of meeting times per day.

The Conference

If you have followed the above guidelines to prepare for parent conferences, strategies for conducting the conference are a natural outgrowth of the efforts you have already made. During the conference, continue to **build on the positive relationship** you have created with parents. Continue to **share specific information about the child** and **listen respectfully to parents** to learn more about the child's behaviors and interests at home. Here are some additional things to remember as you conduct your conferences.

✓ **Hold the conferences in a comfortable, quiet setting without the distraction of phones ringing or people walking in and out.** Your classroom is a natural place to hold conferences since it is the environment that you will be discussing with parents as you share information about their child. To continue the two-way dialogue you have established with parents, **remember to seat all of you on the same physical level.** This shows them they are equal partners in this discussion.

Successful Parent Workshops

Workshop sessions for parents are an excellent way to enhance the partnership between school and home. In these sessions, teachers gain information about parents' goals for their children and may suggest ways in which parents can support their children's learning at home. For parents, the workshops can be an opportunity to relax and socialize while learning about child development and the High/Scope approach.

Workshop sessions may be held in the setting itself, in a meeting room (in the same building or elsewhere), or at someone's home. Holding the workshop in the actual early childhood setting has the special advantage of allowing parents to use the children's play materials. This experience often leads to a better understanding of the program. For example, in one program's parent meeting, a group of parents worked at the children's sand and water table. Having constructed a sand castle with connecting bridges, they decided to add water, which they planned to have flowing under the bridges. But the sand bridges collapsed. This led to a long discussion of why this had happened and how to solve the problem. When the teachers later posed the question, "What did you learn from the activity?", the parents answered that they learned about construction techniques, properties of sand, and the process of working and solving problems cooperatively. Parents then connected this experience with what children learn from using sand and water. The insight came as a great surprise to those parents who thought their children were just playing!

Encouraging this kind of active learning by parents is the goal of parent workshops. Here are some tips for effective workshops:

• Involve the whole family in parent meeting plans. Before a workshop, talk to children about what their parents will be doing at the meeting, and afterwards explain what parents did. If anything is produced by parents at the meeting, leave it on display to share with the children the next day.

• Plan to provide refreshments at the beginning of a meeting to offer an informal start and give parents something more to do than just take a seat and wait. In some groups, parents may enjoy bringing the snacks, or the whole meeting may be structured around a potluck.

• Parents are more likely to participate in a meeting if you have involved them in choosing topics. Find out which topics are of most interest to parents by talking to them informally or posting a checklist of possible topics near the entrance to the school, with space for parents to add ideas to the list. Another good time to ask about possible workshop topics is at the end of a successful parent meeting, when parents' enthusiasm is high. Typically parents choose topics such as *discipline, helping children learn everyday routines, and preparing children for grade school.*

• To encourage parents' attendance, carefully consider both the timing of the workshops and parents' needs for child care. Ask parents for their preferences. If many parents live at a distance from the school, they may prefer having meetings right after the day's session. If distance is not a problem, they may feel more relaxed in an evening session. In either case, you will probably have to arrange for child care for your students and their siblings during the meeting.

• Once topics and times for parent meetings are selected, send them to parents. Follow through with reminders to parents one or two days before the meeting. Right before the meeting, write up the agenda and post it in the reception area or entrance. In this way, parents can see and discuss the agenda, and staff can draw attention to it and answer any questions.

This kind of advance preparation will lead to livelier, better-attended meetings.

As you talk with parents, refer to the materials you have prepared—the anecdotes on the parent report form and the work samples you have collected. Rather than reading the parent report form to the parents, use the anecdotes and work samples as springboards for natural conversation.

✓ **Pause frequently to encourage parents to share their own stories** about their child's experiences and interests. This helps you to see how home experiences relate to school experiences, leading to a better understanding of the whole child. With this information in hand, parents and teachers can **develop strategies together to support the children's learning.** Keep a pad of paper handy on which to **jot down ideas for following up on your discussion.**

At one parent/teacher conference, Andy's mom and his teacher were discussing the following anecdote, which appeared on Andy's parent report form in the social relations *category: "After Danny took the shovel that Andy was using, Andy went to the teacher and told her what happened. When the teacher brought together both boys to talk about the situation, Danny agreed that he took the shovel. When the teacher then asked Andy if there was something he could tell Danny, Andy didn't say anything. Then the teacher asked Danny if he was finished using the shovel, and Danny said he wasn't. Then Andy said, "Give it back," and Danny returned the shovel." The teacher explained to the parent that this indicated that Andy, as he developed skills in social problem solving, was at the stage where he would usually request an adult's help in solving conflicts. She pointed out that once the adult offered ideas and encouragement, Andy was usually able to talk directly to the other child about the conflict, rather than just walk away from conflict situations. The parent said that, at home, she had observed Andy handling conflicts with his brothers in similar ways. Together the parent and teacher agreed that they would continue to encourage Andy to let other children know, in his own words, what he wanted, and that they would help in this by supplying some of the language if needed.*

This friendly exchange between a parent and teacher illustrates the positive parent/teacher relationships that contribute to successful conferences and to a shared effort to develop ways to support the child. Your day-to-day efforts to strengthen ties with parents and to gather and share specific observations about children are the most important factors behind successful conferences.

Involving Parents in Curriculum Planning: A Head Start Story

By Nita Banks

• •

We are a 23-classroom Head Start program located in a 9-county area centered in Appleton City, Missouri. Six years ago, the parents and staff of our program chose High/Scope as the curriculum approach.

The shift to the new approach went smoothly. Learning to use the active learning ingredients, take anecdotal notes, and plan as a team around children's interests, strengths and cultures all felt like a natural transition for us. Our biggest challenge was figuring out how to involve parents in the curriculum process.

The Head Start Performance Standards state that parents of children in the program "must be invited to become integrally involved in the development of the program's curriculum and educational approach,...provided with opportunities to increase child observational skills and share their assessments with staff, ...[and] encouraged to participate in staff-parent conferences and home visits to discuss child's development and education." (HSPS 1304.21a2)

We believed in these standards. In addition, we were determined to offer parents options for participating that were practical and doable *for them.* We wanted to involve parents in meaningful activities that they would get excited about, learn from, and see as valuable for their child. Tracking our progress and success in involving parents was another key point. We knew we had to have a way to assess the effectiveness of our efforts.

A Possible Solution: Parents as Observers and Note Takers

We have said it a thousand times in Head Start: *Parents are children's first and best teachers.* We decided to put that principle to the test by involving parents in anecdotal note taking and team planning.

As is recommended in the High/Scope approach, our teachers take anecdotal notes during the normal course of classroom activities. (Anecdotal notes are brief, objective descriptions of children's actions and behaviors.) We use these anecdotal notes in our daily team planning sessions, to help us as we assess children's development and interests and plan corresponding classroom strategies. During this process of planning and discussion, we refer to High/Scope's child assessment instrument, the High/Scope Child Observation Record (COR) for Ages 2½–6 (see

Parents can help in the process of noting child observations.

right), to guide us in interpreting and summarizing developmental information about each child.

To help us be attentive to each child's individual needs and interests, our program has developed a special way of organizing the planning and assessment process. Each week we focus specifically on four or five children. We call it their "target week." (Each child's "turn" for a target week comes up about once a month.) During the target week, we make sure we take anecdotal notes on the classroom behaviors of the focus children; we plan around their strengths, interests, and cultural backgrounds; and we update their portfolios and COR forms. (The other children in the classroom are also included as we make observations and plan, but the focus is more intensive on the four or five target children.)

This planning and observation process is a demanding one, but we knew that parents could take part in it, with a little training and ongoing feedback. We decided to ask parents to be "co-teachers" in this process by observing their child at home and sharing that information with the teaching team. In turn, teachers and parents would use the information from the notes to "brainstorm" strategies for supporting the child in the classroom and at home. Teacher and parents would also score the COR form together and plan around the goals they had decided on for the child.

Next step: Getting Parents to "Go for It"

Our next challenge was getting parents involved in our new planning process. We knew there were many factors that might affect parents' willingness to participate. Some of our parents had had negative experiences in school. We were afraid the process of taking notes on children's home experiences might feel an awful lot like homework to them! We were also aware that some parents had literacy issues that they were working on; we anticipated that these parents might not feel comfortable writing down notes and sending them in to teaching teams. In addition, welfare reform had put a good percentage of our parents back to work or school. As a result, parents had heavy work and school responsibilities, and we were concerned about the additional demands our planning process would place on them.

For all these reasons, we knew we had to make the process as user-friendly as we could. Training parents at the start of the year so that they would feel relatively comfortable with the process was important, so we gave an overview of the process at our orientation night. We then provided actual practice at the first home visit, and gave formal training to parents at the first parent meeting in October. In these training experiences, parents learned what an objective anecdotal note was and how it fit into the COR, and they brainstormed with teachers (using what had been learned from the anecdotal notes) to find ways of increasing children's key experience opportunities.

To encourage parents to begin making observational notes, we gave them "Curriculum Notebooks" that explained the process, provided examples to illustrate it, and had blank pages for their notes. Note pages listing the key experience categories were also included for those parents who felt confident and wanted to go to that next step of classifying their observations.

Invitations to participate in daily team planning went out to parents the week before their child's "target week." We were careful to give parents who could not attend meetings a choice of several other ways to participate

About the High/Scope COR

The Child Observation Record, or COR, is High/Scope's child assessment instrument. The COR translates everyday observations of children into developmental terms. Teachers classify child observations into six categories of child development, then use the COR instrument scales to identify children's developmental levels in each area. This results in a developmental profile for each child. This child's writing efforts would fall in the COR category **Language & Literacy.**

in planning, including phone conferences, sending in a poster that parent and child would make together reflecting the child's current interests, sending in ideas for classroom activities, and/or sending in anecdotal notes taken at home.

"Home Activity Sheets" with suggestions on how to give children opportunities for specific key experiences were also sent home with the target children. These sheets were among the most-used of the materials we sent to parents. The suggestions given were not for extra activities, but rather for simple ways of enhancing the learning opportunities that occurred during everyday routines. For example, an Activity Sheet might suggest that parents ask children to choose a story to read together at bedtime, or that parents include some of the child's favorite activities when planning their day's schedule. In this way, parents didn't have to obtain outside materials or set aside a lot of time to complete a "project" with their children. Room for anecdotal notes was provided on the back of the Home Activity Sheet.

An Example of Cooperative Parent/Teacher Planning

Let's follow the process as it worked for one child, 3-year-old Atien. It was Atien's "target week." At the beginning of the school year, the teaching team and Mae, Atien's mother, had set goals for Atien. The main focus had been her abilities in the COR category **initiative.** They were hoping that by mid-year Atien would be *participating in program routines without being asked* (COR item D-4). However, the teachers had noted recently that Atien, like many young 3-year-olds, was not yet following routines consistently and often moved rapidly from one interest to the next during work time, rather than focusing on one play idea for any length of time. **Initiative** was chosen as the COR category to focus on for the week.

The week before Atien's target week, an invitation had gone out to Mae, her mother, asking her to take part in daily team planning. However, Mae's job prevented her from coming in for meetings, so she and the teachers agreed to communicate through phone conferences (scheduled during Mae's coffee breaks at work) and by sending notes back and forth. To help the teachers get ready for Atien's week, Mae sent in some notes on Atien that she had already taken.

Mae's notes let teachers know about Atien's current play interests. Mae had written:

"Atien went around the house today smelling everything. She said: 'This smells like apples!' (I was making apple pie). 'This smells like Daddy!' (She had climbed up on the dresser and gotten his after-shave!)"

Mae also reported on Atien's interest in water play:

"Atien has played in water several times this week. She refused to get out of the tub. She helped me by rinsing dishes, and then wanted to rinse them again when we were done. On two different days, she ran water in the bathroom sink and washed all her dolls."

Teachers sent home an activity sheet that listed opportunities for Atien to participate in home routines. For example, the sheet included these suggestions: Encourage your child to help set up for family times (meals, household chores, etc.); create a daily schedule using your child's interests as clues for each part of the routine (for Atien, different smells might work—orange peel for breakfast time; toothpaste for toothbrushing; Mom's cologne for bedtime, etc.); make affirming statements each time your child participates in family routines ("You helped set the table!" "You got ready for bed the first time I asked! Thank you!" etc.).

Parents are dedicated observers of their children!

To encourage Atien's active participation in the classroom, the teachers used what they had learned about Atien's interests in water play and smells. They made sure there was water in the sink in the house area. They set up the water table as a "bath station" for babies. They added scented play dough made with Kool-Aid to the play dough area. The teachers planned one small-group time to focus on "smelly jars." Children guessed what was in them and ideas were charted on poster board. During the transition to meal times, teachers encouraged children to sniff the air and guess what would be served. The teachers charted children's guesses, and the group revisited them at circle time. Teachers asked Atien to hold the chart and lead the cheer when a guess was correct. Songs, fingerplays, and stories about water and smells were also included at circle time.

At the end of the week, Mae and the teaching team compared notes. Atien not only had participated in routines at school but also had reminded teachers when it was mealtime ("I can smell it!"). After breakfast, Atien led

Supporting Parents as Note Takers

I would like to involve parents in the anecdotal notetaking process, but many of our parents are concerned about their writing skills (spelling, punctuation, and grammar). Can you give me some ideas for ways I can reassure them and help them feel comfortable enough to get started?
—A Head Start teacher

Obviously, if parents are sharing their apprehensions with you, they trust you already and feel that you are there to help. The fact that they are asking to be involved shows you have already overcome a major hurdle. So, use what you already know about providing support to help the parents feel comfortable about sharing their observations. Some ideas:

- **Share control.** Ask them for ideas about what would feel comfortable. Do the parent's observations have to be shared in writing? Does the parent want weekly calls from you? Some parents may feel more comfortable being "mentored" by another Head Start parent. Others may ask you to come by for home visits more often to get a better idea of the environment they are writing about.

- **Focus on parents' strengths.** For example, if the parent has kept a baby book on their child, and feels proud of it, suggest she approach note taking with the same attitude. Point out that just like their baby book, their anecdotal notes will be a record of the child's milestones, "cute quips," and everyday activities. This could take the pressure off and make note taking feel less like school work.

- **Provide positive feedback.** Acknowledge all efforts. Reassure parents that notes are just a means of communicating between classroom and home, with both teachers and parents sharing the child's wonderful moments; assure them that they're not going to be graded on their work. Jot down positive comments on the notes parents do send in. Be sure to mention the key experience reflected in the note! (Nothing is more reassuring than concrete proof that what one is doing provides worthwhile information.)

- **Practice "reflective listening."** Draw out the parent. Is the parent asking for help in improving writing skills? If so, are there opportunities in your area to help with this? Many areas have various family literacy projects going on, so check them out and be able to provide information on them to the parent.

children in taking their places for circle time and held the chart high ("I said sausage—I was right!"). She had given detailed plans for work time ("I'll use the cherry play dough and make two pies for Mommy!"). She had also organized complex play sequences around favorite materials. She had laid out a baby blanket next to the water table ("Babies get dry here!"), used another blanket to dry the dolls, then set them on a table to dress them ("I'll put your clothes on!"). At home, Atien had helped Mae set the table and wash dishes afterward. Mae reported that sitting through a meal had become easier for Atien, because she knew that when she was finished, she got to rinse dishes. Bedtime was also easier, Mae said, because at 8:30 p.m. Atien knew that she would get to play in the tub until the kitchen timer rang, when she would brush her teeth and read a book that she wrote with Mom about the lake.

Mae and the teaching team added the following scores to the **Initiative** section of Atien's COR: *A. Expressing Choices, (4) Child indicates with a short sentence how plans will be carried out.* (Said, "I'll use the cherry play dough..."); *C. Engaging in complex play, (3) Child, acting alone, carries out complex and varied sequences of activities.* (Carried out doll bathing/dressing sequence); *D. Cooperating in program routines, (4) Child participates in program routines without being asked.* (Reminded teachers of mealtime; arranged children in circle).

Mae and the teachers agreed to keep using Atien's interests to encourage her to continue to participate in routines. They also decided to begin to look more closely at Atien's progress in **Social Relations,** another COR category. Mae said she would start taking notes on how Atien interacted with family and peers, so that by the next target week, teachers would have more to go on.

Mae and the teachers also reflected on the time they had spent focusing on Atien. Mae estimated that she had spent about 15 minutes at the end of each day taking notes and reflecting on what her child had said and done, plus about 15 minutes for each of the two phone conferences. The extra time invested by the teachers included giving written feedback to Mae. The lead and co-teachers had worked together to balance the workload to accommodate the phone conferences. Through these extra activities plus the daily planning sessions, they accomplished a lot: In addition to updating Atien's COR and adding to her portfolio (snapshots and anecdotal notes), they found that ideas for lesson plans came flooding in, once the interests and developmental levels of Atien and the other four focus children were brought into focus.

Outcome: Is It a Keeper?

Each week, parents are asked to sign a report stating that they received their invitation to daily team planning. At the end of the week, teachers check off the parents who actually participated in some way. This report is mailed to the Head Start central office monthly. Parents are also asked to write comments directly on the lesson plan that is mailed to the central office and reviewed weekly by the education coordinator. At the end of the program year, teachers ask parents to complete surveys asking for feedback on the planning/assessment process.

Parent Comments

Parents from the Appleton City, Missouri, Head Start program made these comments about participating in anecdotal note taking and curriculum planning.

- "I think the weekly home activity sheet helped because it showed me there are different ways to teach. You don't just have to use pencil and paper."

- "My child enjoyed my paying attention to him and writing about him."

- "It forced us to spend quality time together and really listen to what our children are feeling."

- "I wanted to help everyone see where my child is developmentally."

- "My other children at home helped take notes too and they were surprised at how smart our child is!"

- "It helped me see more of the good things he does."

These tracking measures were used each year. The third year showed the most participation. Some classrooms had 95–100 percent parent participation; some had 50–60 percent; the overall average was 65 percent.

On this page are a few actual comments from parents' surveys. You decide—were we successful? We think we were. By the way, that third year was a Peer Review year. The federal review team thought so, too.

Answering Parents' Computer-Related Questions

By Charles Hohmann

• •

Parents who see their children using computers in school or at child care often have questions for teachers. They may ask for help in choosing equipment or software for home use, or they may need ideas for working with children at the computer. Here are some typical parent concerns about computers and some suggestions for providing help.

Software and Equipment Tips

Parents often ask for software suggestions. Don't hesitate to include in your recommendations the same software you use at school. Children who have the same programs at home seem, if anything, more involved with them at school.

If parents tell you they are considering new equipment for children's use at home (or for the parent's own use), you might point out that now is a good time to buy. Today's fully-equipped multi-media computer systems are well suited to the many available CD-ROM-based educational software programs as well as to the home productivity software parents may want for writing letters, balancing a checkbook, or preparing income tax returns. With their modems and built-in software, they're also ready for surfing the Internet for vacation information and exchanging e-mail with friends and relatives.

You can facilitate children's use of a home computer by recommending to parents the use of a children's menu pro-

You can post software suggestions for home use on the parent bulletin board.

gram. A children's menu provides large, colorful, single-click icons that allow children to find and start their favorite programs as soon as they are able to use the mouse. A children's menu will also prevent children from getting into programs designed for adult use or from deleting files from the hard disk drive.

Parent Support Ideas

A few tips for parents can help make home computer learning activities a success for children and adults. While children can and should learn to use computer activities independently, advise parents that children's success with software can be greatly enhanced by parental guidance and support. Young children often need a brief introduction to a new computer activity—what choices are available and what's to be accomplished. Also, many children's programs provide opportunities for shared experiences like playing a game, adding labels to a picture, or discussing words in a story.

Children especially enjoy using software programs at school that they've already played with at home.

Help parents understand that even when children's home computer experiences are mostly independent, the occasional adult suggestion or comment can lead to discussions or experiences that offer additional learning opportunities. Such questions/comments might include ones like "When you finish, let's try printing one of your pictures so we can send it to Grandpa" or "What was your favorite part of the tale of *The Tortoise and the Hare*?"

Parents may also want to know where they can find good information about children's software. Help them by suggesting print resources like *Young Children and Technology* (Hougland, S. & Wright, J., New York: Allyn & Bacon, 1997). Children's software reviews are also available on the Internet.

Finally, remind parents that computer activities are just one kind of learning experience they can share with their children. Computer activities should be balanced by physical activities such as walking, riding, sledding, and swimming; creative activities involving blocks and building sets, paper, and all kinds of art materials; and language experiences, such as bedtime stories, visits to the public library, and everyday conversation.

Chapter Eight

Team Planning, Assessment, and Staff Development

• •

*T*eam planning, child and program assessment, and staff development are key ingredients of the High/Scope educational approach. Each teaching team must design an individual system of planning and assessment that works for them, and that incorporates observation of children and anecdotal note-taking (as part of the High/Scope Child Observation Record known as the Preschool COR), daily planning sessions, and development of strategies for future interactions and activities. This chapter addresses these issues and highlights the important role mentoring can play in the area of staff development.

In the first article, "Note Taking: You Do Have Time!," Nita Banks provides suggestions for how you and your team can find time each day to take notes and plan as a team around them.

The second article, "Planning Around Children's Interests," by Michelle Graves, outlines an approach to planning in which teachers incorporate their observations of children's interests into every aspect of the preschool day. Focusing on the interests children reveal through their actions and language helps teachers learn about the activities and experiences that offer particular children the greatest opportunities for learning.

In the next selection, "Toys From Home: One Teaching Team's Dilemma," Michelle Graves focuses on the experience of a teaching team at High/Scope's Demonstration Preschool and how team members worked through the toys-from-home issue by using a team process guided by High/Scope Curriculum values. Graves expands on this topic in the article "Child-Inspired Classroom Plans," which describes how the teaching team at High/Scope's Demonstration Preschool supported and built on children's expressed interests by adding materials and planning experiences related to the play themes generated by toys brought from home.

The next article, "The High/Scope PQA: Assessing Program Quality Through Classroom Observations," by Polly Neill, takes you step by step through High/Scope's Program Quality Assessment (PQA) process. The PQA is a program assessment instrument designed to be used in all center-based preschool and child care settings, not just those using the High/Scope educational approach. To complete the PQA, staff take notes, underline relevant descriptors, and choose a score. In the next article, "Using the PQA to Improve Your Program," Beth Marshall provides examples of how participants in the 1999 High/Scope Ypsilanti Training of Trainers Program (YTOT) used the PQA to identify their programs' strengths, target training needs, and communicate to outsiders about their goals and needs.

In the next selection, "Mentoring in the High/Scope Preschool Classroom," Linda Ranweiler explains how teachers who have the opportunity to attend High/Scope teacher-training programs can use the process of mentoring to pass their new knowledge on to their co-teachers. Ranweiler provides the basics of mentoring and offers tips on how to share the excitement of new ideas in a positive way that acknowledges the feelings of those left behind to "hold down the fort." In the final article, "Administrators—How You Can Support Mentoring," Ranweiler encourages preschool program administrators to support the mentoring process for their teachers by providing training in communication skills and time for the process to take place.

Note Taking:
You *Do* Have Time!

By Nita Banks

• •

A necdotal notes are brief, objective, written observations of children's actions and language. High/Scope teaching teams use daily anecdotal notes to gain information on children's individual abilities and interests. Teachers use the information highlighted in the notes to guide them as they plan classroom experiences, make changes in the physical setting and materials, and choose adult/child interaction strategies.

When anecdotal notes are used in daily team planning, they are a valuable tool for preventing problems, assessing children's developmental levels, and building on children's strengths and interests. Finding time every day—both to take notes and plan as a team around them—can be a challenge. Below are a few suggestions that have worked for us.

→ **Focus on four or five children each week.** While you should always remain open to observing and taking notes on every child, target a few children each week for extra attention. This narrows the playing field and makes the task of note taking less formidable. It also insures that the child who gets along with everyone, doesn't act out, and always follows directions isn't overlooked.

Make a list of the children in your classroom and divide them into groups for targeted observations. You can use almost any criteria for these groupings: classroom arrival times, similar interests, developmental levels, etc.

→ **Once you've decided how to choose the target children, divide the workload.** For example, if there are two teachers on the team, start by dividing the class into two groups of eight to ten; then have each teacher focus on two or three children from their group each week. Each teacher has primary responsibility for his or her group of children, including taking notes, scoring the COR, keeping up portfolios, and so forth. In High/Scope classrooms, the lead teachers and co-teachers are partners in the entire daily routine. Make sure this includes equal sharing of daily team planning and assessment responsibilities!

↪ **In your efforts to attend to the target children, be careful not to pass over the other children** as opportunities arise for anecdotal notes and related lesson plan ideas. Outstanding notes will jump out at you once you have on your anecdotal eyes and ears! Be sure to record ALL of these and to consider them when setting up the learning environment.

↪ **To get started in note taking, decide how and where you'll record observations.** One system that works well is to make an anecdotal notebook for each teacher. Include a group of pages for each child, with one page for each COR or key experience category. If confidentiality is an issue, use codes for children's names. Notebooks can be left on shelves, or any other convenient surface. Throughout the daily routine, teachers can quickly step to these spots and record notes. For example: *1/23/98 WT - BLE sorted and handed out correct name cards to four children at the art table.*

↪ **Catch it while it's hot!** Sometimes as you work with children, a great idea pops into your head for a possible activity for the next day. If you can, share it with your co-teachers immediately. After they add their personal "two cents," one of you can dash over to jot down your ideas on the lesson plan. For example, after hearing children pretend to "catch the bus" in the house area, one High/Scope co-teacher thought of some materials to add to the area for the next day (a few extra chairs, materials to make bus tickets, and road maps) as a way of encouraging children to expand on their idea.

↪ **Get it on tape!** Sometimes you can glean information you would not normally catch just by turning on a tape recorder during small-group time or some other time when you notice that children are very absorbed in their activities. For example: *Atien at work time: "I'm going to put all the babies up at cleanup time." "Babies get dry here!" "I'll put her clothes on!"* When you review the tape later, these comments will trigger your memory and you will be able to jot down more about a child's activity.

↪ **Enlist a parent to help take notes in the classroom.** If parents are taking notes at home and sharing them with teaching teams, you will be way ahead. Chances are good that some of these same parents have the time to help, would be really good at it, and are eager to expand their horizons. Invite them in during work time, identify children to focus on for the day, and ask them to share in the note taking. Giving them a certain area to work in as an option might help. Narrowing the focus might also make it easier to involve them. For example: *"Thanks for volunteering to help with the notes! We're looking for evidence of children working together to complete a project. Would you mind floating between the block and house areas today, and jotting down what children are saying and doing there?"*

↪ **Prioritize.** When it comes to daily team planning, it's easy to say "I just ran out of time." In many cases, for example, the co-teacher is also the bus driver for the program and bus routes can be long. So, it's important that both teachers realize and believe in the importance of discussing what worked and what didn't, focusing on what children are doing and talking about, and using

Jot down ideas as soon as they come to you!

that information on a daily basis to make sure children have plenty of opportunities to develop in all areas. All teachers must first make daily team planning a top priority—then they can begin to solve any problems that are keeping them from it.

Teachers play many important roles. One of the most important is to be an *investigator.* This involves gathering *evidence* of children's current interests and strengths and using it to provide more *opportunities* for them to show what they really can do. If you're a good investigator, and use the information wisely, children will grow and develop far beyond what you thought possible.

Planning Around
Children's Interests

By Michelle Graves

· ·

F or the past few weeks, Rachel has been engrossed in making things with string. One of her favorite work time activities is making "Home Alone" traps, which she creates by attaching string to the classroom climbing structure and winding it around a closet doorknob several feet away. She continues winding the string back and forth between the structure and the doorknob until she has many layers of string. Then she hangs toys from the string layers "so there will be noise if someone tries to open the door." Rachel has also used string at the art area, creating interesting effects with paint by using pieces of string as paint-brushes. Today at work time, she finds a new use for string; she cuts three lengths of string, gets out three brightly colored wallpaper scraps, and tapes one to each piece of string. When she finishes, she takes her work to the teacher and says, "Help me make a mobile so I can take it to Jeremy's school crib." (Rachel has a 12-week-old brother who has just joined the program's infant room.)

§

Leah and Megan, who are pretending to be dogs, crawl into the block area where Daniel and Victor are building. They crawl up to Daniel and Victor and make loud barking noises. Daniel says, "You need a dog house," and he and Victor begin reshaping their block structure so it encloses Leah and Megan. The girls continue to bark and howl. Soon Alex comes over and says, "Hey, let's have a dog show." He goes to the art area and returns with paper, scissors, markers, and tape for making "prize ribbons." While he is working, Daniel and one of the teachers join in making ribbons.

§

As Rachel experiments with string and the other children create a play "drama" centering on dogs, they are expressing their personal interests and ideas. While these interests reflect general play preferences that are typical of preschoolers (pretend play, making and building) the *specific form* these interests take on this particular day is unique to these preschoolers.

Learning how to plan based on such unique child interests is the focus of this article. To many teachers who have already set up their classrooms and daily routines around High/Scope guidelines, the notion of "planning around children's interests" may seem obvious. "Of course we plan around children's interests," they may say, pointing to an environment designed around activities that preschoolers typically enjoy. "We have role-play materials, blocks, a sand table, lots of books and small manipulatives, computers, and a great playground. What more could we possibly do to plan around children's interests?"

Planning: From General to Specific

These teachers, of course, have planned in a **general way** around the interests of children. When we organize our classrooms into interest areas, we are using what we know about child development to choose materials that

If children have been re-enacting their camping experiences in the classroom or center, you might decide to hold small-group time outdoors in a tent, encouraging the group to make up a story about camping.

will be attractive and engaging to preschoolers. Within this environment, the plan-do-review process and other elements of the High/Scope daily routine give children countless opportunities to pursue their personal interests. But setting the stage for children's choices in these ways is only the **first step** in planning around children's interests. This article looks at the **next step,** the process of examining the **specific interests** children express in their play and making plans to support and build on these

interests. For by building on these specific child interests, adults encourage children to expand the depth and complexity of their play. In these expanded play experiences, children use and strengthen a wide range of social, intellectual, and physical abilities.

If we look again at the two play examples that open this article, we can learn many specific things about the children's interests. Rachel is interested in making traps like those she saw in a movie, in working with string and paint, in crib mobiles, and in her new baby brother. The children in the other scenario are interested in dog shelters, in dogs who do a lot of barking, and in pet-show prizes. The teachers who worked with these children attended to these particular details in developing strategies to support children's learning during these play experiences and during related play experiences on the days that followed.

Strategies for Building on Children's Interests

The following strategies will help you plan around the particular interests of children in your classroom.

• **Take notes on your observations of children in order to gather specific information on children's activities.** To support children's interests, you have to know what children are doing in the most specific terms possible. Documenting your child observations daily through anecdotal note taking helps you remember the details of children's activities and enables you to share what you've observed with your teammates. **Anecdotal notes** are brief capsule summaries of a child's behavior during a specific incident. They include information on the activity and materials the children chose, how they worked with the materials, the language they used, and how they interacted with peers and adults. Some examples of anecdotal notes from Rachel's classroom are presented on page 352.

• **Meet daily to share and interpret your observations with your team members and to make plans for the next day's program based on your observations.** Daily meetings are a necessity for teammates to stay attuned to children's shifting interests and their needs for support.

• **Use a child development framework to interpret your observations and learn more about how individual children's interests relate to their abilities.** The various **High/Scope key experiences** identify the specific cognitive, social, and physical abilities that are emerging in the preschool years. By looking at a child's play interests in terms of the key experiences, adults learn which abilities are reflected in a child's actions at a given time and garner ideas for supporting the further development of these abilities. In the pet show example, the children's teacher had the key experiences in mind as she worked alongside the children, pretending to get ready for the pet show. Hoping to learn more about the children's thinking in relation to pet shows, she casually remarked, "I wonder what kinds of prizes the dogs will be awarded." Daniel then suggested that prizes should go to "the loudest dog" and "the one that sleeps the most." Then, after the

Typical Anecdotal Notes

2/4 After building a "trap" out of string and hanging objects at work time, Rachel explained its purpose: "So there will be noise if someone tries to open the door."

2/6 At work time Rachel got out three pieces of each of the following materials: wallpaper scraps, pieces of string, and pieces of tape. She then used the tape to attach one piece of string to each of the paper scraps.

2/7 "Rachel made a mobile but I don't have a baby, so I'm just going to make a picture," said Samuel when provided with mobile-making materials at small-group time.

2/8 At small-group time on the playground, Theresa took a streamer and wove it in and out of the openings in the chain-link fence. After she finished weaving with one streamer, she got a second one and commented, "Look, I made a long color line."

5/10 When asked for her work time plan, Megan said, "to be a dog again."

5/10 Daniel worked with Victor to make a doghouse-like space to enclose Megan and Leah, then worked with Alex to create prize ribbons for a dog show.

5/11 Leah responded to Megan's plan ("to play with Leah and make a ribbon") by walking hand in hand with Megan to the art area.

ribbons were completed, Alex asked the teacher to write Daniel's words on the ribbons. Because of her familiarity with the key experiences, the teacher recognized that Daniel and Alex were using **classification** and **language and literacy** abilities as they formulated their ideas for dog prizes. Thus she continued to support this activity by encouraging them to come up with additional ideas for prizes, by assisting them in writing their words on the ribbons, and by supporting their interest in writing during other parts of the daily routine.

• **Use adult-child interaction strategies in support of children's play interests.** The verbal and nonverbal strategies you use as you work directly with children communicate to them the importance you place on the play interests they are expressing. In the example above, the teacher's nondirective comment about prizes is an illustration of effective use of an adult-child interaction strategy to encourage a child to elaborate his ideas.

• **Add materials to the classroom and outdoor play area to support children's interests.** These additional materials may enable children to expand their thinking by adding detail to their artwork or role play or by repeating a familiar process with a new material. Observing her interest in tying and stringing, Rachel's teachers added a simple loom and weaving materials to their center, as well as wooden dowels and plastic coat hangers for making mobiles. Similarly, the teachers who worked with the pet-show players added additional prize-related materials to the art area. These materials included award certificates (both used and blank), strips of satin and velvet ribbon, hole punches, cardboard discs, safety pins, and paper clips.

- **Incorporate your observations of children's interests as you plan experiences for the adult-initiated parts of the day—planning and recall times, small-group time, large-group time.** For example, in Rachel's classroom teachers used her interest in *"Home Alone* traps" (an interest she shared with several other children) as the basis for a **planning** strategy. The teachers tied several small toys to a string so that shaking the string made a jangling noise. As the other children covered their eyes, the child whose turn it was to plan carried the "trap" to the area she planned to work in and then shook it. The other children then tried to guess where the sound came from. Once the correct interest area was guessed, the child described her plans. Similarly, after the pet-show pretending described above, teachers developed a related strategy for the next day's planning time. Using heavy paper and strips of ribbon, they made interest area symbols that looked like prize ribbons. They asked individual children to select the prize ribbon that stood for the interest

If children have been enjoying using shovels indoors at the sand table, build on this interest by providing opportunities for different kinds of shoveling experiences outdoors.

area they planned to work in and then to discuss their plans. Rachel's teachers also planned a **small-group experience** to build on Rachel's interest in tying and stringing, an interest which quickly spread to other children in the classroom. The teachers planned this experience for outdoors, providing the children with yarn, string, and crepe paper streamers.

What About Pre-Planning for Children's Interests?

For the next two weeks at school we've planned to have children learn all about insects and bugs. Isn't that the same as planning around children's interests? After all, children do like bugs.

—A preschool teacher

It is true that you will have some children in your classroom who are fascinated by bugs and insects, and there are many activities you could plan for this unit that would actively involve children in the learning process. Nevertheless, there is a difference between a 2-week unit on insects and what we call "planning around children's interests" in the High/Scope approach.

Our approach to planning begins with specific observations of children rather than with a predetermined topic or set of topics. When teachers observe and interact with children, they look at the activities and materials children choose and how they interact with the adults and children around them. During the day and after the children leave, teachers jot down anecdotal notes describing these observations, and then develop plans based on these notes and the High/Scope curriculum framework.

We would recommend storing up your ideas for bug-related activities until children's interest in bugs surfaces in the classroom. In some climates, this often happens during the spring or early summer when insects become active. At these times, note and **build on children's specific interests.** Some children may be fascinated by spider webs; others, by mosquito bites; and others, by the buzzing sounds of bumblebees. Still others will be more interested in the soggy, muddy ground as it thaws, or the feel of the newly mowed grass on their favorite rolling hill. Be sure you take children to places where they have the opportunity to make these kinds of discoveries. Then watch their reactions and try to build on the interests you observe in all the children, rather than those of a select few. Through this process you will create many "learning moments" for children—times when they are most receptive to internalizing new information and connecting it to their previous experiences. You will also notice that this approach to planning has an added benefit—that of watching children's confidence grow as you send them the message that they are capable people who have control over their learning environment.

The children enjoyed weaving the materials in and out of the links in the chain-link fence; some children tied them onto the slide, the tree house, and other playground structures.

• **Use the interests of individual children as a springboard for introducing new ideas and experiences to the rest of the group.** All educators wrestle with the issue of how to introduce new experiences to children. We find that introducing a new play idea that another child has already experimented with in the classroom makes the activity especially attractive and engaging to children. After observing the pet-show play, the teachers planned an imitation experience for **large-group time** that built on the **classification** language Daniel and Alex used when they discussed the pet prizes. The teachers asked individual children to take turns naming a pet and providing a title it might win at a pet show, for example, the dog who is the loudest barker, cat with the softest fur, squirrel who is the fastest nibbler. As each child shared an idea, the group acted it out. The ideas the children generated enabled their teachers to understand and record additional information about the children's abilities in the areas of **classifying, naming attributes,** and **initiating ideas.**

§

In this article, we've outlined an approach to planning in which teachers incorporate their observations of children's interests into every aspect of the preschool day. Why is planning around children's interests so important? When we focus on the interests children reveal through their actions and language, we are learning about the activities and experiences that offer them the greatest opportunities for learning. As teachers, we need to know and use the details of children's interests if we are to be effective supporters of their social, intellectual, and physical development.

Toys From Home:
One Teaching Team's Dilemma

By Michelle Graves

• •

Classroom teaching is a daily adventure filled with joys and opportunities—as well as challenges and problems. Resolving the many issues that arise in day-to-day teaching is part of the responsibility we assume as classroom teachers. Some of these issues are relatively clear-cut. For example, few teachers or parents would argue against a policy of serving healthy, nutritious food, even though children might prefer the taste of cupcakes and lollipops. Other issues and problems—involving conflicting needs and viewpoints—are less easy to resolve. In such cases, teaching team members often fear that any solution they choose will disappoint or frustrate either children, their parents, or the teachers themselves.

In this article, we deal with one such complicated issue—what to do when children bring toys from home to the preschool classroom or center. This article focuses on the experience of a teaching team at High/Scope's Demonstration Preschool and how team members thought through this issue as it surfaced during the first week of school—the decisions they made, and the outcomes of those choices. Our intention in sharing this experience is not to imply that all programs should handle toys from home exactly as we did. Instead, our goal is to illustrate a process you can use to examine the choices you make about any issue that arises in your work with children. By using this process, you and your team can work out solutions that are compatible with your curriculum principles and respectful of the needs of both children and adults.

Jessie looks for classroom materials to use with the doll she brought from home.

Toys Arrive: What to Do?

The issue of toys from home surfaced the first week of school at the High/Scope Demonstration Preschool. On those beginning days, children entered the classroom with various favorite objects: blankets, stuffed animals, dolls, and a variety of action figures, including monsters and dinosaurs. Our interactions with children and parents the first week of school made it clear that bringing toys from home was an emotional issue for many of them. In some cases parents apologized about the toys their children had brought in, telling us that children had cried when asked to leave their toys in the car or at home. In many cases it seemed that the toys represented a link to home that helped children feel comfortable in the classroom: children would some-times talk to us "through" a special toy (pretending it was the toy talking) or use favorite items as conversation starters with peers.

While we understood the emotional importance of these toys to chil-dren, we still felt a dilemma: Should we allow children to bring in their favorite toys, knowing we had no control over the quality and appropriate-ness of these play materials? While we wanted to meet children's emotional needs and support their choices and interests, we felt that the presence of toys from home in the classroom could raise troublesome issues. Were we ready for the conflicts that could erupt if children were pressured to share their special toys? Would children's play get rougher if toy weapons and action figures were brought into the setting? If we allowed the toys from home, would children play with them exclusively, missing out on the many play options offered in our carefully planned setting? We also wondered whether, in setting a policy on toys from home, we should make a distinc-tion between security objects (like blankets and stuffed animals) and other kinds of toys.

As the team approached these issues we used a team process **guided by curriculum values.** As we describe throughout this article what hap-pened, we'll discuss both the **aspects of the High/Scope Curriculum** that guided our thinking and the **details unique to our situation** that had to be considered as we made decisions.

To resolve the toys-from-home issue, the first big hurdle we had to overcome was our own newness to each other as a teaching team. While we both had experience in the High/Scope approach prior to working together in this setting, we still worried about the effects of our decisions on our just-developing working relationship. Would one person's opinion carry more weight than another's? Would we be able to reach a compromise if we did not agree? Would we be able to effectively communicate the rationale for our decisions to children and parents?

As we resolved to delve more deeply into the issues surrounding toys from home, we realized we had to **focus on our own teamwork.** Two teamwork strategies emphasized in the High/Scope framework are **communicating openly** and **respecting individual differences.** Thus, in our discussion of this issue, we tried to learn as much as we could about everyone's experiences and points of view. We took turns talking about our previous experiences—a school where the policy was simply "No toys from home allowed," and another school where bringing toys was permitted but where children's use of them was limited to short segments of the morning. We also talked about our experiences with another common type of toy policy, one that permitted security objects like stuffed animals and pacifiers (because of their obvious emotional importance to children) but barred other kinds of toys.

An "Old Maid" game brought from home offers an opportunity to play cards like an older brother does.

We also listened carefully to the reasoning behind the various policies we discussed. The school with the "No toys" policy served families in a wide income range, which set up a potential "haves" versus "have nots" situation; teachers in the school that allowed the toys, but only for short time periods, had set this policy because they felt the toys interfered with the children's ability to make detailed plans (they had observed that sometimes children held off making their plans because they were waiting to see what the "toy of the day" would be). We also shared our experiences with "security objects only" policies. One team member said that while the policy seemed clear-cut in theory, in practice it was sometimes difficult for teachers to make this distinction. Sometimes a child's security object was not a cuddly toy but a hard plastic action figure; at other times literal-minded preschoolers could not understand why some toys were allowed and some were not.

Reaching a Decision

Through this respectful process of sharing and listening, we allayed our initial concerns that one person's opinion would be given more weight than another's. This freed us to focus on the children and other aspects of the curriculum.

Children's Personal Toys:
Two Approaches

Cathy Albro, a High/Scope certified trainer who was formerly the owner of Creative Learning Center in Grand Rapids, Michigan, shares the following account of how children in this full-day preschool center helped to shape the center's policy on toys from home:

Initially, we had a blanket rule that toys from home were not allowed in the classroom, but children brought toys in anyway. As a result, the staff found itself policing the environment, reminding children of the rule, and expecting them to put personal toys out of sight until it was time to go home. Teachers were committed to promoting children's ideas and interests, so children's pleas ("Could we just share it instead of putting it away?" "It's too long to wait") were hard to resist. These experiences influenced the staff to begin to rethink classroom policy; eventually children were permitted to bring toys from home.

As they came to a decision to change the policy, staff members identified issues they would have to resolve to make the presence of the toys from home a positive learning opportunity for everyone. Some of these issues included encouraging sharing, dealing with fragile or consumable toys, and developing a policy to cover toys that were obviously modeled after weapons, such as plastic guns and swords.

Much as the teachers at High/Scope's own Demonstration Preschool have found, the Creative Learning Center teachers found that solutions to these issues came from both the High/Scope approach and from the children themselves. Staff found the following curriculum strategies to be especially useful: *acknowledging and labeling children's feelings* (about sharing), *helping children predict outcomes* ("That toy is delicate. What do you think will happen to it if you toss it off the climber and it hits the ground?"), and *including children in the problem-solving process.* The concern about toy guns and swords was resolved when the **children** themselves decided they were causing too many problems and agreed on a rule that this kind of toy should stay at home.

Karen Molinario, Director of the Discovery Preschool in Gretna, Louisiana, and a High/Scope certified trainer, reports that teachers there have had similar experiences in dealing with toys from home in the classroom:

Taking cues from children is a central part of Discovery's policy about toys from home. For example, Molinario relates that children's miniature metal cars were "the big craze" at her center. Molinario explains that the children arrived at 6:30 a.m. and immediately started to play with their cars. Breakfast starts soon after this arrival time, and this led to problems for some children: they found that the cars can get in the way of eating and they sometimes spilled juice on the cars. Since the children expressed concern about the spills, the teachers one day asked them for ideas about preventing this from happening. One child quickly volunteered that putting the cars in his pockets would keep them safe. However, another child then pointed out that her clothing did not have pockets. "Our bins. They'll be safe in our bins," this child suggested. Since this discussion, children's pockets and their individual bins have become the two options for storing the cars once breakfast has started.

Molinario adds that miniature cars are not the only special items children have brought from home. One child was especially (and literally) attached to his favorite backpack. For the first two weeks of his school experience at Discovery, he wore the pack on his back the entire day. Only when he felt comfortable in his surroundings did he choose to hang it on his personal hook!

After considering all the issues, we decided that most important to us was a single curriculum principle: **Positive interactions with others are an essential element of supportive environments for children.** Our training in the curriculum had stressed the importance of being sensitive and responsive to parents' and children's emotional needs. Keeping this principle in mind, we considered our observations about children's attachment to their toys, knowing that for many children this was a first experience outside of home.

Together, these factors helped us decide to allow the children to keep their personal toys with them at school. We saw this as an important way to develop trusting relationships with children and their parents. Our decision to permit the toys included not only security objects but also other kinds of toys. In setting this inclusive policy, we were influenced by the team's previous experiences with "security toys only" policies. Another factor that contributed to our decision to permit a wide range of personal toys was this key curriculum principle: **responding attentively to children's interests is an important strategy for building relationships with children.** We knew these favorite toys from home were an expression of the interests children valued most.

The Impact of Our Decision

Having agreed on a toys-from-home policy, we faced another question: "What now?" To deal with classroom issues that might arise as a result of our decision, we again looked to the curriculum for guidance. In the following discussion of how we implemented our decision, each section begins with the curriculum principle that was key to resolving the issue discussed.

✓ **Teaching adults use a problem-solving approach to deal with everyday classroom conflicts.**

We realized our decision to allow toys from home might result in additional conflict in the classroom. Rather than view possible conflicts in a negative light, however, we decided to use them as opportunities to help children learn to solve problems. As expected, conflicts did arise! Certain kinds of toy-related situations were frequent sources of conflict. For example, sometimes children wanted to use other children's special toys; at other times, toy owners wanted to share their toys with certain children while excluding others; and occasionally, a treasured personal item was lost, misplaced, or damaged.

In situations like these, we maintained our commitment to the principle that, **with support, children can resolve interpersonal conflicts.** In the beginning we spent a lot of time using High/Scope's **conflict resolution process** (see Chapter One article, "Encouraging Group Problem Solving") with children who were upset or fighting about a toy. Typically, for example, a classroom adult would **calmly approach the children having the conflict,** sitting or kneeling at the children's level. Then, holding the disputed toy to keep it "neutral" and keeping voice and body language calm and reassuring, the adult would **acknowledge both children's feelings.** *("You're really upset." "You wish you could hold it, too." "It's hard to give up your special toy.")* As the children calmed down, the adult was able to **gather information about the conflict** *("You just want to hold it until cleanup"),* **restate the problem from the children's perspectives** *("'Till cleanup seems too long?"),* **ask them for solutions** *("How long can he hold it?"),* or **offer suggestions** if children were unable to think of solutions on their own *("Maybe while you wait, you could hold one of the school dinosaurs?").* Once

During a break in classroom activity, Jake keeps his hockey stick in hand. Jake's interest in hockey soon spreads to the other children.

children had returned to their activities, the adult would **stay "on alert," ready to offer follow-up support and encouragement,** if necessary.

As children became familiar with this process, we noticed that conflicts over toys brought from home began to decrease. Some children decided, through experience, that they would prefer not to share their toys and so chose to leave them at home. Other children became skilled in resolving their conflicts over toys. As the school year went on, certain children even began to take on a mediating role. It was not uncommon to hear Jake say, "Uh-oh, we have a problem—but I think we can find a solution."

✓ **Adults and children form partnerships with one another and engage in a process that leads to unexpected discoveries.**

Our decision to allow toys from home created a partnership that led to many positive (and often unexpected) results. The items children brought from their homes gave us many insights into what was truly

Allowing Comfort Items From Home

I just started working in a preschool program. The approach is child-centered, but one thing puzzles me. There is a strict policy against pacifiers, "blankies," and other personal comfort items from home. Our director says those items are not allowed because they spread germs (the children suck and drool on them) and prevent children from becoming independent. I don't like to take these comforting things away from the children, and I know they are not very happy about it, either. What do you think?
— *A first-year preschool teacher*

We believe that such a policy does not serve the best interests of children. In an active learning setting, caregivers respect children's choices, are confident of their ability to solve problems, and understand children's need for trusting relationships. Thus, they accept the fact that some children may choose to keep personal comfort items close to them at all times of the day or during parts of it, such as nap time or greeting circle. Whether the child's special object is a particular striped blanket, a special soft dolly with all the hair worn off, a pacifier on a green ribbon, or a miniature car that was a present from Daddy on his last visitation day, caregivers understand that children feel more at home when they can have the item at hand. Such items can give children the courage, for example, to stop crying, feel less agitated, or take an interest in their non-home setting. However insignificant or "grubby" the item may seem to the adult, holding it or having it nearby often gives the child a greater sense of control and independence. Children trust caregivers who respect their feelings about their personal comfort items. On the other hand, they learn to mistrust people who routinely take their comfort items away.

important and of interest to them. We found that children were often better informed than we were about topics related to these items, and these child-owned materials often led to classroom conversations in which children had the opportunity to be the "experts." For example, when Jenna and Elia brought in their own plastic velociraptors, they told us a lot we didn't know about these small dinosaurs. The day Rebecca brought in a plastic lantern from home, she shared what she knew about her family's experiences with winter camping and the proper equipment needed to stay outdoors in cold weather.

In addition, we were relieved to discover that our approach to personal toys did not open up a floodgate; children brought in relatively small numbers of toys. We also found that, for children, these home materials didn't supplant the materials already in the classroom; instead children usually chose to use the toys from home in conjunction with classroom materials (for example, using the classroom blocks to build an elaborate structure for a favorite action figure from home).

✓ Observations of children form the basis for assessment and guide adults in making plans for the next day.

Our decision to accept toys from home in our classroom had a continuing impact on program activities throughout the year. We learned a great deal about how children negotiated the social issues of sharing and solving problems, as well as about their continuing development in other important areas. We reflected on these behavioral observations in our daily planning sessions, interpreting them in terms of High/Scope's **preschool key experiences** and **child assessment instrument,** the High/Scope Child Observation Record (COR) for Ages 2½–6. Based on these discussions, we were able to develop specific strategies for supporting the development of individual children. Children's experiences with toys from home also inspired us to select additional, related materials for the classroom and to plan related activities.

These added materials and plans are among the many ways our program was enriched and changed as the result of our decision to include children's toys from home. While your teaching team may ultimately arrive at a different policy for dealing with personal toys, we recommend that you follow the team process illustrated here to explore this or any other classroom issue. Through this process you can arrive at solutions that reflect an active learning approach to education and meet the specific needs of your children, parents, and teaching adults.

Child-Inspired Classroom Plans

By Michelle Graves

• •

In High/Scope classrooms, daily team planning sessions are an opportunity for adults to discuss the interests and themes they see emerging in children's play and to plan ways to build on these experiences. After we decided to allow toys from home in the Demonstration Preschool, for example, we observed to see what kinds of play would develop around these personal toys. We noticed that toys from home were often used as props for two play themes that were becoming especially popular: dinosaurs and sports.

Because of their importance to children, we decided to support and build on children's expressed interests in these play themes by adding related materials and by planning related experiences. Our intention in doing this was not to impose the interests of a few children on the rest of the class, but rather to highlight these play ideas and make them available to the entire group. Individual children could then choose to explore them further or ignore them. Some of the plans we made to build on these interests are described next.

- **Adding materials to the classroom.** Zachary's habit of bringing in a toy dinosaur every day, Elijah's com-

What We Learned About Children

Here are some examples of anecdotes we recorded about children's classroom experiences with toys brought from home.

At greeting circle, after bringing a red dinosaur into the classroom, Zachary made this suggestion: "Hey, guys, I know! Let's all move like velociraptors to the planning tables." He then demonstrated his idea by crouching down low, roaring, and holding his outspread fingers in front of him.

Jake arrived at school with a hockey stick in his hand. He announced to the other children: "My Dad got me a real hockey stick just like the Red Wings use. I watched them on TV last night and they won 3 to 2."

After her family went on a winter weekend camping trip, Rebecca brought a plastic lantern into the class. She told the children that it was "to help see when it got dark." Then she made a "tent" with blocks and blankets, set the lantern next to it and pretended to go to sleep.

ments about dinosaurs being extinct, and the other children's interests in these toys and conversations prompted us to add books about dinosaurs to the book area. Two favorites were *It's Probably Good Dinosaurs Are Extinct* by Ken Raney and *Time Flies* by Eric Rohmann. We also added plastic dinosaurs in various sizes and colors to the block area, along with cone-shaped pieces of cardboard. Children used the blocks to build "dinosaur houses" and used the cardboard as "mountains for the dinosaurs to climb." In the toy area, we added small plastic dinosaur counters to the container that already housed plastic teddy bear and kitty cat counters.

Jake often brought in sporting goods, for example, a hockey stick and a towel with a sports logo. This stimulated the other children's interest in sports events of all kinds. To support and extend these interests, we added football jerseys and athletic shoes (house area), brochures and glossy programs from sporting events children had attended (book area), and bats, balls, and hockey sticks (outdoor play area). Children who had been playing "hockey" and "football" indoors enjoyed bringing these games to the larger outdoor space where there was more room for running and rolling.

- **Planning field trips.** To expand on the dinosaur theme, we scheduled a field trip to a nearby museum of natural history. We arranged for children to have opportunities to touch and examine dinosaur bones, footprint fossils, and dinosaur eggs at the museum. Children also had the chance to view full-sized skeletons of some of the dinosaurs they had talked about in class.

To support children's sports interests, we planned a walking field trip to a high school football field, where we had the opportunity to appreciate the length and width of the playing field. The bleachers not only provided a climbing option but also offered a brand-new vantage point from which to observe the field, trees, and sky.

- **Planning small-group activities.** After the field trip to the museum we planned a small-group experience in which children worked with paint and the plastic dinosaurs from the block area. Some of the children painted entire dinosaurs a new color, while others painted only the feet, then made prints on white paper to represent dinosaur footprints like we'd seen at the museum. (At the end of this activity, the children washed the paint off the dinosaurs.) For another day's small-group time, we provided plastic pull-apart eggs and small plastic dinosaur counters hidden inside balls of modeling compound. Some children pretended the dinosaurs were hatching out of the eggs while others rolled and re-rolled the compound to cover and hide different parts of the dinosaurs.

- **Planning large-group activities.** At large-group time we played a stopping-and-starting movement game about dinosaurs. First we asked a child to choose a dinosaur and demonstrate its movements. Then we played a musical selection. Next, the group imitated the child's ideas until we turned off the music. Then it was another child's turn to present a movement idea for the group to imitate.

Jake brought from home a tape of two local football fight songs. During work time, we played it during some of the children's pretend football games. Once the song became familiar to the children, we added it to our song book as a large-group singing option.

- **Creating planning time strategies.** To continue building on children's interest in dinosaurs, we told the children at their planning time: "Roar like a dinosaur to the area you will work in, then bring back something you'll use."

The children's interest in sports was also the inspiration for some additional planning strategies. One day, for example, we initiated planning by telling children: "Skate to the area of your choice, then tell us what you plan to do there." On another day, we used a basketball-related planning opener: "Toss this beanbag through the hoop that has the sign for the area where you plan to start work time. Then tell us what things you will use there and what you will do with them."

The above plans were inspired by the children's activities with the toys they brought from home and the reactions of other children to these toys. We arrived at these ideas by planning around the framework of the High/Scope daily routine and preschool key experiences, integrating this framework with what we knew about children's interests. Note that we also recommend applying the same planning process to the other interests and ideas generated by children—whether or not they involve toys from home.

A "Ken" doll brought from home becomes a pretend football player.

The High/Scope PQA:
Assessing Program Quality Through
Classroom Observations

By Polly Neill

• •

For most of us, evaluating the quality of products and services we use is a common concern in our daily lives. But because we're not always sure how to measure quality, we often look to outside resources for help. For example, if we wanted to know about the quality of our local drinking water, we might get a test kit from the State Health Department.

But suppose it's an early childhood program that we want to evaluate? Are there any tools we can use to size up the program? How do we know which program features to look for? How can we be sure our evaluation will be fair and objective? Perhaps most important, how can we be sure that our evaluation will provide useful information to program staff? Can the evaluation results be presented in a form that staff can use to recognize their program's strengths and identify improvements they want to make?

What Is the PQA?

High/Scope's Program Quality Assessment (PQA) is a program assessment instrument for early childhood settings that is designed to answer concerns like these. The PQA can provide an objective evaluation of a program's effectiveness in **seven key areas:** *learning environment; daily routine; adult-child interaction; curriculum planning and assessment; parent involvement and family services; staff qualifications and staff development;* and *program management.* Individuals who may find the PQA useful include directors and staff of preschool centers, Head Start personnel, evaluators of state-funded preschool programs, college and university teachers, early childhood researchers, and parents.

PQA assessment starts with direct observations of a program's facilities, materials, and the interactions among children and adults.

The PQA is designed for use in *all* center-based preschool and child care settings, not just those using the High/Scope educational approach. It reflects "best practice" in the early childhood community—a consolidation of current theory, decades of practice, and ongoing research on the elements of programs that help preschool children develop to their full potential.

The PQA instrument includes 72 items distributed among the seven key areas listed above. The individual performing the assessment completes the instrument by observing the program firsthand and conducting interviews with program staff. Each item is scored using a 5-point rating scale, from a low (1) to a high (5) level of quality.

Over the past year, High/Scope staff have trained a number of early childhood professionals in using the PQA and have learned a great deal about the practical issues that arise as staff use it for the first time. Drawing on these experiences, this article provides suggestions for using the classroom observation portion of the PQA. These suggestions are not intended to substitute for PQA training (which is recommended for all beginning users), but simply to provide a better understanding of the instrument for those already using it or considering getting started.

In the rest of this article we'll walk you through the PQA process, starting with a visit to two typical preschools, then demonstrate how the observations from these visits are used to answer some of the questions that are included in a PQA evaluation.

Visiting the Program—The Beginning of PQA Assessment

Assessment with the PQA always starts with a personal visit to observe the preschool program in action and interview key staff. So let's imagine you're visiting two typical preschool programs—some of the things you might observe on these visits are noted in the vignettes on the next pages.

Observations like these are typical of those made by individuals in daily contact with early childhood programs. Such observations are the "raw material" of PQA assessment. As you read through the rest of this

Visiting the Rock Creek Child Development Center

You arrive early at Rock Creek Child Development Center. As you park, you notice how attractive the obviously new building is—beautiful cedar shingles with bright white trim. It also appears that each classroom has its own fenced-in outdoor play area with a swing set and sandbox.

The center director gives you a tour of the center, proudly pointing out all the unique features that they were able to include because the center was designed especially for them. You admire the skylights, freshly painted walls, bright murals, and the multi-colored kites hanging from the cathedral ceiling in the lobby. When the director takes you into the classroom you immediately notice all the new wooden tables, chairs, and shelves; another colorful mural along one entire wall; and the floor-to-ceiling windows.

Bright banners, made by a local artist, hang from the ceiling. Shelves, tables, and covered bins are placed around the perimeter of the room, leaving a large open space in the center. Around the water table are four pairs of colorful footprints painted on the floor to indicate how many children at a time can use the water table. On the shelves are covered plastic tubs in a rainbow of colors. On some of the higher shelves are art materials and more covered tubs. You also see a baby doll in the cradle, a milk crate of wooden blocks, and a child-sized police uniform and bridal dress. After you are introduced to the teacher in that classroom, you talk for a bit longer with the center director and then leave.

article, you'll see how the PQA's criteria and procedures are used to shape such raw material into a clear and focused picture of a program's strengths and weaknesses. We'll refer back to these observations as we review three steps you'll follow in completing a PQA item.

Taking Notes: Step 1

An easy rule of thumb for completing the PQA is "Start at the bottom of the page (the space left for taking notes), and work your way up." Remember to fill the bottom of the page with careful notes and study them *before* deciding on a score. Once this is done, go to the top of the page and begin scoring.

Your **first step,** then, is to **observe the classroom and record what you see in the form of supporting evidence/anecdotes.** These notes provide the foundation for the next two scoring steps, so it's critical to thoroughly document what you see in the classroom. We use the term *evidence/anecdotes* because your notes become exactly that—a set of "verbal snapshots" capturing important *observations and facts* that will back up the score you will select for a particular PQA item. Depending on the PQA sec-

Visiting the Osage Avenue Preschool

When you called the Osage Avenue Preschool, the director told you it was located in the old Osage Avenue Elementary School, but it had a separate entrance that you would see if you drove around back. As you park your car, you notice that this parking area is reserved for preschool staff and families. You also see quite a large fenced-in area with swings, balls, tricycles, wagons, a sandbox, a climbing structure, and a small locked shed. On the gate to the play area is a sign that reads, "Osage Preschool Goes Outside" with additional decorations added by the children.

As you pass under the purple awning into the preschool, you notice children's artwork everywhere—on the walls at both adult and child levels, in the glass-fronted "trophy cases" in the school hallway, and on the tables in the lobby. You stop at the "Parents' Bulletin Board" and see the menu for the week, pictures from a field trip, and a note about the vision screening scheduled for next week. The center director gives you a quick tour of the entire center and then takes you to one of the classrooms and introduces you to the teachers. They invite you to come in and explore the classroom. They are planning for the next day, but urge you to ask questions. As in the lobby, the walls have displays of children's work. You also see paintings hanging from clotheslines. Drying on top of some of the shelves are more of children's creations, made from a wide variety of art and scrap materials.

The classroom has a northern exposure and the windows are placed high up. As a result, the room does not get a lot of natural light. The tables, chairs, and shelves are well used and scratched from years of wear. In the house area, you see what appear to be real utensils, pots, and pans, as well as a real cowboy hat, construction worker's hat, football helmet, numerous pieces of adult clothing, and pairs of shoes and boots.

The art area appears to have plenty of materials as well—stacks of paper, open tubs of yarn, ribbons, buttons, macaroni, even an entire bin full of staplers and one full of bottles of glue. The block area has lots of different kinds of blocks—large, small, wood, and cardboard. There are open bins full of small and large vehicles and a separate shelf reserved for the fire trucks. You look over the classroom for a few minutes more. As you leave, the teachers encourage you to return any time for another visit.

tion and item, your supporting evidence/anecdotes may include lists (materials, furniture, labels), brief notes on situations you observe, or actual language from children or adults.

The notes you record under each PQA item are necessary for scoring; they also provide additional, objective documentation the program staff can use later for observation/feedback, inservice training, and other aspects of their program improvement efforts.

A sample of some of the PQA notes you might record about the two centers, based on the observations described, is shown on the next two pages. These sample notes are intended as supporting evidence that might

Sample Notes From
Rock Creek Child Development Center

Block Area:

- Wooden blocks in a milk crate (no label)
- Multi-colored covered tubs stacked on the floor, holding smaller manipulatives and toys
- Low shelves (reachable by children)—
  small vehicles, farm animals,
      wooden people in separate
      covered tubs
  one large wooden truck, one barn,
      one fire engine

House Area:

- Low pantry-like shelves—
  toy food
  toy tea set
  plastic silverware
- Separate laundry baskets—
  dress-up clothes
  stuffed animals
  small kitchen items

Art Area:

- One small shelf with box of markers, box of crayons, two glue sticks, a tray of paper

Toy Area:

- Covered tubs in tub storage shelf holding
      Duplo blocks
      shape sorters
      Lotto games
      Memory card games
- Low bookshelf, four books and two puzzles

Also:

- Higher shelves have small handwritten labels.
- No other labels observed.
- High shelves (out of children's reach) holding
      other art materials
      small manipulatives
      toys with many pieces

appear under PQA Item I–E, *Classroom materials are systematically arranged, labeled, and accessible to children,* from the PQA's Learning Environment section. Because this section focuses on the physical setting, many of the notes needed to complete it may be recorded when children are not in the classroom.

As you can see from the examples, PQA notes are specific, objective, and factual; they contain no judgmental words like "attractive" or "inadequate." Another thing you may notice is that much of the supporting evidence is organized in lists, which provide a lot of information in a simple format. Lists are particularly useful in the Learning Environment section of the PQA; in other sections, such as Adult-Child Interaction, it may also be useful to record information in the form of brief anecdotes about children's actions and language. As you become more familiar with the PQA, you'll find that the evidence/anecdotes you collect for one item or section may be used again to support scores for other items in the same or different sec-

Labels (All Types):

Examples of labels—

- Catalog pictures:
    Duplos
    markers
    teddy bear counters

- Tracings:
    dishes
    blocks

- Actual items:
    small dinos
    feathers
    ribbon

- Drawn pictures:
    glue sticks
    crayons
    beads

House Area:

- Real pots, pans, plates, bowls, and cooking utensils
- Empty food boxes and cans
- Adult clothes hanging on a child-sized coat rack
- Real shoes, boots, and hats in baskets on the floor

Art Area:

On separate shelves—

- Markers, crayons, chalks, and colored pencils
- Feathers, ribbons, cardboard tubes, wallpaper pieces
- Play dough, rolling pins, cookie cutters
- Tape, staplers, glue bottles, masking tape, and glue sticks

Block Area:

- Large hollow blocks, cardboard blocks, large and small vehicles, and carpet squares on floor
- Divided shelf with unit blocks, each shape in own compartment
- Fire trucks on separate shelf

Toy Area:

On same shelf—

- Duplos, Duplo people, Bristle Blocks
- Cuisenaire rods, washers, nuts and bolts, pegs and pegboards, stringing beads
- Teddy bear counters, small and large farm animals, small and large dinos, and small and large wild animals
- Low bookshelves with a variety of books
- 6 puzzles, 1 large floor puzzle

General:

- All shelves are about 2½ feet tall and open.
- All materials are labeled.
- At work time, child got scissors, paper, and glue off shelf.

tions—a process called cross-referencing. For example, you might want to refer to some of the notes taken for Item I–E when looking at Item I–F, *Classroom materials are varied, manipulative, open-ended, and authentic and appeal to multiple senses (sight, hearing, touch, smell, taste)* or at Item I–G, *Materials are plentiful.*

Underlining Relevant Descriptors: Step 2

After you have thoroughly reviewed your notes related to a PQA item, the **second** step in PQA scoring is to read the **descriptors** for each level and underline the phrases in them that match the supporting evidence/anecdotes. The PQA's *descriptors* are specific, concrete statements of the exact criteria for each score. On each PQA item, descriptors are provided for levels 1, 3, and 5; they are listed in the three columns under these numbers. These brief statements are one of the outstanding convenience features of the PQA, since they contain much of the information you'll need to rate each program element. As a result, there's no need to constantly refer back to the manual to check how a particular aspect of a program should be rated—you have the information you need right on the page with your notes. Just compare your notes to the descriptors for that PQA and underline those statements that match with observations you've written down.

The example below shows how this underlining procedure was completed for Item I–E, based on the sample notes from the Rock Creek program.

You'll note that under the column labeled **1,** for the lowest implementation level, we underlined "Materials are not labeled," because the only labels that could be observed were the ones written on the high shelves for adults to use. Under level 3 we underlined the sentence, "Similar items are placed together" because the notes say that the farm animals, small vehicles, and wooden people each had a separate tub and that the dress-up clothes were all placed in a laundry basket. We also underlined the last sentence, "Children can reach and get out some of the materials without adult help," because while some of the materials are indeed accessible to the children, some are out of reach (most of the art materials and small manipulatives).

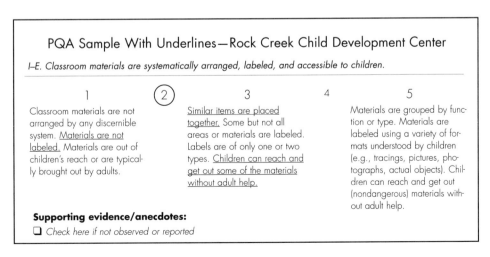

PQA Sample With Underlines—Rock Creek Child Development Center

I–E. Classroom materials are systematically arranged, labeled, and accessible to children.

1	(2)	3	4	5
Classroom materials are not arranged by any discernible system. <u>Materials are not labeled.</u> Materials are out of children's reach or are typically brought out by adults.		<u>Similar items are placed together.</u> Some but not all areas or materials are labeled. Labels are of only one or two types. <u>Children can reach and get out some of the materials without adult help.</u>		Materials are grouped by function or type. Materials are labeled using a variety of formats understood by children (e.g., tracings, pictures, photographs, actual objects). Children can reach and get out (nondangerous) materials without adult help.

Supporting evidence/anecdotes:

☐ *Check here if not observed or reported*

Choosing a Score: Step 3

If you've done your work properly in the first two steps, scoring, the final step, should go smoothly. To choose a score for a PQA item, do one of the following:

- If **all** the criteria are met, circle level **1, 3,** or **5**

OR

- If the criteria for a lower level have been exceeded but all the criteria for the higher level are not present (that is, you see *some, but not all,* the criteria), choose one of the "in-between" levels with no descriptors (either a **2** or **4**).

To score Rock Creek Development Center on Item I–E, we circled the **2.** Why? Because one of the sentences under level *1* is underlined and some of the sentences under level *3* are underlined. In other words, they exceeded the first level, but were not quite high enough on this item to receive a *3.* The availability on the PQA of these "in-between" scores permits a more accurate assessment of each program's features.

Now it's time for another try at underlining and scoring. This time, review the criteria for Item I–E below, but use the observations noted for the Osage Avenue Preschool. Now do the underlining and scoring for item I–E.

What did you underline this time and how did you score this center?

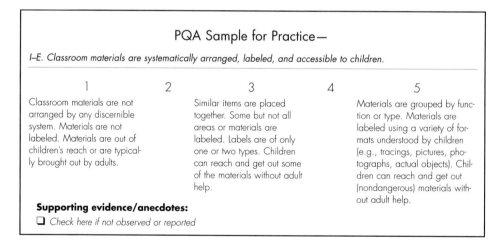

PQA Sample for Practice—

I–E. Classroom materials are systematically arranged, labeled, and accessible to children.

1	2	3	4	5
Classroom materials are not arranged by any discernible system. Materials are not labeled. Materials are out of children's reach or are typically brought out by adults.		Similar items are placed together. Some but not all areas or materials are labeled. Labels are of only one or two types. Children can reach and get out some of the materials without adult help.		Materials are grouped by function or type. Materials are labeled using a variety of formats understood by children (e.g., tracings, pictures, photographs, actual objects). Children can reach and get out (nondangerous) materials without adult help.

Supporting evidence/anecdotes:
☐ *Check here if not observed or reported*

§

We hope this short practice session with a single PQA item gives you a feel for how the instrument works and a glimpse of its potential usefulness in the programs you have contact with. Used with care, the PQA can be very helpful in evaluating early childhood program quality and identifying staff-training needs. It can also be useful in explaining to parents, non-educators, and other members of the community what kinds of early childhood practices work best for children, families, teachers, and administrators. For an in-depth look at the entire instrument, we recommend that you enroll in High/Scope PQA training.

Finally, when you use the PQA, remember these three things:

1. *Looks can be deceiving! Don't be misled by superficial aspects of the facility—for example, brand-new furnishings, expensive tuition, or a long waiting list for admission. Studying the PQA carefully helps you to separate the real factors that contribute to program quality from superficial indicators like these.*

2. *The score is only as good as the evidence/anecdotes you assemble.*

3. *Scoring the PQA is as easy as 1, 2, 3!*

Using the PQA to Improve Your Program

By Beth Marshall

. . . .

Want to evaluate your own classroom program or other classrooms in your center? You'll find that the High/Scope PQA is a handy tool that aids in self-evaluation of any early childhood program. Below are examples of how participants in the 1999 High/Scope Ypsilanti Training of Trainers Program (YTOT) used the PQA. Their experiences illustrate how programs can use the PQA to identify strengths, target training needs, and communicate to outsiders about their goals and needs.

Assessing Training Needs

Staff of many classrooms and centers complete a PQA at the beginning of the year as a baseline measure, to get a sense of their strengths and weaknesses. As one participant noted, "The PQA is a way to notice what areas of the program are not being implemented as well as they should be. . . but equally important, it points out to the staff the areas in which they are successful. It is an opportunity for staff to take pride in their accomplishments and know that they are striving to provide a quality program."

In several classrooms in this participant's program, teachers noticed that they didn't really understand PQA Items III–K and III–L, which deal with independent problem solving and conflict resolution by children. Previously, the teachers said, they had believed that conflict was "something bad that had to be stopped." Not until they read through these items on the PQA did they realize that conflict actually provides positive opportunities for learning. At the request of these teachers, several of their staff development workshops for the upcoming year will focus on both conflict resolution and supporting children who encounter problems during play.

In another program, the staff realized that they needed more information on what kinds of materials to provide and how to label them so chil-

dren could find the materials and put them away independently. The teachers asked for and received workshops on these topics.

As a result of these workshops, the teachers contacted community members to ask for donations of authentic items like pots and pans, old telephones, and computer keyboards. The team invited parents to a labeling party in which parents and teachers created a wide variety of labels. (Before this, their classroom had just a few labels, mostly made from catalog pictures.) The teachers were thrilled with the results. Their PQA evaluation, by identifying genuine needs, had helped them reach out successfully to both community members and parents and improve the learning environment as well.

The PQA helps program staff evaluate each element of a program against objective criteria. It helps staff answer questions like "Does our block area provide a variety of play opportunities?"

When the team members at this center looked back at their baseline PQAs, they were really excited to see concrete evidence of their progress in implementing changes in their programs.

Making Curriculum Decisions

Classroom teachers find that the PQA can also serve as a useful road map that helps steer them in the right direction about specific classroom issues. For example, in one classroom, one teaching team was considering whether to spend time and resources making bulletin board displays for the classroom on topics such as "Weather changes" and "Welcome to the new school year." While they knew they didn't want to buy commercially produced products, they were unsure about whether "home-made" versions would be appropriate.

Using a Low PQA Score as a Catalyst for Change

We use the High/Scope PQA and are concerned that we got a low score in the outdoor play area item. Our classroom is housed in an elementary school. We don't take the children outside because all the playground equipment is for older, larger children and isn't really safe for our little ones. Also, we are concerned that the older kids will knock down the preschoolers. Because these circumstances are really out of our control, we don't think it's fair that we got a low score in this area.

—*A Head Start Teacher*

It sounds like you've really thought through the decisions that you've made for outside time, given your circumstances. However, the PQA is not meant to be punitive. Instead, it offers an honest look at the quality of the program you provide for children. While you indeed may believe that you have no other alternatives in your situation, that belief doesn't change what you score for item I—D, which requires an outdoor play space that provides for varied play experiences.

Rather than see your low score as a negative, you might try using it as a catalyst for change. For example, show this item to your program director and do some additional problem solving about how you can provide outside experiences for your children.

Perhaps you could organize a fundraiser (possibly involving the local PTO) to purchase portable and/or stationary equipment that would be appropriate for preschoolers. Show the item to the principal at your school. Maybe you could take your children outdoors at the beginning of the day, when the other classrooms are not out, so the older children won't bother your children. Maybe there is a way to carve out a safe play space on the existing playground, by sectioning off a portion with temporary orange construction fencing, or by designating a different field as the preschool playground. The point is, the PQA could actually help you involve others in coming up with solutions, and ideas that will result in an appropriate play space for your children.

Deciding to consult the PQA for assistance, they looked over Item I–I, *Child-initiated work . . . is on display.* Under the descriptor for level 1, they found a reference to "adult-made or commercially produced products." This led to a discussion among the teaching team members about why this situation warranted a level 1 rating (which indicates the lowest level of quality).

After some discussion, the team decided that if they wanted to help children develop a better understanding of the weather and the changing seasons, it would be more appropriate to take advantage of how children *experienced* weather on a daily basis. As a result of this shift in outlook, the team made several plans: they would photograph children outside over the course of the year and continually add the new photos to a classroom album; they would listen to and acknowledge children's comments about the weather ("It's cold this morning, and I got to wear my new yellow sweatshirt!"), and they would support children's understanding of weather with their own comments about ongoing weather conditions.

They also made various plans as alternatives to the "Welcome" bulletin board. To prepare the classroom for the first day of school, they posted photos of the children and their families taken during home visits before school started. They thought this display, showing familiar faces and children's homes, might offer a comforting connection between home and the new school.

In the end, the team was quite happy with the curriculum decisions they made. They decided to continue to use the PQA on an as-needed basis, to help guide their decisions about how to accomplish classroom goals using an active learning approach.

Mentoring in the High/Scope Preschool Classroom

By Linda Ranweiler

• •

Loosely defined as the gentle guidance and nurturing of another person through stages of growth and development, **mentoring** is a complex and challenging process. In High/Scope programs, mentoring often works something like this: teachers participating in long-term High/Scope teacher-training programs (such as the 4-week Lead Teacher Training Program or the series of 8 two-day workshops) are typically members of a classroom teaching team that consists of two teachers working with 15–20 preschoolers. When funds for training are limited, many agencies or schools are able to send only *one* of the teachers from a classroom team to the training. However, to make the High/Scope approach work, *both* members of the teaching team must understand the curriculum approach and share equally in the teaching responsibilities. Somehow, then, the content of the training must be passed along to the team member who does not attend the workshops.

Because this situation is so common, questions like the following are very frequently heard from High/Scope training participants: "How is my assistant teacher supposed to plan and lead a small-group activity/write objective anecdotes/understand active learning [or whatever] when she's never attended a High/Scope workshop?!"

One answer to such dilemmas is **mentoring.**

The successful mentor...

- Is willing to listen
- Is sensitive to her co-teacher's needs
- Is able to initiate and maintain the relationship
- Communicates feelings of acceptance
- Demonstrates willingness to share ideas and materials
- Is receptive to learning from the co-teacher
- Is nurturing and supportive
- Respects the uniqueness and strengths of the co-teacher
- Is confident, secure, flexible, altruistic, warm, and caring

In some educational settings, particularly in public schools, mentoring is a *formal* program. In such settings, a seasoned, experienced teacher, who has been teaching for 10 to 15 years or more and is recognized as an excellent educator, agrees to work as a mentor to a newly hired teacher or group of teachers. In regular meetings, the mentor helps the new teacher or teachers learn more about school policies and procedures, classroom organization and management, curriculum, assessment, and so forth.

The typical High/Scope mentoring relationship, however, is quite different from such formal arrangements. In these High/Scope mentoring teams, the level of education, knowledge, and experience varies in every situation. The **mentor**—the teacher who is attending (or has attended) High/Scope training—can be a brand-new teacher, a former elementary teacher who is now teaching preschool, or a paraprofessional who has many years of experience working with children. The experience and prior training of the **co-teacher** who is not involved in the training can vary just as widely.

In some High/Scope programs, too, the need for **administrative support** for the mentoring process is not recognized. To support a teaching team in which one member is attending High/Scope training, for example, a supervisor could make adjustments in budgets and time schedules to allow mentoring meetings to take place. However, since mentoring is not usually a *formally recognized* program in most High/Scope classrooms, administrators often don't see the need to provide this kind of support.(For more information on administrative support for mentoring, see the next article in this chapter, "Administrators—How You Can Support Mentoring.")

Given the loose and informal nature of so many mentoring arrangements in High/Scope programs, then, it's not surprising that the teachers involved experience many challenges. This article offers strategies for facilitating this process of learning together about the High/Scope approach.

Mentoring Basics

To understand some fundamentals of effective mentoring, let's look more closely at a situation that typically occurs at the beginning of a mentoring relationship. Often the teacher who is the trainee returns from a 2-day or week-long workshop full of new ideas and eager to make immediate changes in the classroom. She may be puzzled to find that her co-teacher doesn't share her enthusiasm—in fact, the co-teacher may be resistant even to *hearing* about the workshop. This resistance is understandable if we look

Communication Skills

Here are some important communication skills that are necessary for mentoring teachers. Co-teachers and administrators will also find them useful.

Nonverbal Strategies

Remember, 93 percent of the information we share is communicated *without words*, through facial expressions, body language, voice pitch, intonation, and timing! *So. . . ,*

- **Listen intently and respectfully**—use your body language to communicate that you are listening by making eye contact, fully facing your co-teacher, leaning forward, and resisting distractions. Help your co-teacher gain insight into a problem by giving her your full attention as she articulates the problem. This will help her sort things out, develop alternative solutions, and gain emotional release when necessary.

- **Match your co-teacher**—in posture, gestures, voice tone, and rate of speech. This shows that you are really listening as you converse together.

Verbal Strategies

- Paraphrase the content—summarize, give examples, translate. This communicates that you are attempting to understand your co-teacher: *"I think I under-stand—you'd like to see how I use a few of the strategies at planning and recall time before you have to use them yourself with a small group."*

- **Paraphrase feelings**—use empathy to acknowledge the speaker's feelings and emotional state. This communicates that you are truly concerned about you co-teacher: *"It sounds like work time last week was really frustrating for you!"*

- **Clarify**—ask for more information from your co-teacher so you can fully under-stand what was meant: *"I'm not sure I understand ... Tell me more about this sit-uation that developed in the block area this morning."*

- **Probe**—encourage your co-teacher to think more deeply about her decisions: *"So after you pass out those materials to your small group, what do you think some of your children might do with them?"*

- **Use positive presuppositions**—use language that implies your co-teacher has already thought about an issue, is knowledgeable in this area, and can talk about it: *"When you use this plan-ning strategy for your group in the future, how would you make it more concrete for Daniel?"*

at the situation from the co-teacher's point of view. Unlike the teacher who attended the workshop, the co-teacher has *not* had a break from being with the children. She has also had to work with a substitute teacher or work alone and take on more responsibility.

This example highlights the need for certain characteristics in a mentor, in particular a **willingness to listen** and **heightened sensitivity to a co-teacher's needs.** Being a mentor is a challenging job, and mentors often need to work on their own **interpersonal and communication skills** first, before they can focus on educational issues.

The challenge for training participants is to bring the excitement of learning new ideas back to their own classrooms and to follow up by making long-term changes in their early childhood programs.

Another situation that can create difficulties in the mentoring relationship is the **level of understanding** participants take away from a workshop. In a few days' time, trainees are introduced to new information, asked to discuss and think about it, and given an opportunity to practice using it. They are also asked to make plans to apply what they've learned in their own classrooms. When they return to their sites, however, they sometimes find that they don't remember some critical piece of information. ("Now, how am I supposed to introduce these materials at small-group time?") Or, they may realize they haven't practiced a new strategy enough. ("I know asking a lot of questions isn't a good idea, but how else can I converse with Jackie, who hardly ever speaks to adults?") Unsure of new skills and strategies, trainees may wonder how they can possibly convey the new approach to their co-teachers.

To overcome such difficulties, it may help both members of the team to keep in mind that **attending a workshop is only the beginning of learning to use the High/Scope approach.** As trainers, we know that most of the learning does not take place in our workshop settings, but back in participants' classrooms, where both teachers can learn together. The co-teacher gains **new knowledge and skills** as she learns about High/Scope practices for the first time, and the mentor gains a better **understanding** of the approach as she explains rationales, mechanics, and strategies to her co-teacher. In addition, the mentor learns from the co-teacher's **professional and life experiences and cultural perspectives.** Thus, it is common for workshop participants to say that they learned more as *teachers* of the approach than they did as *learners!*

Two basics of successful mentoring relationships, then, are a commitment to **develop and use good communication skills,** and a willingness to **learn from each other.** Keeping these fundamentals in mind, here are some concrete steps the mentor can take to get the mentoring relationship off the ground.

Steps for Getting Started

A good place to start is to sit down with your co-teacher to **define the relationship.** Learning together about the High/Scope approach should be considered a continuing aspect of your *partnership* as team teachers. Explain that you will be sharing information and studying resources acquired in High/Scope workshops, and make plans together to meet on a regular basis to solve problems and discuss aspects of the educational approach. Assure your co-teacher that you are willing to coach, observe, and model/demonstrate new strategies for her as needed.

Next you might discuss or write down (whichever is most comfortable) your answers to these questions: What are each of you willing and able to invest in the process of learning High/Scope practices? What outcomes do each of you expect? As you answer these questions together, remember that the process of working together to implement changes in your program involves a **shared dialogue,** a reciprocal turn-taking process, and continued study.

Building trust is another essential step in the development of a successful mentoring relationship. This takes time, obviously—but there are some specific things the teacher who has attended training can do to facilitate trust-building. Try the following steps when you return from your next High/Scope workshop.

• At team planning time, **ask your co-teacher how things went** while you were away. Encourage her to share stories about the children, the substitute teacher, the routine, and so forth, and **acknowledge her feelings** throughout the discussion. Like the teacher in the earlier example, your co-teacher may have resented the extra responsibilities she had to take on while you were at the workshop. By giving her a chance to vent and by acknowledging her negative feelings, you are building a trusting relationship.

While teachers attend a training workshop, their teammates may be left behind to "mind the store" and often must take on extra responsibilities.

• After you have spent some time really listening to your co-teacher, **focus on the positive things** that happened while you were away. Ask her to show you

Peer Support Provides Training Follow-up

A successful example of peer support is the program developed by **High/Scope certified trainers Janell Shain and Julie Curry at the Loess Hills Area Education Agency, Council Bluffs, Iowa.** (Shain is an early childhood consultant and Curry is an early childhood special education consultant at that agency.)

Most of the 15 teachers in Shain's program had participated in two or more High/Scope training workshops. Yet, when they returned to their home schools and centers, which are spread over seven counties in southwestern Iowa, many found that their teaching colleagues or administrators lacked knowledge of High/Scope and therefore could give them little support in implementing changes based on the High/Scope approach. To counter this isolation, Shain and Curry invited the teachers to attend six follow-up meetings spaced 2 weeks apart.

These meetings were not intended to be training sessions conducted by Shain.

Instead, the goal was for participants to take responsibility for their own learning by organizing the content of the sessions. Participants used a study team approach involving group planning of the agendas, networking, and reflection leading to further learning. The responsibility for hosting meetings also was shared; meetings were held at various participants' centers.

Shain says that the teachers responded well to these follow-up sessions, which often provided the support they needed to make changes in their classrooms. By sharing problems, strategies, ideas, and experiences, participants became more reflective about the changes they were making, deepened their understanding of the educational approach, and developed a support network they could call on in the future as they continued to develop their skills as teachers.

something a child made at work time, or to tell you something cute or funny that a child said. Find a way to authentically comment on her strengths: "You know, Marsha, I never have to worry when I go away—I know that in spite of all the unexpected hassles, you will manage to stick to our daily routine, so the children will have that consistency even when there's a change in teaching staff. I really appreciate your ability to do that—I know it's not always easy."

Now that you've laid the groundwork for your relationship by defining your roles and building trust, you are ready to "get down to business" and **focus on specific aspects of the High/Scope approach.** The following strategies work well for mentors who are currently learning about High/Scope, and just as well for mentors who have already completed the training and have been implementing the approach for a number of years.

• **Ask your co-teacher where** *she* would like to begin. You might show her the list of topics covered in your training session (or the High/Scope preschool "wheel of learning," if you have completed all the training). What particularly interests her—what does she want to learn more about? You may think she needs to learn more about adult-child interaction strategies, but if she wants ideas for making recall time more interesting, that's the place to begin. Follow her lead. Remember, the principles of **intrinsic motivation** apply to an adult's learning process, just as they do to a child's.

Since High/Scope teaching team members share teaching responsibilities equally, both team members must learn the approach.

• **Together, decide which methods will work best for the topic you choose.** Your co-teacher may want to **read** about the topic first: make sure she has easy access to the High/Scope preschool manual *Educating Young Children: Active Learning Practices for Preschool and Child Care Programs*, (Hohmann & Weikart, 1995), the participant guides used in your training sessions; the *Supporting Young Learners* (Brickman & Taylor, 1991) and *Supporting Young Learners 2* (Brickman, 1996) books; and any other relevant resources. Or she may prefer **talking** about it with you. A third method might be **modeling**—for example, she may want to watch you use several planning strategies with the whole group before she tries any with her own small group of children.

• **Explore *Educating Young Children* together.** Look at and discuss the **photos,** then relate them to the children in your own classroom. Read and discuss some of the **child anecdotes,** comparing them with anecdotes you've written about your own children. Find some teaching **strategies or ideas** that you'd each like to try. Afterwards, discuss how things went, and return to *Educating Young Children* and other training materials for further study as your understanding of the High/Scope approach continues to deepen.

The Learning Never Ends

Mentoring is sometimes temporary (you get a new co-teacher in January, and she'll only be with you until March), sometimes longer term. As your time together progresses, and you both learn more—about the children, the curriculum, and each other—the mentoring relationship will change. Your co-teacher may start out very dependent on your knowledge and expertise, but your goal is to help her become an autonomous, self-reliant, and successful High/Scope preschool teacher. Someday she may find herself taking on the mentor role, when she is assigned to work with a new co-teacher who knows nothing about High/Scope!

It's helpful to recognize quite early on that even if your mentoring relationship is temporary, the learning process never ends—for either of you. You can continue to use this process in all your professional relationships.

§

The mentoring process just described is one answer to the question of how to encourage continued, on-the-job learning. See below for another approach—organized **peer support** or **coaching.**

REFERENCES

Hohmann, M., & Weikart, D. P. (1995). *Educating young children: Active learning practices for preschool and child care programs.* Ypsilanti, MI: High/Scope Press.

Brickman, N. (Ed.). (1996). *Supporting young learners 2: Ideas for child care providers and teachers.* Ypsilanti, MI: High/Scope Press.

Brickman, N., & Taylor, L. (Eds.). (1991). *Supporting young learners 1: Ideas for preschool and day care providers.* Ypsilanti, MI: High/Scope Press.

Administrators—
How You Can Support
Mentoring

By Linda Ranweiler

· ·

Mentoring in a High/Scope preschool classroom can be a tough job, no matter what the circumstances. Administrative support can make all the difference between a very successful and a not-so-successful experience for the teachers involved.

Another article in this chapter suggests that in many High/Scope programs, there is little or no **administrative support** for the mentoring process. We believe this lack of support stems more from lack of knowledge than from lack of interest. Who wouldn't want to double the impact of their limited training dollars?

For administrators who truly want to see their High/Scope-trained teachers mentor the co-teachers they work with, the first step to take is to **recognize and understand the mentoring process.** Having only one High/Scope-trained teacher in each classroom almost *necessitates* mentoring, if you truly expect both teachers to use the same approach. Then, to make mentoring happen, make your expectations clear to everyone involved by adopting the following strategies.

Communicating Your Expectations

For your **existing staff,** explain the mentoring process as you understand it, and get their input on the kinds of support they will need from you to make mentoring work. Explain that you see the process as a **learning tool for everyone,** not as a case of "experts" passing knowledge down to "beginners." Be especially clear in stating your expectations for those **staff members currently enrolled in a High/Scope training project.** Tell them you expect them to discuss the training's content with their co-teachers, and to practice applying their new knowledge together. Explain that curriculum

Time for mentoring is just as valuable and necessary as time for attending workshops and other training sessions.

resources should be shared with their team member throughout the training period, and any decisions about changes in their classroom should be made jointly with co-teachers.

• When you hire **new staff,** let them know that mentoring is part of your staff development process. If the new teacher doesn't know about High/Scope, inform her that she will be placed with a co-teacher who understands the High/Scope approach and will serve as her mentor. If the new teacher has had High/Scope training and/or experience, let her know that you may eventually expect her to become a mentor for another teacher.

Providing Training and Logistical Support

For mentoring to work in your agency, you'll need to **provide training for mentors in the communication skills required** for mentoring. Workshops on communication skills are available almost everywhere. You may be able to conduct a session yourself, or arrange training for your teachers through a local community college, continuing education agency, or outside consultant. A workbook that may be helpful if you are doing the training yourself is *Mentoring: A Practical Guide,* (Shea, 1992).

Another way to support your teachers is to **schedule the time needed for the mentoring process to take place.** You already provide time for teachers to attend workshops and other training sessions; remember, time for mentoring is just as valuable and necessary. Does your staff have a regular team planning time? Since they still need to be recording anecdotes and discussing their plans for the next day, is there some way you can extend team planning time for mentoring purposes? If they do *not* have a designated team planning time, can you sub for them in the nap room occasionally or hire nap room staff so your teachers can be free of distractions while they work together? Can you help them find time at the end of the day for mentoring discussions?

A final way to help out your mentoring teams is to **substitute in the classroom occasionally, allowing the teachers to observe.** You might do this for the co-teacher, so she can observe her mentor using various interaction strategies during a small-group time, for instance, or observe how a particular planning or recall strategy works. You might also *take the mentor's place for a short time*, so she can observe a child, write a narrative, and then discuss classroom interactions with her co-teacher.

The mentoring process benefits everyone—you, your staff, the children, and their families—because it helps teachers become more knowledgeable, skilled, and professional. It deserves your full support!

REFERENCE

Shea, G. (1992). *Mentoring: A practical guide.* Menlo Park, CA: Crisp Publications, Inc.

Appendix:
Related High/Scope Press Materials

Early Childhood Curriculum

Print Materials

Educating Young Children: Active Learning Practices for Preschool and Child Care Programs, M. Hohmann and D. P. Weikart, 1995

A Study Guide to Educating Young Children: Exercises for Adult Learners, M. Hohmann, 1997

High/Scope Extensions—Newsletter of the High/Scope Curriculum, N. Brickman, Ed., 6 issues/year

Getting Started: Materials and Equipment for Active Learning Preschools, N. Vogel, 1997

High/Scope Program Quality Assessment (PQA): Administration Manual, PQA Form, PQA Head Start User Guide, 1998

Supporting Young Learners, N. Brickman, Ed., 1991

Supporting Young Learners 2, N. Brickman, Ed., 1996

Tender Care and Early Learning: Supporting Infants and Toddlers in Child Care Settings, J. Post and M. Hohmann, 2000

High/Scope Child Observation Record (COR) for Ages 2½–6 (kit), 1995

High/Scope Child Observation Record (COR) for Infants and Toddlers, 2002

High/Scope Preschool Key Experiences Series: Creative Representation, Language, Literacy (booklets & videos), 2000, 2001

Let's Go Outside! Designing the Early Childhood Playground, T. Themes, 1999

Daily Planning Around the Key Experiences: The Teacher's Idea Book, M. Graves, 1989

Planning Around Children's Interests: The Teacher's Idea Book 2, M. Graves, 1996

100 Small-Group Experiences: The Teacher's Idea Book 3, M. Graves, 1997

The Essential Parent Workshop Resource: The Teacher's Idea Book 4, M. Graves, 2000

Making the Most of Plan-Do-Review: The Teacher's Idea Book 5, N. Vogel, 2001

A School Administrator's Guide to Early Childhood Programs, L. J. Schweinhart, 1988

"You Can't Come to My Birthday Party!" Conflict Mediation With Young Children, B. Evans, in press

Movement in Steady Beat, P. S. Weikart, 1990

Movement Plus Music: Activities for Children Ages 3 to 7, 2nd Ed., P. S. Weikart, 1989

Movement Plus Rhymes, Songs, & Singing Games, 2nd Ed., P. S. Weikart, 1997

Round the Circle: Key Experiences in Movement for Young Children, 2nd Ed., P. S. Weikart, 2000

Other Media

High/Scope COR for Windows 95/98, COR-PC, and COR Mac for Ages 2½–6 (software packages)

Plan-Do-Review: Visiting High/Scope's Demonstration Preschool Video Series
1. *How Adults Support Children at Planning Time,* 1997
2. *How Adults Support Children at Work Time,* 1997
3. *How Adults Support Children at Recall Time,* 1997

Supporting Young Artists Video Series

    1. *Exploring and Creating With Clay,* 2000
    2. *Exploring and Creating With Dough,* 2000
    3. *Exploring and Counting With Paper,* 1997
    4. *Exploring and Creating With Drawing and Painting,* 1997

Adult-Child Interactions: Forming Partnerships With Children (video), 1996
The High/Scope Approach for Under Threes, U.S. Ed. (video), 1999
The High/Scope Curriculum: Its Implementation in Family Child Care Homes (video), 1989
Setting Up the Learning Environment (video), 1992
The High/Scope Curriculum: The Daily Routine (video), 1990
The High/Scope Curriculum: The Plan-Do-Review Process (video), 1989

Small-Group Time Media Package (videos), 1988

    1. *Counting With Bears*
    2. *Plan-Do-Review With Found Materials*
    3. *Working With Staplers*
    4. *Representing With Sticks & Balls*
    5. *Exploring With Paint & Corks*

Supporting Children's Active Learning: Teaching Strategies for Diverse Settings (video), 1989

Elementary Curriculum

Print Materials

Elementary Curriculum Guides

    Foundations in Elementary Education: Overview, C. Hohmann, 1996
    Foundations in Elementary Education: Movement, P. S. Weikart, 1995
    Foundations in Elementary Education: Music, E. B. Carlton, 1994
    Learning Environment, C. Hohmann and W. Buckleitner, 1992
    Language and Literacy, J. Maehr, 1991
    Mathematics, C. Hohmann, 1991
    Science, F. Blackwell and C. Hohmann, 1991

Elementary Program Implementation Profile (PIP) Administration Manual, 1997
Literature-Based Workshops for Language Arts—Ideas for Active Learning, Grades K–2, K.
    Morrison and T. Dittrich, 2000
Learning Through Sewing and Pattern Design, S. Mainwaring, 1976
Learning Through Construction, S. Mainwaring and C. Shouse, 1983

Elementary Science Activity Series:

    Life and Environment, F. F. Blackwell, 1996
    Energy and Change, F. F. Blackwell, 1996
    Structure and Form, F. F. Blackwell, 1996

Teaching Movement & Dance: A Sequential Approach to Rhythmic Movement, 4th Ed., P. S.
    Weikart, 1998

Guide to Rhythmically Moving 1–5, E. B. Carlton and P. S. Weikart, 1996, 1996, 1997, 1999, 2001
Cultures and Styling in Folk Dance, S. Longden and P. S. Weikart, 1998

Other Media

Elementary Curriculum Video Series
> *Active Learning,* 1991
> *Classroom Environment,* 1991
> *Language & Literacy,* 1990
> *Mathematics,* 1990

Foundations in Elementary Education: Music, Recordings, E. B. Carlton and P. S. Weikart, Coproducers, 1995
Rhythmically Moving 1–9 (records, cassettes, CDs), P. S. Weikart, Creative Director
Changing Directions 1–6 (records, cassettes, CDs), P. S. Weikart, Creative Director
Beginning Folk Dances Illustrated 1–5, (5 videos), P. S. Weikart, 1988, 1989, 1991, 1996
Teaching Folk Dance: Successful Steps 1 (video), P. S. Weikart, 1998
Teaching Folk Dance: Successful Steps 2 (video), P. S. Weikart, 1999

Adolescent Education

Print Materials

Learning Comes to Life: An Active Learning Program for Teens, E. M. Ilfeld, 1996

Program Guidebook Series, S. Oden and D. Weikart, et al., 1994
> 1. *Introduction*
> 2. *Workshops*
> 3. *Work Projects*
> 4. *Evening Programs*
> 5. *Room Groups*

For and About Parents

Print Materials

You & Your Child—(a series of 12 child development newsletters for parents), 2001
All About High/Scope—(a series of 10 information-packed fact sheets), 2001
Designing, Leading, and Evaluating Workshops for Teachers and Parents: A Manual for Trainers and Leadership Personnel in Early Childhood Education, J. Diamondstone, 1989
A Guide to Developing Community-Based Family Support Programs, A. Epstein, M. Larner, and R. Halpern, 1995
Community Self-Help: The Parent-to-Parent Program, 1983
Involving Parents: A Handbook for Participation in Schools, P. Lyons, A. Robbins, and A. Smith, 1984
Involving Parents in Nursery and Infant Schools, B. Tizard, J. Mortimore, and B. Burchell, 1983
Getting Involved: Workshops for Parents, E. Frede, 1984
Good Beginnings: Parenting in the Early Years, J. Evans and E. Ilfeld, 1982
Activities for Parent-Child Interaction, J. Evans, 1982

Other Media

Involving Parents in Active Learning Settings (video), 2001

Troubles and Triumphs at Home Series (videos)
     1. *When "I've Told You a Thousand Times" Isn't Enough*
     2. *Converting Conflict to Calm*
     3. *Let Them Do It*
     4. *Let Them Say It*

Public Policy & Research

Print Materials

High/Scope Monographs

Longitudinal Results of the Ypsilanti Perry Preschool Project, D. P. Weikart, D. J. Deloria, S. A. Lawser, and R. Wiegerink, 1970 (reprint 1993)

Home Teaching with Mothers & Infants: The Ypsilanti-Carnegie Infant Education Project—An Experiment, D. Z. Lambie, J. T. Bond, and D. P. Weikart, 1974

The Ypsilanti Perry Preschool Project: Preschool Years and Longitudinal Results Through Fourth Grade, D. P. Weikart, J. T. Bond, and J. T. McNeil, 1978

The Ypsilanti Preschool Curriculum Demonstration Project: Preschool Years and Longitudinal Results, D. P. Weikart, A. S. Epstein, L. J. Schweinhart, and J. T. Bond, 1978

An Economic Analysis of the Ypsilanti Perry Preschool Project, C. U. Weber, P. W. Foster, and D. P. Weikart, 1978

The Ypsilanti-Carnegie Infant Education Project: Longitudinal Follow-Up, A. S. Epstein and D. P. Weikart, 1979

Young Children Grow Up: The Effects of the Perry Preschool Program on Youths Through Age 15, L. J. Schweinhart and D. P. Weikart, 1980

Changed Lives: The Effects of the Perry Preschool Program on Youths Through Age 19, J. Berrueta-Clement, L. J. Schweinhart, W. S. Barnett, A. S. Epstein, and D. P. Weikart, 1984

Significant Benefits: The High/Scope Perry Preschool Study Through Age 27, L. J. Schweinhart, H. V. Barnes, and D. P. Weikart, with W. S. Barnett and A. S. Epstein, 1993

Lives in the Balance: Age-27 Benefit-Cost Analysis of the High/Scope Perry Preschool Program, W. S. Barnett, 1996

Lasting Differences: The High/Scope Preschool Curriculum Comparison Study Through Age 23, L. J. Schweinhart and D. P. Weikart, 1997

Supportng Families With Young Children: The High/Scope Parent-to-Parent Dissemination Project, A. S. Epstein, J. Montie, and D. P. Weikart, in press

IEA Preprimary Project Series

How Nations Serve Young Children: Profiles of Child Care and Education in 14 Countries, P. Olmsted and D. P. Weikart, Eds., 1989

Families Speak: Early Childhood Care and Education in 11 Countries, P. Olmsted and D. P. Weikart, Eds., 1994

What Should Young Children Learn? Teacher and Parent Views in 15 Countries, D. P. Weikart (Ed.), 1999

Early Childhood Settings in 15 Countries: What Are Their Structural Characteristics?, P. Olmsted and J. Montie (Eds., with J. Claxton and S. Oden), in press

Other High/Scope Research Studies

Into Adulthood: A Study of the Effects of Head Start, S. Oden, L. J. Schweinhart, and D. P. Weikart, 2000

Training for Quality: Improving Early Childhood Programs Through Systematic Inservice Training, A. S. Epstein, 1993

Challenging the Potential: Programs for Talented Disadvantaged Youth, S. Oden, M. Kelly, Z. Ma, and D. P. Weikart, 1992

Models of Early Childhood Education, A. S. Epstein, L. J. Schweinhart, and L. McAdoo, 1996.

Other Media

High/Scope International Videotape Series: Sights and Sounds of Children (15 videos— Belgium, China, Finland, Greece, Hong Kong, Indonesia, Italy, Nigeria, Poland, Romania, Slovenia, South Korea, Spain, Thailand, United States), 1994

High/Scope Perry Preschool Study Through Age 27 (video), 1993

**To order any of these High/Scope® publications,
please contact**

High/Scope Press
600 North River Street
Ypsilanti, MI 48198-2898
800-40-PRESS
Fax 800-442-4FAX
www.highscope.org

Index

adult strategies for, 89
interest in, 88
long-term perspective of, 89
starter plants for, 88
"A Garden Journal," (Clegg
Hawkins), 91–94
Gardner, H., 187
"General Teaching Strategies for
Children With Special
Needs," (Gerecke),
251–54
Gerecke, Katie, 218, 231, 241,
251, 255, 410
"Getting Excited About Art,"
(Brickman), 291–92
Godinez, Lucinda, 217, 219, 224
"Going Beyond 'Follow the
Rules,'" (Graves), 27–30
Graham, Pam, 317
Graves, Michelle, 2, 5, 13, 19, 27,
53, 55, 96, 113, 121, 125,
344, 349, 357, 365, 410
Greeting time, 135, 155
movement strategies at, 129
Group times, and special needs,
236–38

Handler, Debbie, 2, 31, 39, 410
Hands-on guidance, 211
Hawkins, Linda Clegg, 58, 91,
410
Harry and the Haunted House
(Schlichting), 135
Head Start, 2, 308
Head Start Performance
Standards, 333
Health, and outdoor experi-
ences, 171
Help, too much, 9
Helping words, 222, 229
Hensel, Nancy, 199
Here-and-now orientation
See Present-oriented
thinking
High/Scope approach, 5, 36, 57,
91, 187, 231, 343, 388
anecdotal notes in, 334
collaborating with parents,
307
and elementary children's
development, 275
encouraging expression,
296–97

in inclusive classroom, 247
and language acquisition,
295
strategies that meet
individual needs, 243
versus traditional
methods, 232
High/Scope Child Observation
Record (COR), 115, 122,
124, 322, 329–30, 334,
335, 336, 339, 343, 345,
346, 364
High/Scope Curriculum, 252,
358
access to, 239
High/Scope daily routine, 95
High/Scope Demonstration
Preschool, 2, 13, 27, 45,
58, 66, 87, 96, 129, 139,
144, 185, 188, 195, 205,
344
language and literacy
development of, 155
at outside time, 326
and toys from home,
357, 358
High/Scope early childhood
approach, 220
High/Scope elementary
approach, 277
High/Scope elementary
classrooms
organization, 277
and workshops, 293
High/Scope elementary
programs
choices in, 296
and parent/teacher
conferences, 303
High/Scope Family Information
Sheet, 251, 313, 316
High/Scope framework
key principles of, 241–42
High/Scope IBM Technology
Demonstration Partner-
ship Project, 66
High/Scope K–3 Curriculum
Series: Science (Blackwell
& Hohmann), 287
High/Scope key experiences.
See also Key experiences
and small-group time,
116

"The High/Scope PQA: Assessing Program Quality
Through Classroom
Observations,"
(Neill), 369–77
High/Scope programs
and reading, 109
strength of, 243
"High/Scope's Approach for
Children With Special
Needs," (Gerecke &
Weatherby), 231–39
High/Scope's Program Quality
Assessment (PQA), 344,
369–70, 379
assessment process, 370–77
and curriculum decisions,
380–82
descriptors, 375
evidence/anecdotes, 372–74
score, 376–77, 381
and training needs, 379–80
High/Scope's six-step conflict
resolution process. See
Conflict resolution
process
"High/Scope Strategies for
Specific Disabilities,"
(Gerecke & Weatherby),
255–66
High/Scope teachers and care-
givers. See Teachers and
caregivers
High/Scope Training of Trainers
course, 44
High/Scope UK, 58, 91, 310
High/Scope Ypsilanti Training of
Trainers Program
(YTOT), 344, 379
Hohmann, Charles, 276, 277,
285, 287, 295, 299, 308,
341, 410
Hohmann, Mary, 47, 57, 58, 59,
77, 95, 96, 105, 144, 175,
246, 411
Home activity sheets, 336
Home visits, 323
"How Does Your Garden
Grow?" (Ansbach,
Lucier, & Gainsley),
87–90
The Hungry Thing (Slepian &
Seidler), 135

About the Authors

Cathy Albro is a High/Scope certified trainer who lives in Grand Rapids, Michigan.

Ursula Ansbach is a High/Scope field consultant and former staff member in the Preschool Department at High/Scope Educational Research Foundation. Ansbach is a founding mother of Harmony School, an alternative school located in Bloomington, Indiana. She also directed a child care center in a New York City shelter for homeless families, under the direction of Homes for the Homeless. During this time she began training her staff, and staff in sister agencies around the city, in the High/Scope approach.

Nita Banks, a former Head Start education and staff development manager, has been a certified High/Scope trainer since June 1994 and is currently endorsed in the High/Scope Preschool Curriculum. Banks has done quality improvement training for a number of Head Start programs and has served on numerous Federal Peer Review teams within Region VII, which includes Missouri, Nebraska, Kansas, and Iowa.

Nancy Altman Brickman is a writer and editor at High/Scope Educational Research Foundation, where she has worked since 1977. She is the editor of *Extensions: Newsletter of the High/Scope Curriculum,* the starting point for the *Supporting Young Learners* series.

Ann S. Epstein is Director of the Preschool Department at High/Scope Educational Research Foundation, where she has worked since 1975. Epstein develops early childhood curriculum materials, directs a team of consultants who conduct inservice training around the country and abroad, and supervises implementation of the High/Scope Demonstration Preschool. Epstein also conducts research and evaluation on a variety of federal, state, and local early childhood programs. She is the author or co-author of nine books including *Supporting Young Artists, Models of Early Childhood Education, A Guide to Developing Community-Based Family Support Programs,* and six research monographs, as well as numerous articles in High/Scope publications and professional journals. Epstein has a Ph.D. in developmental psychology from the University of Michigan and a master of fine arts degree from Eastern Michigan University.

Betsy Evans is a High/Scope Foundation adjunct trainer who conducts Lead Teacher Training Programs throughout the United States. Evans is a trained adult mediator, and Founder and Program Consultant for the Giving Tree School in Gill, Massachusetts. She has worked with young children since 1974, and she has been instrumental in developing High/Scope training materials on conflict resolution, including a video and a book on conflict mediation with young children published by High/Scope Press.

Suzanne Gainsley has been a teacher in the High/Scope Demonstration Preschool since 1998. She has also worked with infants, toddlers, and preschoolers in various child care settings as a teacher and assistant director.

Katie Gerecke is a High/Scope certified trainer, a preschool consultant, and professor of early childhood development at Mt. San Antonio Community College, Walnut, California.

Michelle Graves is an educational consultant and staff writer at High/Scope Educational Research Foundation. Graves has teaching experience in early childhood special education, preschool, and elementary school programs, and formerly directed the child care program for employees of Veterans and University of Michigan Hospitals in Ann Arbor. At High/Scope, Graves conducts a variety of training projects for early childhood educators. She developed High/Scope's *Small-Group Time* video series and authored *The Teacher's Idea Book: Daily Planning Around the Key Experiences; The Teacher's Idea Book 2, Planning Around Children's Interests; The Teacher's Idea Book 3: 100 Small-Group Time Experiences,* and *The Teacher's Idea Book 4: The Essential Parent Workshop Resource.*

Debbie Handler has more than 27 years of experience in the management and administration of early childhood programs in both the public and private sector. She also has enjoyed an association with High/Scope Foundation for 16 years. Handler has conducted training projects for early childhood, Head Start, special education, and kindergarten programs throughout the United States and in several foreign countries.

Linda Clegg Hawkins has worked for 27 years as a nursery head. She has used the High/Scope approach for the last 14 years and has helped in the training of nursery nurses and early years teachers for a variety of colleges and universities in the U.K. In the 1990s, Hawkins began the first High/Scope Outdoor Classroom in the U.K., while working with the Groundwork Trust, South Tyneside. The "Garden" is well known and has frequent visitors from all over the U.K. and Europe.

Charles Hohmann has been a leader in the development of the High/Scope approach to elementary education since 1972. During this time, Hohmann has been deeply involved in elementary staff development through such projects as National Follow Through, Native American School Improvement through the Bureau of Indian Affairs, the High/Scope IBM

Technology Demonstration Partnerships, and various High/Scope teacher education programs. He is the author of the *Overview* and *Mathematics* volumes in High/Scope's elementary curriculum series and coauthor of the *Science* volume.

*M*ary Hohmann, an educational consultant at High/Scope Educational Research Foundation, has conducted a variety of training projects for preschool educators throughout the United States and overseas. She has written numerous articles for High/Scope publications and is co-author of the High/Scope preschool manual, *Educating Young Children: Active Learning Practices for Preschool and Child Care Programs* and the *Study Guide to Educating Young Children.* Hohmann is also co-author of the High/Scope infant-toddler manual, *Tender Care and Early Learning: Supporting Infants and Toddlers in Child Care Settings.*

*D*iana Jo Johnston is an educational consultant at High/Scope Educational Research Foundation. A former elementary teacher and administrator, Johnston conducts High/Scope training projects for both preschool and elementary teachers and administrators throughout the United States and internationally. She also develops High/Scope Training of Trainers materials and has conducted various Training of Trainers projects.

*P*am Lafferty, a former preschool and elementary teacher, has been involved with the High/Scope approach since 1987. She is a staff consultant with High/Scope UK and has conducted training in the U.S., the Netherlands, Turkey, and Ireland, as well as extensively around the U.K.

*R*osie Lucier is a certified High/Scope teacher and current co-teacher in the High/Scope Educational Research Foundation Demonstration Preschool. Before coming to High/Scope, Lucier served as both teacher and Assistant Director for Army Child Development Services at Fort Knox, Kentucky, and Schwabach, Germany. She has also taught pre-kindergarten in the Killeen Texas Independent School District.

*C*arol Markley, a former High/Scope educational consultant and Demonstration Preschool teacher, currently works as a data collection coordinator in the Research Division at High/Scope Educational Research Foundation. She hires and trains High/Scope's data collectors to use a variety of assessments and coordinates the collection and processing of data for several early childhood research projects.

*B*eth Marshall is an educational consultant at High/Scope Educational Research Foundation and former Demonstration Preschool teacher. Marshall develops the content and support materials for High/Scope training workshops. She also conducts High/Scope workshops and long-term training projects for teachers, trainers, and administrators throughout the United States and internationally, including the High/Scope Training of Trainers Project and the High/Scope Trainer Certification Project.

Polly Neill is a research associate and trainer at High/Scope Educational Research Foundation who works primarily in the area of assessment. Neill is one of the developers of the High/Scope Child Observation Record for Infants and Toddlers and is helping to develop the High/Scope COR for Children Ages 5–7 and the 2nd edition of the High/Scope COR for Children Ages 2½–6. She is also part of the team that develops training workshops for High/Scope's various assessment tools.

Jacalyn J. Post is an adjunct lecturer in early childhood methods and early childhood policy courses at the University of Michigan in Ann Arbor. Post also supervises student teachers in their early childhood and elementary student teaching placements. She is co-author of the High/Scope infant-toddler manual, *Tender Care and Early Learning: Supporting Infants and Toddlers in Child Care Settings.*

Linda Weikel Ranweiler, a former preschool teacher and quality improvement trainer, has been a High/Scope educational consultant since 1994. Ranweiler has conducted training projects for preschool teachers in the United States and internationally; worked on the development and improvement of High/Scope training materials; and is now writing a book on supporting emergent literacy in High/Scope preschool classrooms.

Eileen Storer worked in Head Start centers, lab preschools, and kindergartens before coming to High/Scope Educational Research Foundation. At High/Scope, Storer taught in the Demonstration Preschool, coordinated a statewide research and training project that focused on supporting local programs in their assessment of program quality and child outcomes, and conducted program evaluations for program improvement. Storer is currently on leave from her position as consultant in the Early Childhood and Parenting Programs division of the Michigan Department of Education to complete a 1-year appointment as a National Head Start Fellow in Washington, DC.

Pam Weatherby has been a special education teacher in the Ontario-Montclair School District in California for more than 30 years. She has been nominated for Teacher of the Year in her district and has served as a mentor teacher and has written numerous program grants. Weatherby has a masters degree in early childhood special education and has been a High/Scope endorsed trainer for the past four years. She is the past president of

California High/Scope Educators and has presented language and literacy workshops at the High/Scope International Conference in Ypsilanti, MI, and in Jalapa, Mexico.

*P*hyllis S. Weikart, Director of the Movement and Music Education Division at High/Scope Educational Research Foundation, is one of the country's leading authorities on movement-based active learning and recreational folk dance. She bases her writings on her ongoing work with students of all ages—from preschoolers to senior adults. Weikart is the author of numerous movement and dance books, including such major works as *Round the Circle: Key Experiences in Movement,* 2nd ed.; *Teaching Movement and Dance: A Sequential Approach to Rhythmic Movement,* 4th ed.; *Movement Plus Rhymes, Songs, & Singing Games,* 2nd ed.; *Teaching Folk Dance: Successful Steps,* a comprehensive guide to teaching over 200 beginning and intermediate folk dances; and its companion book *Cultures and Styling in Folk Dance,* written with Sanna H. Longden. With Elizabeth B. Carlton, Weikart is also co-author of *Foundations in Elementary Education: Movement and Foundations in Elementary Education: Music.* In addition, she has developed the *Rhythmically Moving 1–9* and *Changing Directions 1–6* international folk dance recording series, the *Beginning Folk Dances Illustrated 1–5* demonstration videos, and the *Teaching Folk Dance: Successful Steps* teaching videos.

In addition to being a nationally known and highly respected educator and author, Weikart is a researcher, curriculum developer, workshop leader, and choreographer. Through her wide-ranging experiences, she has developed an approach to teaching folk dance that ensures the success of both teachers and students of all ages.